THE STORY OF SLAVE AUREUS
BOOK TWO

AS TOLD BY SLAVE AUREUS
AND WRITTEN BY
MISS MARIE CLAIR ORMAN

authorHOUSE

AuthorHouse™ UK
1663 Liberty Drive
Bloomington, IN 47403 USA
www.authorhouse.co.uk
Phone: UK TFN: 0800 0148641 (Toll Free inside the UK)
   UK Local: (02) 0369 56322 (+44 20 3695 6322 from outside the UK)

© 2024 Slave Aureus and Marie Orman. All rights reserved.

No part of this book may be reproduced, stored in a retrieval system, or transmitted by any means without the written permission of the author.

Published by AuthorHouse 07/19/2024

ISBN: 979-8-8230-8872-5 (sc)
ISBN: 979-8-8230-8873-2 (e)

Library of Congress Control Number: 2024914483

Print information available on the last page.

Any people depicted in stock imagery provided by Getty Images are models, and such images are being used for illustrative purposes only. Certain stock imagery © Getty Images.

This book is printed on acid-free paper.

Because of the dynamic nature of the Internet, any web addresses or links contained in this book may have changed since publication and may no longer be valid. The views expressed in this work are solely those of the author and do not necessarily reflect the views of the publisher, and the publisher hereby disclaims any responsibility for them.

FOREWORD

Slave Aureus has been an Ambassador to the British BDSM society lifestyle and through active participation has helped surface and thereby trying to make safe such activities under the Safe Sane and Consensual ideology for those new and learning the lifestyle parameters, however slave aureus learned the hard way. This is that story of how she came to be

Slave aureus is known by many lifestylers worldwide as an active participant, a leader by example if you wish.

The operation that she is drawn into operated by previously establishing false names, so the names used are the ones known to slave aureus but not real names of those that took part. The importance of this is because slave aureus was taken to levels where truth would be paramount and so all had to be about a truth that she would come to know by the usage of pain and tortures.

Slave aureus was trained by the methods used in the story and did take place in the late seventies.

Book Two is the continuing story for another 3 months, each book will cover about 3 months of time and now we also will add what we now know to be how it comes to and end but in reality it should be at the end of book 6, but because of Marie has serious health issues and might be able to complete books 3, 4, 5 and 6 so the Endgame that details how the captive environment came to a swift end and will be in every book from book 2, just in case, so that readers are not left in the dark as to how the end came. health issues we will list it in all books incase she cannot write more

There is information on www.slave-aureus.com website www.fetlife.com is a website that offers friendship and help for those that share in the BDSM proclivities. This is not an endorsement but we have written permission to quote the line above

This Story is for ADULTS only
As told by Slave Aureus
And Written by Miss Marie Orman

SEQUENCE 8

RETURN TO HOME BASE

As I awoke in the unusual surroundings of this posh luxurious room in a state house in grounds somewhere in the UK, light is shining in the windows and now Istra is also awakening. I am reflecting on last night's adventure. Istra yawns and stretches a bit and says "hello Aureus it seems we both survived last night, I am looking forward to going home, back to home routines I know and the routines you need to get to know." "Yes home base" I said. Then Istra said "it might be an idea to leave your doubts about yourself here and start afresh back home Aureus." "Yes I kind of felt a change taking place lately and you have more experience than me so I will follow your lead."

"My own serious doubts are that I am sure I can not stop my foot tapping to the many songs we hear on the speakers and that can let me down" "yes Aureus that is because you are a musician as well as a female slave, just like the rest of us." Istra said. At that point in time four domestic girls appeared and the leader spoke "come on you two lets get a wiggle on The Master wants to get going, think he wants to be back home by a certain time," "you two look after Aureus we will see to Istra."

I had forgotten the morning procedures and so the bathing and brushing of hair took place. The Domestics did most of the talking, but maybe they could. "We will serve breakfast on the aircraft," the leader of the domestics said. Then Ahmed and Niobi appeared. Niobi spoke "have you domestic ladies finished with these two?" "Yes Sir" the Domestic leader replied. Then Niobi spoke again. "Leader I see you have not noticed both need their hair roots dyed again and slave Aureus needs a pubic area shave!" "Yes Sir I had planned to do it on the aircraft today going back to base" the leader of the Domestic girls replied. "Make sure you do Domestic leader, if I see these jobs have not been done by the time we get back to base you will be on report Understood?" Niobi added grumpily and the leader replied. "Yes Sir!" Then the guys positioned themselves into their usual position to pick us up and then we were off. It did not take long before we was outside in the cold morning air and soon we was on the coach footplate and struggling to get up the stairs and to our seats for the trip back to the airport to board the aircraft.

I was not sure how they planned to do this as it was now mid morning and there will be some risk of us naked slaves being seen as we transfer from the coach to the aircraft or so I thought.

As we approached the airport we were waved through the airport gates. Master Mussons airplane the giant DC10 was set over to one side all on its own and I could see the rear loading ramp was down so as it happened there was enough of our Guards and trainers to block anyone looking as we stepped off the bus and then picked up by our various carriers' up into the airplane which was a lot warmer than the coach or the UK weather.

It was not long before all the doors were secured and we was off down the runway and soon into the air, I noticed Istra was holding my right hand with her left quite tight like. "Are you alright I asked" "Yes she said, it's because I know what is coming and I am scared." "Scared of what I enquired and she just said" "Sssh" putting her fore finger to her lips.

Then I saw Master Musson and Niobi approaching. They collected two portable chairs with them as they glided down the aircraft isle to where Istra and I sat for the take off. They placed their chairs onto the floor and sat down then Master Musson spoke in his broken English voice.

"Aureus its important for you to realize that you are my slave now and even though we have a different attitude towards you and the others is because that was the beginning, now this is for the rest of your life, however there is a problem. The Colonel wants you for one of his whore houses. Now I will not give you up and he is making all sorts of threats so we may have to move home bases in time. In the meantime you will both have Guards 24/7just outside of your cell. Plus there will be extra security during your training programs and the

Doctor will always be on hand. Plus I shall be stepping up the training as its our standard practice at this stage because its still all fairly new to you, I am sure Istra will help you as will the others because you are now apart of my family.

I have enquired if I might lease or purchase the House we was at in the UK last night as a backup, plus I have another in the USA. This also means that we may all do a lot more traveling if the Colonel does not back down. We may also set up a base in Saudi Arabia as I have friends there as well, which will enable us to stay within the middle east locations.

Master Musson then stood up and went back to the front of the aircraft and Niobi picked up and folded both their chairs and followed.

Now I know why Istra was scared I think, I am not sure what she expected me to do as I can not do anything as I realized a long time ago escape was impossible other than my 'sleep escape.' Also now a part of me is here, that part that I can not control but it can control me.

Then the domestic girls appeared with the breakfast bowls of porridge and a metal cup of milk on little trays. I could see that all the Men were still with us even what I thought was Istra favorite, the Lathander guy, Master Robert was still with us, some military guys all in uniform, they all seem to be stretching their legs walking down one side of the aircraft across the back and up passed where we was sitting. A few more of our Guards were with us; the rest went back to the other aircraft that was hired as I learned later that Masters two spare 747's were in service and were not available for flight. So he hired another for this special event at Gatwick which did round trips to base at Tripoli and back to bring all the Domestics and Guards. So it's likely they all went back the same way so it's probable we will arrive first at base.

Istra sitting on my right was very quiet and I was worried that something was on her mind, "Are you ok Istra," I said, Istra replied "I am worried that base has been virtually empty whilst we was away and I am frightened to say the least for us to arrive back first, I think Master is too," Then Niobi appeared and said "The Domestics have placed a plastic sheet over the beds in the tent so they can shave slave Aureus pubic area and then they will do your roots that need re-dyeing. You can then both rest on the beds for a while?" "Yes Sir thank you Sir." Istra said then she added "Master Niobi Sir I am frightened for us to arrive back at base before the others can get back and secure base if things are so bad with the Colonel?" "Niobi responded with "Yes the Master is equally concerned. He plans to make an overnight stop over in Saudi Arabia, so the other aircraft can overtake us and arrive in advance of us. Thus making sure the base is secure long before we arrive, so it going to be a longer trip home than was originally planned so I suggest you and Aureus get plenty of rest Istra." "Please Sir I need to use the bathroom first?" "Yes do that first then join Istra in the bedroom tent?" "Thank you Sir" so I hobbled to the aircraft toilets which were better than the holes in the ground but still a nightmare with these chains, I felt sure the chains clanking against the china bowl would crack it and managed to empty my bladder, then gingerly washed my hands with the same fear of cracking the wash basin. Then I left the toilets and hobbled up the aircraft back to our seats and that was bad enough on my ankles. I had to rest a bit and sat down, now I know why they carry us a lot.

With that Istra stood up and with her left hand grasps my right hand and indicates for me to stand and we hobble slowly up the aircraft towards the middle wall where the beds were behind the heavy black curtains. After we slipped through the curtains Istra let go of my hand as she approached the far side of the bed and she pointed towards the other side the right-hand side of the bed with her right hand indicating for me to climb on to the bed with the plastic sheeting.

As the aircraft seemed warm there was no need to use the sheets and blankets. As I lay there I heard the music playing in the background, not as loud on the aircraft as was at base, but enough for me to forget myself and loose my feet to the foot tapping.

I turned my head to my right and said to Istra, "Now do you feel happier that Master will make an overnight stop so the others can overtake us and secure base before we get there?" "Yes" she said and then added "I am also worried that you will not understand Master's plan to basically retrain us both to a deeper level, I had been expecting this for some years now, though relations with the Colonel were acceptable and this is the first time he has applied the hard word on Master," "Hard word I enquired what is that?" Istra smiled and said "It's when a human uses pressure or applies pressure to get what they want, better known as the 'Hard Word!'".

"Master will effectively take us both back through another breaking training program so as to deepen his command structures in our minds so the indoctrination command structure will be second to none and hopefully the Colonel will realize the futility of pursuance of either of us for his whore houses." "This time though Aureus it will be with love from Master, not a battle of wits and sadly you will probably weep again, but then so will I, but we shall have to try to do it quietly and in return Master may well ignore us messing up the floors." She said smiling and added in a whisper "don't bank on it."

"When will this begin Istra?" I asked and she said "oh probably the day after we get back, Master understands that we need to get plenty of rest and get comfortable back at base as we have had a busy few days away, and you Aureus have showed Master some real promise in this thing that Master Lathander has in mind."

"I don't think you realize that you are now a part of Masters Slavery family, even if for some reason we are separated you will always now be Musson slave aureus." Istra said kind of glaringly at me.

"Yes sweetheart I had realized that, but as I am still learning all this like a new wife might in an arranged marriage, you have had some years to get used to this life, I am not sure how long I have been here now, I have completely lost track of time and dates." "Yes Aureus I am sorry I forgot you have only been with us now for about 8 weeks, but you have covered a lot more ground than some of the others ever did in the same time period, I believe Mista took longer to settle in, but Master loves us all in the ways that he does." Istra said.

"Well I think I need some sleep escape," I said and Istra replied "You're the only one that voiced that and kept it up, we all understand the concept and in a way I think its helped you to settle in with us, plus it shows you have humor still which makes you human. For now its sleep escape for us both," she said. However before we could get truly into sleep escape mode.

Four Domestic girls arrived with a bucket of water and a box like a tool box and the leader of the Domestics said" we are here to do your roots on your heads and slave aureus requires a shave in the pubic area as none of us are allowed to have any hair other than on our heads as you know slave Istra, I am surprised you did not notify one of the daily Domestics? Slave Istra! It's not good for Master Niobi to have it pointed out to us in that way!"

"Slave Aureus please lay on the bed there and these two girls will do that whilst I and one other will start on your roots slave Istra" the leader of the Domestics said.

The girls applied some cream to my pubic area and then began to shave my pubic hairs, "I usually do it without any creams or soap and as I am used to doing it, can I not do it?" "NO!" the Domestics team leader said in an aggressive tone "Slaves are not allowed to have any sharp objects at all, that is why we keep everything in the locked tool box and we do these jobs with extra eyes to make sure you do not get hold a anything sharp! Its part of the security protocol!"

It did not take long for those girls doing my pubic area and they were very thorough I was scared stiff that one of them might nick me in my genital area, which is why I wanted to do it myself. Then the team leader spoke again "Now that you two have completed that task, get the stuff you need to re-dye slave Aureus hair roots. Slave Aureus please sit up on the corner of the bed so the girls can work on your hair roots from both sides!" After about an hour or two maybe had passed the Domestics now had to rinse our hair and I was wondering just how the planned to do that.

The team leader spoke "Slaves Aureus and Istra its time to rinse your hair so if you can both lay on the bed side by side with you heads at this end so that we can rinse your hair into buckets!"

So Istra and I maneuvered ourselves into the requested positions and I was thinking I need some more sleep escape, though I really could just not drop off whilst the girls were working on my long hair and no sooner had they completed that part and now using electric hair dryers to dry our hair and when they had finished all that, the domestics removed all the plastic sheeting and thus left Istra and me to rest on the beds and eventually dropped off into sleep escape.

These beds were like two king size bolted to the floor and there was gaps between each one and basically covering the centre section of the aircraft with the headboard up against the centre wall and the foot of the beds was leading towards the back of the aircraft.

Some where while asleep I was unaware that Master Robert had snuck onto the bed on my left side as I lay on my left side. I realized very quickly that a Male had joined us when he whispered to me, "Roll over Musson slave Aureus to sleep position one." In a bit of a daze I rolled on my back legs spread as doing the move. The said "Now sit up and slip your wrist chains under your legs as I want your wrist chain underneath your body," I replied "Yes Master Robert Sir," and did as was told. Master Robert then promptly climbed on to me so his legs were in between mine and realizing he was naked totally I shut my eyes closed tight as we are not allow to see a Male below his waist. At the same time he slipped his left foot onto my ankle to ankle chain link to administer control and then reached out to Istra and touched her left shoulder until she awoke, saying "slave Istra assume Musson sleep position one on my left." Almost directly awaking she moved over on to her back like I did, then he spoke again "Musson slave Istra now sit up and place your wrist chains over your ankles so your wrist chains are behind you as well!" "So her left leg touched my right ankle and our anklets clunked and then he put his left arm across slave Istra's belly and laid his head my left shoulder and promptly dropped off so I thought. I thought he had something else in mind and

I was scared stiff to move a muscle, I managed to look at Istra and I am sure she could see my fear if I moved he would know as the same applied to Istra with his left arm across her belly.

Then two Domestics that Master Robert must have brought with him covered us with a white sheet and then left. Master Robert then said in a jolly sort of way "slave Aureus you are all wet and leaking on my leg!" I immediately said "sorry Master Robert Sir" and he replied "Its alright slave Aureus its nature in action, no need for apologies, besides it shows you are settling in to the family unit with us," "Then he exclaimed Ahh now I detect slave Istra is as well is leaking. As he had moved his hand to between her legs It was at that point I had remember to climb into these beds with the wrist to wrist chains behind my back without being told by Istra, which was just as well as it would have been very awkward now. Then Master Robert spoke "Musson slave Istra see if you can hold Musson slave Aureus right hand with your left hand because I'm going to reposition myself and fuck the slave!" Istra did as she was told. Master Robert kind of slipped his equipment soon into my vagina a lot easier than them damned electrodes I thought, its was not long before I could feel his rhythm and using my breath control to help with his penetrating thrusts, "Raise your legs Aureus!" This I did which for me seems to make it grip the Male member more but now my ankle chains were on his back and I was scared he was going to tell me off. Now I was scared of what to do next as no-one have explained what

I should do in this situation and Istra was squeezing my hand so I knew she knew I was worried, but I was just trying to obey Master Robert. Then he said "Don't you dare orgasm slave You do not have permission!" he must have read my mind because I was so close and so I had to try to kill it, ignore it I thought maybe might work now this was a hard lesson to learn, but I managed to lose it somewhere. Even though I wanted to come, not been fucked like that before, these guys really know their stuff. I think that was my initiation here as it was my first time under these conditions, since this whole event took place and I started to weep, quietly but not through pain it was some kind of pleasure I had missed. Then he said "prepare your self slave Istra!" and again like a precision operation Master Robert was out of me and into slave Istra. Initially our hand hold broke loose and Master Robert said "I gave no permission for you to stop holding hands reconnect both of you now! Slaves" and like scolded children we fumbled a bit and then found each others right and left hand then reconnected, I was so scared, scared, of what I do not know as not done the sex side with anyone here and so knowing we can be punished in ways I would rather not think about. Plus with the power and control they have over us I was just scared of doing the wrong thing by ignorance. After a short while Master Robert said to Istra "ok slave Istra you may come" as it seemed Master Robert did, then he said "both close your eyes and keep them shut" Then he said "Istra lick me and clean it," Master Robert said; then he moved across the bed on his knees I presume as I felt his legs straddling across my legs as he moved back to my position, then he said "Aureus Lick it! Clean me up," I knew I was licking his penis. "Musson Slave Aureus I am impressed you held off orgasm-in when ordered, your turn will come." "Now I must go clean up, I will send the Domestics in!" and with that he left us somewhat collapsed on the bed.

Soon two Domestics appeared with two buckets of water for us to have our bucket baths and clean up, and then another Domestic appeared with the hair brush to brush my long hair.

The Domestic leader said to Istra "we have flown over home, on our way to Riyadh, Saudi Arabia. The Master and some of the other Men will be staying at one of the palaces there for the night, so we shall have the aircraft to ourselves, the guards and the flight crew. Saudi police will Guard the aircraft outside.

Istra replied with how long before we land then?" and the Domestic Leader said "About 90 minutes time." Then two of them left while the third brushed both of our hair.

Without thinking I said "I think I can handle tonight's supper!" then Istra and the Domestic girl both looked at me and laughed quietly.

Then when the Domestic left, I said to Istra, did I do it right with Master Robert," "Yes Aureus I am sure Master Robert was happy with your efforts and your obedience otherwise he would have put you on a punishment report and he would have said, so you could worry about it. I would say you used common sense,"

Istra said. "I just know I was scared to death of getting something wrong." "Now I feel hungry and tired not sure in what order."

Then we hobbled back to the seating areas that's where our allocated seats were, then a few moments later the Domestic girls appeared with the usual stewed lamb and potatoes with some greens possibly cabbage in it and a glass of milk.

Strangely I really enjoyed the evening meal, unfortunately seconds are never available probably because the Domestic girls have lot of mouths to feed and really they do a great job.

After our evening meal both Istra and I took turns going to the toilet to do our toiletry needs because we never knew what was going to happen next so we had to fit these things in as and when, not sure what we do if needed a wee in the middle of training or a session event. So I asked Istra.

"Istra what happens if we need a wee whilst in training or whilst Master is doing a demonstration session event?" "Oh one of the guys will hold a bucket between our spread legs and we would be ordered to pee into it, but not get any on Masters nice clean floor" Istra said. Then added "Also do not wet the bucket holder's hand!"

The humming of the aircraft engines was broken by the sound of Captain on the Tannoy PA system. "Master's, Gentlemen and Ladies.

Please return to your seats and buckle up. We are about to land at Riyadh International Airport, Saudi

Arabia." "Please extinguish all cigarettes and smoking paraphernalia."

Soon afterwards was a gentle bump as the wheels touched down and our aircraft taxied to a special isolated area where the aircraft could be connected to external power and other utilities whilst on this parking stand. Then the front stairs could be heard lowering down. Masters Musson Robert and Niobi plus several other Gentlemen in fine dressed suits and with their traditional head-dresses on came through from the front of the aircraft on their way to the garage at the rear of the aircraft. Master Musson said "Goodnight all see you all tomorrow" and then disappeared into the area we know as the garage. Some car doors banged shut and engines fired up and then dwindled until you could hear the back door ramp closing again.

It was noticeably getting dark outside and so for the rest of us that was bed time and a drink of hot milk could be had at night supposedly to help us all to sleep.

I was told at some point that there was some more beds in the front section on the other side of the centre separation wall that the Men or Guests used, when more sleeping arrangements were needed the sofas and some special seats doubled as sleeping couches as we was always segregated from the Men except when they wanted to bed us purposely so the Men mainly used the front section beds, the 6 Musson slaves got priority to the rear section beds and the Domestics used seats sofas and the adjustable coaches to sleep on.

A couple of hours later the hot milk came and that

was a nice drink to have in the evenings, most of the main aircraft lights had been dimmed or switched off to darken the aircraft although there were our internal security guards and various watches of aircraft staff. I believe there were at last two complete sets of aircraft staff on the aircraft anytime that it was in service. Master Musson never tried to do things on the cheap, I had heard that the aircraft was regularly inspected and serviced.

After a fairly restless night I was awoken by the Domestic do their daily chores, the Domestic leader woke Istra and saying "Come along Istra lets get a wiggle on the Master will be here soon and we need to have everyone ready for flight. Then Istra asked the leader "What is the news, did the others get home safe" "Yes the others arrived back at base late last night and all is well."

"Good Istra said I kind of get home sick when we are away for any length of time." After our bucket baths and one of the girls brushed my hair, Istra and I hobble back to our traveling seats, leaving the Domestic girls to change the bedding and clean up where needed.

Then one could hear the rear garage door ramp opening and some people coming up the front steps. Then the front steps were whirring which meant they were coming back into the aircraft just below the main front and rear cabin doors. Soon after that the garage door ramp was whirring as it closed and Master s Musson, Robert and Niobi plus a couple other guys came through the service door to the garage section. Master said "Morning everyone are we ready for home?"

Soon the aircraft engines engaged and the seat belt and no smoking signs were illuminated, then the Captain said over the aircraft tannoy drowning out the constant flow of music. "Masters Gentlemen and Ladies please retire to your traveling seats and strap yourselves in, please extinguish cigarettes and all smoking paraphernalia for take off."

Then moments later the aircraft was moving slowly towards a runway until it got to the footings of a runway as the engines roared and the brakes released as we moved forwards and into speed down the runway until the aircraft was in the air and soon after the seatbelt signs went off and the Captain again came on the tannoy systems saying "Masters Gentlemen and Ladies please feel free to move about the cabin."

Then within about 30 minutes the Domestic girls appeared with the bowls of porridge and metal cups of milk for breakfast. Istra was feeling better for being on the way home to base, she had a smile that I had learned that she did when she was happy, on the other hand I was worried about what was to come and ok I survived it all once I hope I can do it again. In the beginning I had hate and aggression to help me fight my way through. Can I now do the same through so called love I pondered?

After breakfast Istra and I hobbled off back to the bed areas and laid down to rest and it was here that Istra felt the need to inform me of what was to come.

SEQUENCE 9

THE SECOND WAVE

I could see Istra was distressed and she again held my right hand as she lay on the bed to my right and we both looked up at the Black tented bed roomed tent which I believe to be based on the concept of the traveling Bedouin Arabs campsite tents.

"Aureus Master believes that by going deeper into you mentally, no other Male or Master will be able to re-break you either into their slavery. With Master doing this for a time you may believe that he does not really care, but you do not know the Colonel, if he gets hold of you, you will not survive. No-one does because he cares little for humanity, a lot is connected with the God or Holy wars that some Moslems believe in and their presence on this earth is to prepare the ground as it were. They then supposedly help themselves to the spoils in advance so I am told, I do not really understand these religions but I do know that Master is going to be really mean, though I think it will hurt him as much, but he must and this time its both you and me because the

Colonel wants me as well as you, he wants you because you are British, not sure why he wants a Croatian slave."

"Oh I see or at least I think I do, what worries me as I have said before if I can not control myself others will suffer in my stead because I have failed, I thought I would have had more time to get more practiced in this life, its all happening too fast again. I do not really want to hurt anyone, but now you are in the pot as well, surely if the Colonel was to have me, maybe it could be that he leaves you alone, do you not think that would help?" Then Istra sat bolt upright and said "Your serious!?" "Yes of course why not, it seems like the logical thing to do rather than create enemies, to appease them."

"Aureus I don't think it would stop there Master has known him for years and they used to be good friends, but that died soon after this operation got underway. Like many Men whom like to see themselves as all powerful would like the powers to own humans, a lot of countries have outlawed it unless it involves something they want or need and I think your gesture is very honorable, but I am sure Master will not allow you to make it, hmmm if I know him he has this bugged and is aware of it now you've said it." "Oh shit that will mean I've gotten you into trouble all ready for talking?" "No Aureus Master told me to try to warn you what is ahead, he has to remain as the Master of our family, even Master Lathander understands that and like you he is a Westerner, everything is done for a purpose, I am making a poor job of trying to make it easier, but whatever happens the rest of us as Master's slaves will support and back you as much as we can or dare." "I just do not want to hurt anyone; I am beginning to feel I have brought evil upon you all." "No of course not, Master has this idea that females are a distraction and have to be punished regularly, for creating that distraction, I believe the ancient Egyptians had a similar notion, though they was all locked away in harems, whether they got punished or not I do not know!" Istra said holding my hand again.

It was not long before we heard the Captain on the Tannoy "Masters Gentlemen and Ladies please return to your flight seats as we approach our destination about 90 minutes time, but there is some turbulence as we commence our decent thank you."

So it was time to hobble in our chains back to our flight seats, unlike when at base where the guys carried us everywhere so as to save time but the rub on the skin and ankles, but on the aircraft because its moving they class it as dangerous for guys to carry us so we have to hobble everywhere.

The 90 minutes passed very quickly and I was with my own thoughts as now Istra was not talking, as we are not allowed to be chatting the times away like women do in real life, I suspect the men must be worried about being 'henpecked' as they say. Anyway I need to prepare myself, not that I have much choice and then we herd "Captain speaking Masters Gentlemen and Ladies please be sure you are in your flight seats for landing, Please extinguish all cigarettes and all smoking paraphernalia Thank you."

With that and within minutes was that gentle bump as we landed presumably back in Tripoli.

After the aircraft had come to a halt, the whole aircraft seem to come alive with activities all the Men from the forward part of the aircraft came through from the front, the guys that secure the cars in the garage part and put them into bondage so the cars do not move about in the turbulence that one can get in flight.

At the same time that Ahmed and Niobi appeared before Istra and myself and other Men for the rest of the Musson slaves, I could hear the rear ramp doors opening and the cars all starting their engines. Then the guys picked us up and off we went towards the door that leads into the garage bay. As it was late afternoon the guys just walked down the ramp to the waiting cars now outside of the aircraft and Guards had the doors opened ready for Ahmed and Niobi to put us down on the ground so all we had to do was step into the car. As it was reasonably warm there was no need of blankets. Soon the cars were full; some other cars and a coach had come from Master's compound to aid in the transporting of all our personnel that was aboard our aircraft.

No-one was speaking and it seemed to be silence by everyone and it was not long before we were out of the airport and in a sort of convoy with other traffic. After about an hour according to the car clock we pulled into Master's compound and as we approached the doors that opened automatically many of our convoy appeared behind our car, then as we approached the area where all our cells were the car stopped at the same time about 6 Guards appeared. Master was first out of the car and talking to the Guards, Niobi was standing outside of the car blocking the door and Ahmed was on the other side. I was not sure if there was some problem or something was not right. Then Niobi turned and opened the door saying "Come Aureus, I'll take you in Ahmed can bring Istra and so I was soon in Niobi's arms and we was off along the various corridors, then I saw Istra in Ahmed arms not so far behind, I think I was frightened that they might split us up again, but that is not how its supposed to go.

Then we arrived in our cell and everything was ready and the Domestic girls were there with supper, which I was looking forward too. Then Ahmed and Istra came through the doorway and we were placed on our respective beds. The music which had been switched off just came on and started again. Ahmed and Niobi left and the Domestics handed down the trays with the bowls of lamb stew with possible cabbage plus a glass of milk.

The Domestic leader spoke to Istra "Istra whatever is planned begins tomorrow so you guys better get plenty rest, our department will be here early in the morning, I am sorry." "Why are you sorry?" Istra was asking, "We have all been advised to work in pairs and make sure we have a Male Guard with us at all times, you will have two Male Guards outside here. The Master has expressed a major security alert and is bringing in more personnel that he has had as alternative back up, and we have been told what they propose to do and why." "Oh I see," Istra said, and then added "Ok well we maybe see you later for the late night hot milk drink." "Istra for what its worth all the girls understand and we will not slip up in our chores." "What was all that about I whispered, and about not slipping up, I don't understand?" I said. Istra spoke in a firm manner saying. "It seems the whole operation knows the plan and all the girls will do their chores with determination so the floors will be properly checked for F.O.D. (Foreign Object Debris) so we don't have a repeat of that!" as Istra points to the special long term plaster I have on my left leg where my femoral artery was cut by flying F.O.D. a few weeks ago!" "Are you mad at me Istra, as your tone seems to be that of someone I crossed or upset?" "Aureus of course not, this has never happened before and it would seem that all our security and safety is now under threat and we are all frightened to be in our home base that we thought was the safest place to be." Then she sought out my hand and grasped it with some grip and carried on, "And NO! We do not want you to be offering yourself to the Colonel to save us; you're our accepted slave sister and a part of Master's family that is US!

SEQUENCE 10

"Strangely I think the Domestics feel they are a part of this family as well, that's never happened before either, some used to be envious of us or angry as if we would cause them hardships because they are not Musson trained slaves."

"Well I am sure this lamb stew gets better or I am getting used to it and I realize that the Domestics do a lot to take care of us all, that can not be easy plus I don't want to hurt them either." "Yes Aureus they know that when you stood behind Carrick when she was punished for your injury, you shocked them all because they must have listened to the Man that claimed you were a nasty bitch that cared for no-one but yourself. That Man wanted you taught some lessons, but Master saw through all his complaints about you, then he decided to keep you for one of his own. Not everyone is a monster!" she said. "Yes I can see that now though you are wrong it would seem that the Colonel has become the Monster."

"Yes" Istra said smiling and added "We must get

some rest, now you may realize why Master Lathander has joined us here for at least a month plus several other Men that you have not met yet. I think the trainers will be Masters Musson, Robert, Niobi, Lathander and Matt. Some others will be joining us later in the month. The operation is a lot bigger than you have been allowed to know, anyways Aureus as you say sleep escape we must." "Hang on Istra; I must have a wee in the damn glory hole." So I got up and hobbled over to the hole in the floor to do my balancing act, trying not to fall in, but with the chains that was easy done, but not tonight as I relieved my poor bladder. Thank the Gods I just needed a wee at this late time. Then as I hobbled back to bed jangling my chains as I hobbled.

Considering we had been at rest for most of the day I still found it easy to fall asleep, I would have preferred not to wake up, but that was done by the Domestic girls switching on a bright white sodium lamp high up in the ceiling and the leader of the Domestic team of 6 said "Wakey Wakey ladies time to wake up, struggling to get to my feet as I know I need a pee in the hole in the floor, but Istra beat me to it so I had to wait. Luckily I did not have to wait long to line up my chains so they do not drop down the hole and get all messy. Lucky for me I did not need a pooh and then three Domestic girls washed me down and dried me, one of the girls had a hair brush to brush the hair and braid it as standard.

Then two more Domestic girls appeared with the breakfast, porridge and a metal cup of milk as standard and I eat that slowly as my nerves were gaining being on edge, but soon that was gone and the milk as well, just enough time to flick the tooth brush and rinse with water that I spat down the hole with an urgency that meant I was not happy.

As Istra was doing her teeth and mouth rinsing Ahmed and Niobi appeared, Niobi saying "ladies are they ready?" directing his question to the Domestics. "Yes Sir!" The team leader replied and the two Men moved on into the cell as the Domestics moved out.

As per usual Ahmed came to me and picked me up and Niobi picked Istra up, then we was off out of the cell and on the way to one of the training rooms, but which one? Then Ahmed stopped outside some doors and waited for Niobi and Istra to catch up and then the doors were opened by two Guards from the inside. Then both Ahmed and Niobi moved on in very quickly.

It was a room I had not seen before or a room that had been altered and in the middle was our favorite merry go around with the T frame on it in a cross configuration so from above it would look like cross, but from my position it was clear it was rigged to take two slaves opposite one another, but you could put 4 on it as in the other plane that could form the 4 corners of a box. As I peered over Ahmed shoulder, behind us were some viewing seats for guests that would pay heavily to be there and watch as Ahmed placed me on one side of the roundabout base, while Niobi placed Istra opposite me and then both used a climbers locking clip and connected to what looked like a spreader bar which also had the same locking clips at each end. Then

I realized that they wanted to keep our limbs apart and the dangling central drop down line was to just support the weight of our chains, I had automatically spread my legs which were clipped to rings in the roundabout stage floor. This meant that neither of us could close legs or arms and single-tails would have free access to all parts of our Bodies.

When the guys had finished connecting us both up to the roundabout monstrosity and then moved away a sound I have heard before like a large relay clanking as 4 search light type lights that illuminated our position a bit like those stage lights you get that high light singers and dancers, but as the 4 lights came on the rest of the house lights dare I say went off or out. The only other place I heard this noise I think was in The James Bond film "Goldfinger" when James Bond was strapped to a table and the bad guys switched on a laser, it has a similar sound which I can only think might be a relay, these are used when one wants to use electrical equipment that prefers a direct feed an so a relay is used. Like spotlights on cars, one switches the relay on with a basic power lead, but the spotlight is fed by high current or voltage wires.

I was aware that the spectators were being led into the seats behind, Master was always keen to have witnesses, especially if they were business Men that he had dealings with or they was happy to pay a lot. Then I heard the old sound of the medical cart being drawn in by the paramedics and the Doctor was sure to be there some where and lastly 4 guys stripped to the waist wearing their keffiyeh or shemagh head dress adornments that unmistakably identifies an Arabic or Moslem Gentleman or in our case a Master.

Master Musson made a bee line directly at me while the other Guys were pushing in the whips cart. Master Musson came up close to me from behind and He whispered into my left ear and said "Slave Aureus I think you know what I got to do to keep you." And I replied "Yes Master"

"So it begins" he said as he went to the cart to choose a whip either a bullwhip or a stockwhip, could even be a signal whip but they tend to be shorter and I am fairly sure he will choose a bullwhip and as usual he would air crack it just to be sure it would break the sound barrier and the cracker not drop off. Either way it made me jump as not been whipped in few days and that always worried me, but then the first one landed and strangely I heard some female count 1. I glanced to the direction of the sound and it was Catricks. They arranged for her to count the lashes, I have enough to do to handle the pain without worrying about counting.

The first I hardly felt but the second was clearly defined as it came down to the left of my spine and the 3rd was on the other side and already I was into my deep breathing because Master was not playing he was making everyone count especially as he quickened the pace, most of the time my eyes were shut but glimpsed seeing Niobi standing behind Istra opposite me and I thought he was effecting a standard training program just waiting for me to lose control.

Catricks was counting away but my brain was gone and just trying to keep on top of the pain was enough for me to be concentrating on as I heard Catricks call 50. Master stops and approached from behind Aureus drink some water as he put a small metal cup to my lips, at that point I heard Master Euan say "lets see if she is wet Sir? God damnit she is." I whispered "sorry Sir" and Master Euan said "No-No No! Do not be sorry, this is a new development for us all and especially for your Master." Then Master Euan said "Master Musson Sir I think you should instruct your slave to indicate that you would like her to have these events because they are a good sign?" "Yes slave Aureus I want you to relax and allow your body to respond in these ways, I believe your body is indicating what we do is ok." And then Master moved in closer and whispered in my right ear. "Aureus I should have said something earlier before we started that any sexual responses you may have are actually adding value to your status and that honors me in a new field of slavery discovery." Then he withdraws and added, "Master Euan is correct!"

Then it begun again, though I wish there had not been such a long gap as I lost the sequence rhythm and now I had to do it all over again, I realized that Niobi was echo-ing Master on Istra, so when Master stopped whipping me. Niobi stopped as well, and now as the third one landed catching my left hip bone and that really did sting and hurt and then he quickened the pace again which I wondered if that made a difference although it also cut down my reaction times and again

I/we seemed to be handling it. I know for a fact that the female brain creates a pain killer for the purpose of birthing children and so I wondered if my brain could re-wire itself to help with this situation as we approach 70 and Master has caught my breast both on top and underneath, between my legs across my stomach area many times on my bum where I do seem to have a lot of erogenous or erogenic zones whereby I almost feel could lead to an orgasm, but Master has sensed something and changed where he wants to land that whip most of the time with this whip it feels a bit like a sting with a thud behind it, some whips are like a bee sting or a pin prick with a hammer behind each lash and some of the very long whips have a thud and a bigger thud behind them so it lands and you feel the sting that seems to grow into a bigger pain. I am also looking for things in the walls to latch my eyes onto as a way of distraction.

I hear Catricks counting at 89 and even though I feel tired and my body feels like it is either leaking sweat or blood, either way it's out of my line of sight. Then again Master stops at 100.

Master approaches with the small metal cup with water in and presses it to my lips, "Drink Aureus" "yes Master," I mumble out. We have not even completed a normal training program and I am worried as to why just as Master Euan pops up monitoring his experiment and places two fingers between my legs and exclaimed "she is sopping wet and you have not been whipping light Master Musson Sir? The slave has not been reacting negatively so I am inclined to think she is turned on to it, what do you think Master Musson Sir?"

The Doctor then says "this is news on me too." Then Master Musson said "so unless anyone has some objections I am going to stop here and let the slaves rest." Then I see Master Euan behind Istra and he seems to be excited, "come over here Gentlemen, Istra is equally sopping wet, so Gentlemen I think we are on the verge of a nurtured discovery and to bruise it by over doing the why that we do not understand could be folly." Then Master Musson added I too concur and think the slaves should rest for the rest of the day and we will begin again tomorrow!"

"Ahmed, Matt release them and get them back to their cells, Doctor if you would care to follow and apply the Iodine stuff to stop infections."

Master Musson commanded.

"Gentlemen I fear we must keep this new development under wraps as I can see the Colonel would be more than keen and he would be one to abuse what we have of truly discovered how to nurture and create a Masochistic female slave."

Ahmed and Matt attended to releasing both Istra and myself, though I was so tired I had difficulty in standing up straight and felt like I was about to collapse when the Doctor blocked my fall saying. "Now! Now! We can't have you fall and damage the Masters property." "Thanks Doctor" Matt said as he grasped my left side while the good Doctor was holding me on my right side.

Ahmed spoke in a sense of urgency "We must carry

these two back to their cell, are you coming Doctor?" "Yes Ahmed I had better come, though I think they need rest more."

Then without any hesitation we were both picked up and off on the trip back to our cell, all I could think about was sleep escape.

When we arrived at the cell there were 6 Domestics on hand to assist the Doctor plus one of his paramedics as they seem to think that this time it required professional hands to apply the smelly stinky stuff, however the Domestics had fresh clean tabards to apply when the Doctors had finished, though I felt like I was drunk or something and very wobbly on my feet.

At that point the Doctor said "I think I better hang around a while, if you have other duties Ahmed and Matt, then you leave the slaves in my care for now, please have a Guard fetch me chair!"

Ahmed and Matt left the cell while the Domestics were trying to spoon feed Istra and myself with the usual lamb stew, but I was not interested in food.

For the first time Master Musson applied every lash with greater force than ever before and I had not broke down or shed a tear and I was frightened as to why, albeit was only 100 lashes all told?

I knew I needed sleep escape.

After a few hours of sleep, I woke up to Istra's clanking as she made her way to the glory hole for a pee "Sorry did I wake you?" she said, "I don't think so, I should be used to it by now, besides I wanted to talk with you about today." Looking around smartly as I forgot we had extra Guards on duty and the Doctor was sitting in a chair when I last had my eyes open.

It seems the Doctor has gone and I have to assume the Guards are outside in the passageway so it's safe to talk quietly.

Istra came back to her bed via the shelf unit that had our now cold stew, "Would you like yours, its cold now but its food?" "Yes please Istra, the girls tried to feed us earlier, I was so tired I could not see what you was doing and I was so scared of what took place I think I was or am numb."

"Istra I am not sure I can explain this, what's in my mind, this getting wet under pain and tortures does it mean I, or, or my body like is, is my body now giving out the wrong signals or am I losing my mind…?" then I felt my eyes swelled and tears started dripping off my checks.

"No! No! not at all Aureus you are not losing your mind, besides it happened to me as well and I can not explain it, this is spooks Lathander's doing, I knew he was going to upset the cart, Aureus look when it happened the first time to you I thought it was a fluke or your body reacting like a safety valve or mechanism, but now its happened to me as well, I can only think something has changed." "Yes I can see your logic but I did not have sex on my mind, far from it, I was more scared of letting you guys down, messing up Masters Floor again." Istra smiled for a bit, "Sorry I did not mean to be humorous," "no its alright Aureus we have only got each other, you noticed even though Master had an audience but the other slaves were not involved and I do not know what happened to them, this is all so new for me too. Maybe to the point to off balance us, but why and I am not sure Master is really onboard with spooks you know who Man." "Aureus we really need to get some more rest whatever they have planned they will not stop now and there's the Colonel to worry about as well." "Ok Istra you don't have to tell me twice I am still exhausted from today." "Aureus whatever happened you was marvelous today," "thanks but can I keep it up." as I drift off back into sleep escape.

SEQUENCE 11

DAY TWO

As I awoke to yet another day, that damn sodium light was on again, which could only mean one thing the Domestics were here again and it was bodily maintenance time once again. "Come along Aureus time to shake a leg" Istra said, "Yes ok" I am waking up I think, need to wee in the glory hole first.

The Domestics were concentrating on Istra, with both our bodies full of cuts and bruises; it was a slow process even with a soft sponge and the delicacy that the Domestic girls took with us. "Ok Aureus it's your turn." The Domestic leader said. I was hurting quite a bit and my body felt like I had been run over by a truck and left alive, I think I am partially terrified of what today will bring. After my bucket bath and the girls patted me dry with the towels, one of the girls began brushing and un-tangling my knotted hair, it seems as I sweat it gets knotted even though it's braided.

Then one of the girls handed me my tray with my bowl of porridge and metal cup of milk, though I seem to be dragging the eating of it out or I was still tired, I had not noticed that Ahmed and Niobi had entered our cell and were standing either side of the open doorway watching. Then Niobi said "Come along ladies have you completed your chores here?" "Yes Sir" the Domestic leader said. At that point the Men moved towards Istra and myself and without another word had picked us both up and we was off on the trip to hell or where ever.

I must have dropped off briefly as we arrived back at the same place we was yesterday, in what seemed to be seconds rather than the minutes it used to take and this was the room with the merry-go-around stage thing in it. The Men wasted no time at all in getting Istra and I connected up in the same way as yesterday. I was aware that the viewing area was also filing up with watchers or voyeurs anonymous I was thinking, but this time the other 4 Musson slaves joined us as I heard their chains clanking as their Male carriers placed them down on the floor in front of the voyeurs. Everything seemed to be moving a lot faster today than yesterday.

Then two guards brought in two sets of pyramids that I had not seen for a while and I knew that today was not going to be fun. The Guards secured the pyramids between our legs, as I could only see what they were doing to Istra I knew the same was going on my side. Then Niobi approached my left side holding an electrode which made me shudder as he said "Just for you Aureus we have got some special lubrication!" as he squirted what looked like a tube of toothpaste and all this clear stuff oozed onto the electrode. I knew why he was making this special announcement is because his gobbing up spit made me fell sick to the point my stomach would go into auto dump and that might delay their plans. Istra got the same lubrication too so it must have been of some benefit. I noticed when Niobi inserted it into my vagina it slipped in a lot easier than the time before. I could see that Istra's pyramid was being wired up so I knew what was to come and I was really frightened.

Soon the parade started with the Doctor and his medical cart and his paramedic guys, followed by the whips cart that 4 Guards were pushing in with all the whips on and then Masters Musson +Master Euan + Master Robert + Master Matt and Master Niobi all in their special head dress apparel and bare chested selves like a pack of lions coming to feed.

Master Musson came up to me and said "Slave Aureus do you recall the last time you sat on the pyramid?" "Yes Master" "Do you recall my telling you that you will fear Men? "Yes Master" "Well slave that day has come; it really is for the best!" He then walked off to my left and around to stand beside Istra; because he was speaking softly I could not hear what was said though I heard Istra say "Yes Master" a couple of times. The thought went through my mind that this might be the day I die and maybe the Doctor will not be able to save us although I am no longer sure that I want to live like this. Then Master Robert approached and said "Slave Aureus we are going to test the electrics, it works by way of if Istra moves you get the shock and if you move she will! Now watch Istra!" I could see

Master Musson prods Istra in the side with the butt end of a bullwhip and she moved and I felt the shock which seemed to move up and down strangely in my vagina, catching me in such a way I moved and I could see Istra reacting as if suffering from the same electrical shocks. Shit slipped out of my mouth. I can see this is going to take some concentration. Then Master Robert, whom had stepped back, stepped forwards again and said "Slave Aureus it's my turn to use the whip on you today, Master Musson will whip Istra and Master Euan will quiz you on some of the standing orders and rules to see what if you have learned anything?"

With that he turned and went to the whip cart to choose a whip, I thought it will probably be a Stock whip as I know that's what he likes, they all hurt equally as much though the longer they are the harder they seem to fall and the shorter the more they sting, the wisdom by an experienced slave, I wish!

I knew when he had returned and got himself comfortable because they always seem to air crack their whips and so we know that. "Aaggh, He's Begun and at the same time I could see Istra wince as Master Mussons bullwhip landed upon her and I thought they will not stop now. Catricks was not counting today so it was just the music that was now louder than usual and occasionally the other slaves would clank their chains and trying to keep still was not so easy, I am sure I was hurting Istra because this was new to me. I have lost count because I am trying to concentrate to not move and looking for things like bolts to mentally unscrew with my eyes, then I saw Istra move violently at the same time I got such a jolt in my vagina if my legs had not been secured to the floor I felt my whole body rise like a reaction as if being ejected. It was then that I started to weep, my nose soon filled with snot as my eyes dripped tears down my checks and down to the floor, I was sure Master Musson was watching with his beady eyes then they all stopped briefly as Master Euan stepped forwards with a cup of water, I saw the Master Matt was doing the same for Istra opposite. I gulped my water in between gasping for air as my nose was blocked and the Master Euan said "Slave Aureus what is standing order 1" "Sir its to always seek a Male or Master to keep me a slave" "Good enough slave carry on Master Robert Sir" "Thank you Master Euan Sir!" It instantly flashed across my mind if they carry on like this, it could resemble a freemasonry type institution they are all into formal declaration and before I could think more Master Roberts whip landed across my hip bones which is where I feel the pain most severely and I moved with such violence I saw Istra almost jump like I did earlier, then again Master Robert picked up speed and he was all over the place, when he landed on my right hips the same thing happened to Istra, I just could not keep still, but Master Musson made sure that Istra got her own back by landing his whip in places that effected here equally as bad as me. Then a tune came on and my damn feet wanted to foot tap too and I was trying to recall its title which in the end I think it sounded like "I'll meet you at Midnight" the song refers to lovers meeting in France. But all that got me was Master Robert must have seen my feet and attacked my ankles or rather just above the anklets which is another sensitive area. And I started to weep again or at least my eyes swelled with water and started pour out, my nose was already blocked and I was breathing and gasping for air through my mouth. I failed to get myself distracted and wondered just how long I could keep this up, though it seemed when it looked like I was distracted another bolt of electric was there and alerting the body so I began to wonder if someone else also had controls to it as sometimes I got a jolt while Istra was still. Then again they all stopped and Master Euan was there with another cup of water. I was all sweaty and glancing down realized my body was bleeding again, not dramatically just enough to see a red floor and where I had to blow out my nose it was somehow hidden by the red stuff. "Drink" "Aureus" "Yes Sir" as I am gasping for air and trying not to choke.

Master Euan then said "What's standing order 2, slave?" "Slave to seek regular training Sir" "Good slave You may continue Master Robert Sir" "Thank you Master Euan Sir" and then it began again, though now I was very tired and not sure the out come thinking this maybe the day I die because the pain of the whip is tiring me and the electrics wakes me up and its like a no rest condition, like being forced to run. And then again Master Robert speeds up his attack and then suddenly I felt strange like I was going to faint, at which point the Doctor rushed up and jumped up onto the merry-go-around stage and used his hand against my left leg where that femoral patch was and suddenly his white coat turned red. Master Musson dropped his whip and rushed forward as I lost it and fainted or passed out.

I came too on what seemed to be a stretcher on the floor a few feet from the merry-go-around, Master Musson was looking down on my right and the Doctor still holding down that plaster he put on a few weeks back, then the paramedics gave him a fresh one. The Doctor was pressing so hard it hurt a lot more than some of these whip impacts, however between them they managed to clean it up and apply another of these special plasters. Master was saying "It seems Master Robert must have wrapped there and lifted the old plaster and re-opened the wound, the Doctor says you will be ok but you will have to be in the medical wing for a few days." "Niobi see that Istra goes there too and have the cell Guards move to the medical wing!" "Yes Sir" Niobi said

"They are in your care Doctor!" "Yes Sir" "and Doctor thank you Sir!"

I must have dropped off again as I was extremely tired and exhausted, but now I find myself in one of the hospital beds in the medical wing and as I look around there is my good friend and cell mate Istra fast asleep in the bed next to me on my right.

Over the other side to my left, beyond the spare bed on my left was the Doctor also fast asleep in his chair, so I guess its still sleep escape time, but just then I saw a Guard cross the doorway and then Master Robert entered the room, he came directly to my bed, I think I was now scared to look him in the face and so shut my eyes.

"Aureus I completely forgot about that injury, it may appear harsh, but what Master Musson seeks to do its very serious, in one way he wants to deepen his control imprint on you and make it harder for the likes of the Colonel to try to steal you for his own uses, plus if your incapacitated by constant training and recovery. Anyone planning to abduct you will need a similar sized operation to what we have here, do you understand?" "Yes Master Robert Sir" "Sir I don't see why I have to hurt the others in my failures to take what the others can?" "You are not failing you are in training and it takes a lot more than a few weeks to become equal to the others, they know that and they accept it because Master Musson wants you in his family, just do your best slave Aureus!"

Master Robert gently shook the Doctors right shoulder. "Yes Sir is there a problem?" "No Doctor, but I think you should give slave Aureus a shot of sleeping drug as the sleep will do her more good," then he said quietly "she feels responsible for hurting the others and that will work against the Masters overall plan, I will inform Master Musson." "If you think that is best Master Robert Sir, I will do it immediately. Please be sure the Master is aware." "I am going to see him right now, thank you Doctor." Then the Doctor swabbed my left arm and injected some stuff into me and I felt like being faint again and sleepy.

SEQUENCE 12

DAY THREE

I awoke from what felt like a whole week of sleep rather than 24 hours, I certainly felt better than I did yesterday, but still had a lot of pain from my cuts and welts which could be seen leaking onto the tabard gown and onto the bed sheets as well.

The Domestic girls arrived with their buckets of warm water and towels and 3 started with Istra "Come along Istra time to get out of the pit" the team leader said smiling, then she said "Aureus you too, just be careful how you get out of the bed because of your wound" "You other 3 girls go and assist Aureus and bath her!" "Hang on girls before you do I need a wee, and I can not make it to the toilet?" The Istra said "Place the spare empty bucket between her legs so she can pee where she stands, that will be safer!" so they did and I was able to wee into the bucket with great relief. Istra then said in a low voice "does anyone know what is on for today?" The team leader then said "you should be going back to your cell after breakfast, it's fairly certain that singletail whipping is not on because of slave Aureus's injury." Then one of the other Domestic girls said

"There is a lot of works being carried out in some of the larger torture chambers. I think they are dismantling it all and packing it all away." The team leader said "yes Master has authorized for a lot of the equipment to be dismantled and transferred to another site, I think it's in Saudi Arabia."

Then after two of the girls had finished patting my body dry, a third produced the famous hair brush and began to brush my long hair, I found myself twirling the ring on my finger left hand third finger, the ring of a snake which signifies Masters singletail whips that bite. I was thinking that all six of us had the same ring and I found myself wondering if he had them all made at the same time. Then the team leader said to Istra "did you know they changed the subliminal code on the first day, that spooks guy seems to want you guys sort of be gagging for a good whipping or the pain," one of the other girls chimed in "we are not sure which it is, but we think the Master is not very happy with it." Then the team leader replied "they have changed it back to how it was as before, it all sounds a bit kinky if you ask me."

Then another two sets of Domestic girls came in with the trays of porridge in the metal bowls and the milk in the metal cups. It was then that the Doctor came in and lowered the beds a bit so that we could sit on the beds with our legs over the side to eat our breakfast. Then he disappeared again through the doorway. I began to feel the need for a pooh, then dawned on me that I had not seen hole in the ground or seen a proper toilet on the medical wing.

"Istra I sense I need a pooh and there is not a hole

here, what do I do?" "Hold on Aureus I will ask a Guard to assist." Istra disappeared through the doorway and then a few minutes later Istra and one of the Guards came into the room. I had not noticed before that the Guards were now wearing holstered guns on their waistline belts. The Guard indicated for me to slip my wrist to wrist to wrist chains over his head and he completed the move by picking me up. Just as we was about to go through the doorway the Guard said "You better come too Istra as you cannot be left alone," then the other Guard came in and within minutes Istra was in the other Guards arms and we was off back towards our cell.

As we arrived I needed to get down quickly and think my carrier Guard was aware of it because he seemed to help. The other Guard had placed Istra over the other side by where the food bowls and water cups etc were stored. Whilst I was busy relieving myself I had not seen the Colonel enter the cell pointing a gun at the Guards. He was saying "I mean to have you two in my service in my whorehouses," and then he said "Guards get over there and face the wall." "Slave Aureus get you out of there!" "Sorry Sir I can't it will not stop, Istra get over here see what she means?" Then there was Niobi shouting out loud "Drop it Colonel Sir! Or I will shoot; then Master Musson also appeared "What is the meaning of this Colonel!" "This is my compound and I pay a lot of money to operate my operation from here, you and your government approved it, you cannot just change the rules to suit your own purposes!"

Then the Colonels gun dropped to the floor with a metallic thud, Then the Colonel spoke in his broken English "Master Sir you know I wanted these two slaves for my operation, you still have the other 4!" "Colonel Sir I has all 6 and they are all married to me and are my family, here are the documents signed by your own Government Ministers.

If you take any of them by force you will break your own laws into the bargain and the Prince he will not tolerate that so back off." "Guards escort the Colonel off the premises; get extra help as he will have some heavies kicking around." Then Master Musson looked at me and shouted "DOCTOR! Where the hell are you? "Here Sir, "Right Aureus seems to be having some medical problem, lets get it sorted" he said. "It looks like massive Diarrhea, Niobi + Matt go get a stretcher and pickup a waterproof sheet." "Master Sir we need to place Aureus on the stretcher and take her back to the medical wing!" The Doctor replied. Then Niobi and Matt were back and placed the stretcher down on the floor and laid out the plastic sheets on the stretcher so some of it were draping over the sides. "Ok Niobi and Matt lift Aureus onto the stretcher and then wash your hands before you touch the stretcher again!" "Yes Sir!" Niobi said and Matt followed in close order "Yes Sir!"

Feeling faint I laid down with my wrist to wrist chains resting on my stomach. "Ok Gentlemen lets go" the Doctor said as we moved briskly away from the cell and towards the medical wing. As we arrived two sets of Domestic girls were on hand in case they were needed. Niobi and Matt placed the stretcher on the floor, then Niobi put his arms under my arm pits, while one of the girls held onto the plastic sheet at my chest area while Matt took hold of my ankles and chain and one of the girls held onto the plastic sheet at the ankles end and between them they moved me onto a waiting prepared bed.

The Doctor was preparing a hypo for some kind of injection, after that one he prepared another and said "This one is a mild sedative as you need complete rest. Do not worry Istra will be right here in the bed next door."

Once again I was into forced sleep escape as I started to drift into sleep I started to worry about the increasing bodily problems now occurring, now twice that Femoral artery has been a major problem, now my bowels was joining in the difficulties and thus stopping the plans for whatever was ahead and my desire for a longer sleep seemed to be now.

SEQUENCE 13

DAY THREE

I awake the next morning to find the Doctor watching over us, as I realized that I was back in our cell and strained to see where Istra was, at that point I felt a crick in my neck and think oh no not more complications. The Doctor stepped forwards and said "here have some of this which will sort your bowel problem out" I was thinking he was goner spoon me castor oil but it was not, it was some kind of syrup in a spoon, "I will return every morning until we resolve the situation slave Aureus" he said as he was walking out of our cell. Istra whispered "he will sort out your medical problems or he'll be on the naughty step" she whispered smiling. "Come on wake up we have breakfast here already and the Domestics will be back in a while to bath us, I think your body must be changing to our way of life and that is why your suffering these difficulties, Master told me early this morning that its normal and your body needs time to adjust, that's why you've overslept" "it probably happened to me, but I had no one to point out those changes so I did not acknowledge them, but I have seen them in all the other s and including you."

"So what are we doing today?" I whispered back, not wanting to incur any negative reactions. Istra whispered "Normal training program I think, also Master was telling me that he has temporarily pacified the Colonel. But he will be allowed to take part in some things but only here!" "So we will continue the training together as Master said when the problem came up?" "Oh yes, Master will not trust anyone to go back to the old training program of singularly practice, I am afraid you is stuck with me" Istra whispered quietly then I thought and said in a low voice "No that's wrong I am afraid its you that's stuck with me" as I gestured a smile, then I added "and I still do not like the Colonel!" "That's alright none of us do, so Master will supervise his visits!"

"Whilst we are at it Master is now setting up bases in all the countries that he does business with and that is mainly where each of us come from apart from the USA which has other reasons whatever that is?" Istra said quietly in a way that I recognized that she was not a keen supporter, like she would poke fun at Master Lathander by calling him spooks anonymous. Just then there was a commotion at the doorway as the Domestic girls arrived with their buckets, towels and clean laundry.

One of them dropped the sheets and tripped over them, the team leader was going SSsh and then she said quietly "You twos are getting too relaxed we could hear you up the hall ways like a couple old women waiting for a bus!"

"My fault Istra said, you best let someone know otherwise if the Guards heard and report us and you've not reported we will all be for it, its my fault I am still indoctrinating slave Aureus and with all the other distractions its slow." The team leader said "Yes that is best, I will report it to my superior and you should do the same, then there will be some balance." Then I thought and said "No that's not fair it's me that is out of order I still forget things and my mouth tends to get carried away." "Sssh" the team leader gestured and then said, "you will get carried a ways if you do not learn a bit faster "she said with a smile so I know she did not mean it as if to be nasty towards me. Then I said "Istra please let me take some responsibility for my actions, maybe I can learn faster by the practical aspects of my actions, realizing there could be consequences, besides it's the right thing to do and they may expect it." "That's a thought Aureus I had not seen that, Aureus I do believe you are seriously accepting the new lifestyle and I am proud of you, you really are one of us, the family so to speak." "Thanks I replied quietly lets hope I do not live to regret it I said smiling back in that humorous bent me occasionally come out with!" And with that the Domestics had done all their chores of changing the beds and flushing the hole in the floor removed soiled pots and left two fresh ironed Tabards for later, they left and the team leader said as she left "have a nice day ladies."

About 30 minutes later Ahmed and Niobi appeared at the door, strangely whilst waiting for the guys to come get us I got really scared of my decision and as soon as Niobi got close, I dropped into the known kneeling position which I know as a Yoga move as ones bum is touching the floor and ones legs are forced apart by one own leg or thigh muscles and I blurted out "Sir I found myself talking to Istra in a loud manner when I-I should not have been, please report it or whatever is the correct procedure is!" I had not noticed Master Musson was standing by the door because of a panel about waist high was blocking my view of the door if I had, had my eyes open.

Master Musson spoke loudly and said "the correct procedure is to tell me at the earliest opportunity then there is is no risk of the truth being distorted by a good story!" Istra interrupted "she is still learning Master." "Yes I can see and I am impressed she had the honesty to declare it, because we was aware of it I thought I was going to have to come up with a devious punishment, but you both have caught me off guard and my dear Istra you were right when you claimed Aureus does seem to recognize being apart of the family so to speak I think you said?" "Yes Master I did" she said.

I could see now very clearly that this operation was very much on the ball and not some thrown together ideal or dream of one Man it was like a military operation and they take everything very serious.

Master Musson then said "I shall have to think about this, but for now its basic training for you both,

Ahmed - Niobi if you please Gentlemen lets go." And with that Ahmed soon had me in his arms and Istra was in Niobi's.

Master Musson followed on behind, though I was still shaking or shivering maybe from my move to lessen anyone else getting any punishment that was my creation, and I hate it when I break down or give way for the same reasons. I have known for years I am not mentally strong when faced with some direct opposition of some kind with Men, my eyes swelled and I was soon crushed into a weeping mess, nothing much has changed.

Soon we arrived in what we knew as was one of the basic whipping rooms. Master Musson spoke saying "I want slave Aureus secured as standard, as she is still weak and the chains need to aid her support. Niobi Sir you might as well apply the same to Istra and we shall have Balance I believe someone said," he remarked smiling, "Yes Sir!" Niobi replied.

I had the odd feeling that we had been set up as Master and the Men seem to be enjoying themselves. Then Master Robert appeared and I always liked to see him, no sooner had he cleared the door opening he air cracked his bullwhip to wake us all up I should think. Then the Doctor appeared followed by his two paramedics and the white trolley.

This was leading into the realms of an isolated punishment program for just Istra and me. I believe a part of me slipped out of our established mental control that took me a lot of pain both mentally and physically and so I realized I must learn control. The Doctor appeared in front of me and the proceeded to wrap a bandage around my waist and eventually down to my left leg and thus covering up that awful looking Femoral Bandage. I guess he did not want me leaking the red stuff all over Masters Floors again. He then spoke "That ought to stop any further mess to either the room or the Masters property Master Robert Sir?" "Yes I just hope I can ignore it as a target Doctor Sir!"

Then Ahmed attending to me and Niobi attending to Istra led me over to one side of this large room and Istra went to the other side, it was then I noticed an inverted T frame being electrically lowered both in front of me and Istra. It was two metal poles the lower one was welded in the middle to create the top Tee piece but upside down with eye hooks or bolts at each end and one in the middle to give a variety of options.

Ahmed used three climbers cleats to clip my wrist chains at either end and took the slack out of the middle of the wrist to wrist chains as Master Musson had ordered and then the whole thing was raised a little and this time I was allowed my whole foot to be on the floor, rather than just the ball of my foot. Obviously they wanted me to avoid stretching the femoral wound, then I realized that I was facing a black curtain about four feet in front of me, because my eyesight is not very good without my glasses or contacts the room just appeared to be a black walled room.

Then the curtain was opened and behind the curtain was a huge Mirror that enabled me to see Istra's back profile and then it was explained to me that Istra had such a mirror to see my back as well.

Then Master Robert Spoke again "Just so you twos are not lonely the other 4 Musson slaves will sit in," "Each side of the room if you please Carrier Gentlemen Guards" "plus of course ourselves!" Meaning the rest of the Men as the Trainers, the Guards, and the Doctor

"Time is a wasting" Master Robert said loudly as he air cracked his bullwhip creating such a noise I actually felt a slight draft from it, not realizing that I had not noticed that before.

Master Robert wasted no more time and within seconds of hearing his air crack, I felt that very distinctive pain up my spine like that zipper was back and on his backwards thrust I heard it land elsewhere which was sure to be Istra's back, Like when I was placed in front of the inverted T frame I instinctively spread my legs and most of the time I close my eyes instinctively as I prefer not to see others whipped.

Master Robert like to play a bit and would try to effect "Tic Tac Toe" on our backs and tell us what he was doing, possibly as one pain would bleed into another, I would never have guessed what he was doing, just trying to control the pain is work enough for me to be doing.

Istra and the others were far better at this than I. Then to see if I was awake he would wrap the whip around my middle and in this one expects the pain to be in a specific area but it depends on how much of the belly of the whip lands on ones body causing me a sharp intake of breath, Then he did the same to Istra as I heard her do a sharp intake of breath too.

Then Master Robert quickened the pace which makes it difficult to keep on top and as I have go into fast deeper breaths I could hear the jangling of the other Musson slaves airing their thoughts which made me smile but also caused me to choke a bit and clearly Master Robert realized I needed a moment to compose myself so he did the same to Istra

Suddenly Master Musson appeared with two more Guards and they each had a box each and suddenly I was filled with dread because we have had the pleasure of Masters Electrodes. Master Musson spoke "We all have to go to Canada on a business trip in the next few days, so I want the training program to be more full filling" he said smiling at the same time. "Here Master Niobi Sir you know how to fit this, I just know how to work them" and with that Niobi approached me and run his fingers in my vaginal area "She soaking wet again!" good I thought might save him using his spit again Yuck I thought I hate Men that spit.

For the first time it slopped into my vagina without Niobi's aid, however Istra was not wet and needed his aid, and then a mount of some type was fitted underneath and slipped into a hole in the floor I did not see earlier. Now I was dreading this. Then Niobi pulled up two ring loops out of the floor close to my ankles and used a climbers cleat to attach my ankle to ankle chains to each side to stop me jumping I guess, I have learned not to close my legs to these guys.

Master Musson spoke to Master Robert "Master Robert Sir I would like for you to look after slave Istra as I really need to spend more time with slave Aureus as she is new to my family, "No problem Master Musson Sir, I fully understand." And with that Master Musson air cracked his bullwhip then he said "Niobi bring the music volume up as with us both using whips the sounds will lessen." "Yes Sir" Niobi said. And before I could think about it there was that pain across my shoulders left side first and then the right followed very quickly and Master Musson wasted no time in laying it on every which way, across my breasts and my belly, the pain level was so high I had not realized the electrode was working below, they had a way to make it seem as though it was goining in and out but somehow it was the voltage that must have been moving and now I was pulling on all the chains to solid connections to try to help me get through this. It was not long before the tears slipped out. I promised myself I would try very hard to avoid this, but I was tired and

Slipping back into my other self when suddenly there was a lot of noise emulating from the other Musson Slaves and then I felt a presence behind me sheltering me from the lashes to my back and I knew it was slave Volga from Russia because she whispered something in my ears that I knew was not any other language and then in her broken English she said "Now we do not want snot all over Masters floor." Master Musson had continued to whip my front and Volga's back when there was another jangling of chains and in the mirror I saw slave Arabela from Saudi Arabia standing behind slave Istra and with that Master Musson stopped and said "Well are you last two going to join us?" and with that a doubling jangling of chains was heard as the other two Slave Zaire from Africa stood behind slave Volga and slave Mista from Canada stood behind slave Arabela and both Master Musson and Robert carried on for a while. Though my whip impacts had lessened the shocks had increased and then strangely slave Volga put her arms around my waist as much as her wrist to wrist chains would allow, at which point I must have passed out.

The whole session then came to an end as I came to on a stretcher on the floor. Then the Doctor was kneeling beside me with his stethoscope and said "it seems slave Volga's wrist chains somehow made contact with the electrode in you and something blew is all I know." In a panic I asked "Is slave Volga alright?" "Yes she's ok; it shorted or blew through you, so you're in my parlor for tonight again." The doctor said smiling.

Two guards picked up my stretcher and we off to the medical wing and it was not too far away as we arrived I could see all the others having their bodies coated in the stingy smelly Iodine and clean tabards placed on them to keep their wounds clean and then I had to stand as it was my turn to be coated in stingy smelly iodine, not sure which was worse the whipping or the iodine stings and then the tabard was on and I had to stay in the medical room, thinking I was going to be all alone when orders came over the phone for Istra to stay with me.

Istra soon returned in the arms of Matt, not seem him in a while and then after leaving Istra with me and the Doctor Matt disappeared, The Doctor said "Not to worry I am acting Guard tonight as all the Men are to and from to the airport loading the aircraft with product." From those times we underwent training in the warehouse all amongst the boxes with Ordinance marked on them so we all knew what Product was in the packing cases and boxes.

"Also the Master is leaving a small security staff here as we are all going again so he wants to take much equipment so it will be no holiday for you my dears," Then the Doctor added "Istra knows what the Master is about. In some ways you have an advantage, but only because he likes to do what he does and you 6 can seemingly handle it, he was planning on 12, but someone stopped it."

Istra and I found each others hand through the lower bed bars on the side of the medical beds and we hung on tight whereupon I drifted off into my usual sleep escape.

SEQUENCE 14

I awoke to presence of the good Doctor checking my pulse and listening to my chest with his stethoscope, Istra was sitting on the edge of her bed with her legs and chains dangling in the breeze as it were. I was as stiff as a board, "What's wrong Doctor I am as stiff as a board" "You need more rest; you will have to remain here." "Now before I forget the Master wants you on the pill and you will be issued one a day at breakfast time like the others." The Doctor said and then added.

"In fact my dear I fear you and I will be spending a lot of time together as the Master plans to re-break again, its for your own good and safety because of the Colonel." "If he got you away from us and into one of his whore houses you will not live long, I am sorry my dear I know it's not what the Master had planned or hoped for." The doctor said in a saddened way.

"Doctor I need to have a wee, so can I have a bed pan or be allowed to get up and use the toilet?" then the Doctor replied "No you are to stay in bed until the Master says you can leave it so it's a bed pan that you now need to conquer" Then the Doctor slipped the bed pan onto my bed so I could get it positioned in the right way as I would hate to wet the bed as that is bound to be punishable even for a poorly slave.

"Tomorrow we shall all be off to the USA and Canada. Now it all begins this afternoon so rest as much as you can." The Doctor said.

Because the Doctor is a Male, I knew I was allowed to speak plainly to him as he needs to have the correct information to preserve our health plus I can ask questions ask questions, but always in a respectful manner. Even the Guards are addressed as Sir." So I just had to lay there in the hospital bed bored stupid. Just hope I can be well enough to get out of here and back to my cell with my cell mate slave Istra.

I did not have to wait long before Ahmed appeared at the door and in his usual fashion waving his left hand in a sort of get up motion as he began to lower the bed side panel so I could swing my legs out to the right and then he indicated to me to put my right arm over his head so my wrist to wrist chains would be on his right side as he then lifted me from the bed into his arms. These guys had got this maneuvering down to a fine art; my feet clearly did not touch the floor. Then we was off down the long corridors passing different rooms as we went and eventually to the door that inter connected with the warehouse, so now I knew we was going to play with the ammunition. It kind of scared me in case something would go off with the static electrics a singletail can produce. I would loose a leg or something or end up a vegetable.

Niobi placed me down on the platform and immediately removed my stained tabard whilst Ahmed connected the ends of the chain between my ankles so as to keep my legs spread even though we know not ever to close them. Then Ahmed lowered the chain that had a spreader bar at the bottom and in the same way my wrist were clipped with those climber cleat to link my wrist to wrist chains to the bar end loops, again to keep our arms spread though we would not close them either because another girl would then be punished for my errors. Then that was raised just enough to have our body at someone's control. The Doctor then re-appeared in front of us and placed a bandage over the femoral plaster and wrapped the bandage ends around my waist as tight as possible. I thought that this must look odd but that was the Doctors job.

There was bright sunlight poking through the roof skylights way above us and it was not long because someone air cracked a bullwhip and I knew what ever was to happen was not very far away. I prayed to whom ever not to let me fuck up as I did not want others to suffer at my expense, even though they were more experienced at this than I. Then it hit that burning sensation as the whip seem to diagonally from my right shoulder to my lower left side, but then the next lash was in the reverse direction, left shoulder to my lower right and because impacts were of a thuddery nature I realized whom ever was using a thicker and longer whip. Then they were up and down each leg and then back to my back. Strangely the pain seemed bearable or my mind was lost somewhere until one came up through my legs and landed on my front belly with such a sting it made me jump a little bit. It was then now I am thinking I need to find some thing to distract my mind to like a screw to undo mentally as then the pace quickened and I heard a voice saying "come on Aureus you should be used to some of this by now," Then a Master I had never seen before

Stood in front of me with his back to the wall and he air cracked a shorter slimmer whip and then I felt that pain across my breast and my belly, then he was attacking the fronts of my legs and it was soon apparent that I was leaking the red stuff from the various wounds and I thought how can I be to blame for messing Masters stage floor as they caused it to happen. It was then that I realized I was actually on my own; there was not sign of Istra and the others. At which point both the operator behind me joined in again and then both increased the pace and it became so bad the pain was almost constant and I knew was getting weepy as I was get close to some kind of limit, at the same time I was wondering just how come I managed to cope with that amount of pain without tears or noise, then the pace quickened even more and when I did look with weepy wet eyes the blood on the floor was more pronounced that it was then the Master stopped the session.

As did the rear operator whom ever that was. And then I flopped into the chains as if I had passed out though it was really tiredness. The Master then said "ok Doctor use the Iodine and replace a fresh tabard and one of the Guards will take her back to the medical wing and watch her Doctor!"

Upon arrival back the medical room, I could see someone in the first bed where I was last night and as we got into room more squarely I could see it was Istra and I could see she had been to a routine training program, I forgot nothing stops here. The Guard a guy I had not seen before did the reverse of Niobi's action earlier and thus placed me on the second bed of the 6 beds, then he put the side bars up and left.

I heard Istra's jangling chains as she reached for the separation curtain and pulled it back, and she whispered I heard you stood up to it again? I replied "What do you mean?" "It looks like you are fighting it again," "No I was seemingly able to handle it though I do not know how, but my brain seems to have changed and this may sound strange I liked some of it or what I thought would please Master," "That's not the impression I got?" "Are you mad at me or something?" "No! Course not silly" Istra exclaimed almost on the point of being commanding vocally.

"Then you must be acclimatizing faster than they thought you would?" Istra said, "Is that good or bad"? I asked. I am not sure" Istra said "We have not seen this before all the others broke easily and only needed to be broke once, though you are something new, but then we know now you have masochistic tendencies!" "Who" I asked "who is masochist" I repeated. "It's a term for someone that is sexually stimulated by pain" Istra said, "Well that's NOT me I hate toothache and the dentists" I added hurriedly. "Ok" Istra said "now put your fingers down between your legs, if you are turned on you will be wet, if not bone dry." I did as she said and in a state of frightened concern I said "Good Lord you're right!" "So now I am a pervert as well?" "No silly its humanity some people are some are not, it's something I think the Master wants in all of us."

Then Istra like she would often do touched and held my right hand and said "you know Master is not all bad, in his way he cares, not like the Colonel, you've not had a long session with him so you do not know him like we all do" "your wrong he beat the crap out of me literally until the Doctor appeared and stopped the session" I said feeling a bit queasy. "Doctor I feel sick can I have a bowl please" I said and thinking its bad enough with the damn femoral artery injury, and the shits now I feel sick. With so many medical difficulties I feel useless and yuck inside.

"We better check this Istra said" "tell me more of how that session started she added" "I can't remember every bit just that a Guard and the Colonel appeared, the Guard said something to Master Robert and the Doctor and they both left me with the Colonel, even had his own bullwhip in a bag, and I think he went nuts as if in a frenzy and I passed out, I vaguely remember seeing the Doctor in his white coat in one of his panic states and he told the Guard to escort the Colonel off the premises and passed out again." "Yes Istra said now you mention it I do vaguely remember something on those lines but that was ages ago." Then to my surprise Istra shouted "Guard where the Doctor is? Guard," then a Guard stepped into the room and said in a low voice "he left, now be quiet or will have to report you!" then again in a loud voice she said "Good now go get Master Niobi we may have a breach of security and if want to live you best do it!" she said, I just wanted to hide under the sheet, now I was terrified I had not seen this in very obedient Istra then she said what are you doing "hiding" I said in a wimpish way, please Istra I don't want any more trouble," "this is important if there is a spy here Master needs to know quick and the only way is to get Master Niobi here." "He won't come he hates my guts for being British you know that, like I done him some evil deed." At which point Master Niobi passed through the door curtain which caused me to shudder like he had caught me doing some prank at school. In his broken English he said "what's all the noise about I need rest as do you twos!"

Then Istra spoke "Master Niobi Sir I think we may have a spy in the compound that is one of the Colonel Men." "EXPLAIN!" he said loudly and so Istra went through it all while I just wanted to die or do sleep escape and then Master Niobi said "Aureus identify this Guard what he look like!!" he spoke it loudly with an emphatically presence as if truly important. Then whilst in a state of fear and trembling as to speak of a Male and that of a Guard was not considered safe, "well Sir all I can recall was that he had a big black mole on his left cheek," using my left hand and fore finger to indicate my left cheek, then Master Niobi spoke again "yes I know the one, GUARD GET IN HERE" he said in a loud voice, the Guard outside the medical wing stepped in through the door curtain and stood there facing Master Niobi with almost the same fear as I was in. Master Niobi spoke in his own Arabic tongue and then the Guard disappeared.

Within some minutes Master Musson in his posh dressing gown appeared along with the Doctor whom had also slipped off to bed and was in his dressing gown as well.

Master Musson then spoke in his broken English "is this a private party or can anyone join in?" then Master Niobi spoke to Master Musson in their Arabic native language. Then he turned to Istra "are you sure about this?" "Yes Master and the Doctor should be able to verify it?"

"Master there was also a Master or Male that I had never seen before and I think it was the Colonel whipping my back while the other was working on my front, sorry Master" "You have no need to be sorry Slave Aureus, you cannot be responsible these incursions, it is up to us to improve security and put a stop to all this, now I can see by the state Your body is in that a non professional has had some attempt to whip you and damage my property Musson slave Aureus" Master Musson said in an angry tone.

Then Master Musson turns to the Doctor says "is this true Doctor? Did the Colonel plus a Male posing as a Master get in against my specific orders?" "Yes Sir" he said reluctantly, "I assumed that you had allowed some special arrangement, it was on my return after we had a message to come see you but Master Robert and I could not find you, Master Robert assumed the Guard had returned slave Aureus to either her cell or the medical wing." Then Master Musson said something in Arabic loudly and then in his broken English "it gets worse" he said and added "I can not trust my own staff to keep that Man out of here. Doctor is slave Aureus fit to travel?" "Yes Sir but she will need to spend time in the aircraft medical wing." Then Master Musson added "OK Doctor keep slave Istra and slave Aureus together, Master Niobi Sir Do not separate them and bring Ahmed into a closer Guarding duty for the flight." "Come Master Niobi Sir we have work to do wake up all the trainers and my personal security staff we need to talk!"

"Yes Sir, but I must report that slave Istra did shout at a Guard to fetch me and it's an offence!" "Yes it is Master Niobi Sir" Master Musson said and then added "leave that one to me I will think of something!" and then they left together leaving the Doctor with us. Then the Doctor said "You two best get some rest I am sure you will need it" "Doctor I need a wee and possibly a pooh," "Yes me as well Doctor!" "Ok then hop into the toilet in there pointing to where is cubical office was and there was a toilet behind that. We took turns on the toilet to clear our system as tomorrow looked like it could be busy. Then the Doctor called in the Guard from outside the door and said "Go get another Guard and return quickly!" A few moments later two Guards returned and the Doctor said "Return these two to their cell I have to get all the medical gear together that I might need on the aircraft tomorrow before I can return to bed, so only needs me to lose a bit of sleep and them two needs more rest than they will get if they stay here and then Guard them until you are relieved." "Yes Sir Doctor one of the Guards replied!"

SEQUENCE 15

I awoke to the sounds of a lot of rustling about and when I got my eyes open sure enough it was the Domestics crew here to give us our daily bucket bath and brush our long hair, then braid it.

"Come along you two Lets get a wiggle on You know the Master does not like to be hanging about on flight days, both aircraft are being fuelled and loaded with provisions as I speak!" "Both? I said quietly"

"Yes! Yes after some event last night Master thought better to move the whole operation to another location so his second aircraft a 747 cargo converted aircraft was made ready and the Men have been working through the night to get everything on board and I mean everything so will a be a whole new start for us all, Now enough chatter lets you two sorted!"

As usual I needed a wee first thing in the mornings, so I said "I need to wee, can I do that while you are getting started with Istra?" "Sure" said the team leader. So I got myself up and hobbled over to the hole and managed to do a wee and then hobbled back to the area the Domestics use to bath us which had a drain channel that took any spill's to the hole in the ground.

It had not sunk in yet that I was just getting used to this place as home and now we was off to find a new one. After the Domestics had done their bit and all vanished. Then Masters Ahmed and Niobi appeared and as usual gesturing for us to place our wrist to wrist chains over their heads to they could pick us up and carry us of to an area I had not seen before, then they put us down on the floor and disappeared out of this room. However it might be a reception area for the Masters business I thought as there were fixed seating to one wall and a sort of counter across the room with windows on one side but the room which looked like it had a dropped ceiling. Looking out of the windows I am sure the room was within the warehouse which was now empty and then I see a lot of Men carrying what looked like the medical wing contents to a van. When the Men stopped flowing passed the window, Masters Ahmed and Niobi was back and as usual they indicated they wanted us in the position to be picked up. Then we was carried to the large Limo that we always traveled in, plus then the usual song and dance as we had to wriggle around to the seats that backed onto the driver, Then Master Musson stepped in, with his full Arabic head dress plus a sort of cloak I think, however Master Niobi was in his work wear as was Master Ahmed so they must have been helping with the moving of equipment and stores.

Then as one of his personal security Men approach the back of the car then said in his broken English "The compound is completely empty and everything will be aboard both aircraft for when you get there Sir. My men will follow shortly after we have secured the compound Sir!" Then Master Musson replied in Arabic something as he closed his window and Master Niobi then closed his door. Master Ahmed then got in the front passenger seat and closed his door as the driver started the car and we pulled away.

In a weird way I was sad to leave the compound and I could see Istra was weeping so risking all I held her right hand with my left and kind of snuggled up to her so we was actually touching. Thinking to myself "to hell with it" if I get into trouble for this blatant show of affection.

However the Men seemed to ignore it so maybe it was understood.

The dawn was glinting on the distant horizon as we entered the airport and there was just Masters two aircraft stood there with loads of security guys on the ground and those trucks that act as generators to keep the aircraft electrics, fans or heater running prior to take off.

The driver headed for the rear of Masters Giant DC10 rear garaging ramp and doors, then without hesitation drove up into the usual spot that Master's car would get its bondage to the aircraft floor. It was very quick that Master Musson was out of his door and disappeared in the aircraft main area while Ahmed and Niobi got Istra and me out of the car and carried us to our usual areas at the back end of the aircraft.

I heard Niobi say something to Ahmed about waiting for the security Men that sealed up Masters Compound, and then sure enough was the sound of clatter bang as two more cars mounted the rear ramp and entered the garage area, followed by the loud clump noise of the ramp being raised to its closed position.

Then there was a rumbling of what I thought was a herd of elephants but it must be the ground crews with their jack boots or whatever they wear coming up the staircases. Soon after the engines fired up one after the other and the staircases were raised to a clunking sound as they completed their travel up into the aircraft. As The security guys now acting as guarding assistants checked all our sear belts were secured and as I looked right I could see all 6 of us were here in our usual paired states. Then we hear the Captain of the aircraft say "Please buckle up your seat belts and extinguish all naked flames and stop smoking!" I thought he sounded just like an American, not heard him before. Then the aircraft was hurtling down the runway and gently lifted into the air and we was off, the aircraft was in climbing mode for quite a longer time that I thought was normal and Istra whispered too me "it must be as Master does not want to risk us being shot at by the Colonel that we have made a steeper long climb out of the airport" "oh shit! I had not thought about him!" I said.

Soon the seat belt free sign was flashing and the Domestics was busy getting the breakfast for everyone and many of the Men seem to be circulating freely.

Then Master Musson approached and said "Istra

and Aureus after you have had your breakfast I want you two to go and rest on the bed in the bed tent" as he pointed to the black curtained tent that covered the middle section of the aircraft and almost in unison Istra and I replied "Yes Master!"

I was not sure why because we had both slept well back in our cell, then I remembered the Doctor saying I shall need more rest in the Aircrafts medical wing if they even have one I thought.

Soon the porridge and milk drink arrived on the little trays from the Domestics also wearing their tabards as well, I was not sure now what went before, but something was nagging at me that something was different and then by sheer accident I saw the changes Mrs. Musson wife no. 1 was on board, but in the front section and it was a chance fleeting few seconds while one of the Domestics held the partition door open that I saw her walk passed the open doorway. I thought yes I might felt awkward to see Mrs. Musson naked like us, so its probable there is an understanding that when she is faced with the inevitable that we are to wear the Tabards and I thought "yes that makes perfect sense" Then Istra broke my train of thought "Come on Aureus lets clean up and go rest" "Yes ok I am coming" then hobbling to our back left where there was a toilet and wash room so we could wash our faces and clean our teeth which I still find difficult in these damn heavy chains I was thinking.

Then as Istra opened the washroom door in plain view was Matt one of Master Mussons security Guards more like his personal minder. "Hi Istra and Aureus I have to make sure you get to the new medical area as the Captain says we might enter into some turbulence and we do not want Aureus to become unduly hurt" he said with a boyish smirk I thought. So with Matt between Istra and me we hobble up the aircraft body to the middle section which has this solid wall across the whole body of the aircraft with doors to the front section on either side and in the middle is a huge black curtain that is like a large U shape I guess but big enough to have beds within it, or that's how it was before. But as we go through the curtain on the starboard or right side of the aircraft they have changed it to have two medical beds and a two double normal type beds. Then Matt spoke again "slave aureus will be in one of the medical beds and Istra you can rest in one of the double beds for now. Who ever is chosen to be Aureus punishment slave will invariably be in the other medical bed, who knows you may all take a turn in it." he said smiling as he helped me into one of the medical beds that I could sense was secured to the aircraft floor but with I think some suspension maybe for the turbulence I thought, then he pulled the side bars up so I do not fall out as I was higher than the double beds. Istra laid on the one closest to me as then Matt left and one of the Domestics came in, one that I come to know she was like the leader or top Domestic that all the others followed her lead. She then lay down on the farthest double bed towards the starboard side of the aircraft and she spoke.

"Well Istra are you going to tell her or shall I,"

"Tell her what Dakota? Istra said in a negative fashion or a disgruntled mood. "Whose Dakota I asked?" "Our lead Domestic is known as Dakota!" Istra said and then added. "I thought I mentioned this before Aureus that everyone here adopted a different name and identity like we changed your hair color to blonde like me because Master prefers blondes where possible. There are no mirrors so you can not recognize yourself and it's the same for the Domestics they all have different names and looks" Then Dakota spoke again even the Master is operating on a different name, I know its not his real name because he is a Bedouin Prince of some Royal blood or other, but who I do not know." Then she added "You hear that noise they are turning the back end into a torture chamber just for you Aureus," trying to be strong I said "I should be so lucky." Then Istra butted in "Ok Dakota you know so much why she should be so lucky?" "Well its simple really since the Master found out that the Colonel had a unscheduled session with slave Aureus he now does not know if she has been compromised by him, some of the our earlier Domestics were compromised by the Colonel and when they were supposed to fly back to the USA they went to the Colonels palace and never seen again." "Oh I understand now!" Istra said and added "have you been given authority to disclose this information to us?" then Dakota stood up very quickly and said "No" in a sheepish way, "You- you won't tell will you she enquired. Istra stood up and said as loudly as she dared "I shall have to think about that now get out as I have to prepare Aureus." Then Istra turned towards me and said "I am sorry you had to find out like this I had an idea something like this might be afoot and I hate to tell you Master will be very nasty like he was in the beginning, its partly because he is hurting inside, which is not your fault it is just what it is and the position we find ourselves in. Also I suspect all and every Male that can fly a singletails will be having a go as he needs to speed this up and I suspect we will all be in it and all be messing up the floor." "Now Aureus try and sleep some as you will need all the rest you can get Istra said in a softly way.

Then Niobi poked his head in through the curtain and Istra turned to him and dropped to her kneeling position and said quietly "Sir may I speak?" Niobi replied "yes within proper limits you know the rules" "is this really necessary it's not Aureus fault like any of us we could not have stopped the Colonel." She said quietly Then Niobi replied "Yes I know but that little bit of doubt has crept in there and we all knew the Master was going for a second break to deepen the first to convince the Colonel that Aureus is not for sale at any price. As you know the Master stumbled onto slave Aureus by accident because she was meant to undergo training for that Man she was with, the Colonels pal. When that guy Peter something took the money the Master offered she was doomed to join your merry gang, Now Istra enough or you'll be alongside her." At which point I sat up and said loudly "Stop Istra leave it!" Then Niobi said "Now you've set her off, now I will have to report this chat to the Master and then we shall see how you discovered the plan?" Then I rolled over facing a ways from them both and closed my eyes and thought I need long term sleep escape.

SEQUENCE 16

THE BREAKING OF SLAVE AUREUS

SECOND ATTEMPT

When I awoke the Doctor was there with his stethoscope and listening to my heart beat race I shouldn't wonder, then the Doctor said "Here is the bed pan as you usually need it when you are staying in my place, better to have it before the girls give you your bucket bath." The Doctor then turned to the Domestic girls saying "Ok she's yours to clean up, fetch some water one of you she's a bit dehydrated." And the Doctor left so the girls could get stuck into giving me a bucket bath which was refreshing. At home I always tried to do a wee and a pooh. Then have my daily shower or bath to start the day clean and fresh. So the same here I would try my best as I could do under the circumstances always to start the day clean and fresh. Do those bodily functions before the bucket bath to at least start whatever was to come fresh and clean. Istra was not in sight and I was not looking forward to the forthcoming evening and on board an aircraft I thought that has to be a first, trying to bump up my humor I was thinking I am sure British Airways would not do this a as an adventure tour. When the Domestic returned with a jug of water and a cup I thought again I am sure I do not want all that. Then she gave me a metal cup as usual and filled it to the brim which I did not hang about I drunk it pretty quickly thinking all I need now are a couple of cyanide pills to swallow with the water.

I then wondered if this was a standing order 4 situation and could I do something on those lines because frankly I was now shit scared and then Master Musson seemingly charged through the curtains indicating with his hands that he was going to pick me up and carry me to where ever. I thought he's never done that before, so we are honored, as we left the confines of the medical area. I could see they had transformed the rear of the aircraft into some kind of dungeon in the air, it was dark apart from lights shinning on to an area where a hook plus what looked like a trapeze bar was hanging but it was not clear as we was too far away at that point then there was a crescendo of chains jangling that could only come from 5 Musson slaves that obviously wanted to vent their disapproval. Then the Domestics joined in by banging their metal cups against their metal wrist cuffs. All the Men stood up and indicated silence. I had not realized till then that there was no music playing in the aircraft, but at that point it began quite loud to cover the din of the slaves, trying to be brave. Then Master put me down and I turned to the audience with his right fore finger to his lips indicating to Sssh or quieten down.

Then Niobi attached them climbers spring loaded cleat type things to the last chain link in my wrist to wrist chains and secured it to each side of the trapeze bar. Naturally I had learned to always have my legs spread so all Ahmed had to do was clip in the cleats from the floor to the last chain link in each of my anklets so as I could not close my legs even if I dared to.

Then I saw on my right which was now the port side of the aircraft as I was facing to the back of the aircraft the trolley with all the singletail whips glinting in the dim light from the oiling they must have been preparing them with and now with a bit of wheel clank on my left the starboard side was the Doctors white trolley. Thinking they really have brought everything and then again trying to brighten my mood I am thinking who will bring in the kitchen sink.

Then Master Musson approached from behind and places my braided long hair over my left shoulder as he had done so many times before so I knew it was soon to begin and the pain will begin.

So I psyched myself up by starting some deep breathing exercises and somewhere in there Master air cracked his bullwhip and I knew within seconds the next would be on me somewhere and it landed right across my back from left to right and then the other way, as I am thinking yes he's doing Tic Tac Toe, though this is not the time for levity then I thought yes lets explore the aircraft see if we can mentally undo a few bolts or something, anything to create distraction although Master knows what I am doing and shit just when I was getting on top he catches me on the hip bone and for some unknown reason it really hurts there maybe because I am skinny.

Then he stops and I can hear him move closer and almost feel his presence behind me then he says "some water here now!" and then I hear another body close by and then Master says "Aureus drink" and I do and then says "Master Niobi Sir your turn!" and Master moves around from my right and forwards and then promptly leans up against the back wall of the aircraft and folds his arms and I assume to watch his fourth in command perform, Then a sting across my bottom tells me he's using a thinner whip which has a stinging effect and can be just as Painful as the thicker whips. Master Niobi usually likes what is known as good grouping and or symmetrical grouping, he was clearly going up and down my legs on both front and back and the more they stung increased the pain like a build up of intensity and then without warning the whip was through my legs and stung my belly with the tip but the body of the whip hurt me between my legs. This bought water to my eyes and I felt my nose start to fill with liquid and I could see it would not be long before we will be making a mess of Masters Floor. "Master please I need to wee!" "Then wee shall give you a bucket to save you messing up my floor!" "Thank you Master as a Guard just gets it in place from behind me but between my legs and the water gushes out of my water works.

After half filling the bucket with yellowish water, Master says "Doctor come get this checked it, a bit smelly and the Doctor carries the bucket away.

Then Master Niobi begins again and quickens the pace, I am not sure if I can still control this as I am pulling on my wrists and they cut in a bit because of the awkward angle. Then Master tells me "Musson slave Aureus I want you to turn and face Master Niobi!" "My feet are secured to the floor Master!" "She correct, Guard releases the cleats and when she turns clip them back in!" Then I am able to turn and now face up the aircraft though with my poor eyesight I can not see much, I sense the Guard replaces the cleats to keep my legs apart and he moves away. Now Master Niobi is all across my belly plus they really sting. Then Master Musson says loudly "Master Ahmed Sir gets over here!" Master Niobi stops. Thus giving me a breather as Master offers me some more water to drink. I can here a lot of moving about then the aircraft hits some turbulence but as I am chained up it has no effect on me just gives me a longer breather. I see Master change from his legs together stance to spreading his legs plus at the same time reaching to grab a handle grab a hold on to and stop his falling to the floor. But then our wondrous flight crew manages to get the aircraft back under control. Then Master Ahmed then air cracks his chosen whip and starts in on me and lands what I can only identify as a thick whip about 6 feet long, he's used that on me before. He knows I can handle that plus get on top of this thuddery pain of a thicker whip, although just when I think I have it in the bag he's attacking my breast and my belly, then he catches in my armpit and that really does hurt. This causes me to really pull on the bar above me thinking it might break and then I happened to glance down and I could see Masters Floor was already a bright shade of red and then I must have passed out through exhaustion.

When I came out of my unconscious state I was back in the medical bed smelling what must have been lashings of Iodine Masters favorite piece of medical equipment and with now a clean tabard on.

"Please may I have some water to drink?" "Sure" the Doctor replied and handed me a metal cup of water. It seemed that it was just me and the Doctor in this make shift medical unit and as I tried to look around I passed out again and dropped the cup spilling water everywhere.

When I awoke again the Doctor was fast asleep and so I just lay there thinking what was to come, next are we really going to feel the whip off every guy here that can fly one and then I had a flash back to one of the James bond films where that awful Spectre woman says "Training is useful but there nothing like experience" or something on those lines but in this situation who is getting what, is it for my benefit or theirs?

Then I heard a jangling of chains as Istra came through the black curtains that separated us from the rest of the aircraft and she lay on the bed closest to me and said "are you alright or as well as you can be" and I said "I don't know you will have to ask the Doctor when he wakes up," and then I said "so what has been happening since I passed out like a weak twat?" "No Aureus you did fine, you've not let any of us down, you handled 3 strong Men one after the other and must have took around 750 lashes, some of the girls was counting, you did fine!"

"So what else has been going on? I am sure you have not been waiting for me to wake up for whatever comes next?" "No but they discovered Dakota told us what was about to happen," "Did you tell on her?" "No! Someone did and she was offered an Administrative punishment or is fired when we reach the USA with no pay and she has accepted that." Istra said and then I replied "Silly girl we would have probably stepped in like before when it got too heavy and she must have known that, so maybe she must have not trusted us, what you think Istra?"

"I think you have figured her out she must have only been in it for the money without caring for anyone, we are better off without that type." Istra said.

"We land in about 3 hours so there will not be anymore training until we are on the ground, but then I can not say Aureus so you better get as much rest as you can." "Thanks I will are you staying?" "Yes I shall be here" "You do your sleep escape" she said smiling then I jumped up to a sitting position "How do you know that I do that?" "You talk in your sleep like a right old chatterbox." "Oh yes my mother said I did that when I was young, I was not sure I was still doing it." "Don't worry I do not think you have given any secrets away yet." She said smiling and then I lay down and dropped off into my sleep escape.

When I woke up again I knew we was on the ground, presumably in the USA. Then the Doctor popped through the curtain and said "ah good you are awake, the Domestics want to come in a clean you up and the usual bucket bath, are you ok for that." "Yes Doctor and I need a wee too as it happens."

Then the girls appeared through the curtain all carrying different things from a bucket of water to a bale of white Egyptian towels from others carrying the sponge and soap to the one carting the hairbrush and comb and its all for me, what have I done to deserve this lot and all that's to come and then the Domestic leader said "Come along Aureus lets get a wiggle on, I know there are plans afoot but that's all we know since the discovery of Dakotas treachery the Masters are keeping all the plans to themselves," "treachery? I was not aware of any such, thought she was in the dog house for leaking to Istra and me the plans of this thing they are on now." "Yes but she was also in cahoots with that Guard the one with the big mole on his face, its now thought they were both moles for the Colonel and Dakota was here when the Master first began this operation with his first Istra." "Good God Istra never said anything about this; she must also feel betrayed then, me I am the newcomer all you guys have had to put up with a fox in the henhouse so to speak."

I was impressed the way these girls would wash over my blood and yellow iodine body with such gentleness as if washing a new born baby, they went to great lengths to not to hurt me any more than the Men were doing and I was aware that many had endured some lesser aspects of the heavy training that Master Mussons personal pain slaves have to go through in training and other times. Then they were done or I was done after a good length of time cleaning me up. Then another couple of girls appeared through the curtain with my breakfast, the porridge and metal cup of milk.

Then I had need to go to the loo and started to head towards the only opening on the starboard side of the aircraft when I was met by Master Niobi "Where are you off to?" "The toilet Sir" I said quietly. Master Niobi thought for a moment and then said "is your need urgent?" "Yes Sir" "Well then you will have to wear a blindfold as we have guests and the Master prefers that you do not see them at this time!" "I am happy to comply Sir" and so Niobi put on a blindfold he happened to have in his trouser pocket and then he picked me up and off we went, I could hear voices and then Master Mussons voice "Where are you taking slave Aureus Master Niobi Sir?" and he replied "respectfully Sir to the toilet as she preferred not to mess on your floors!" and Master Mussons response was "Yes she very good at making messes on my floors and we do not have the time to do more cleaning, Carry on Master Niobi Sir!"

It all sounded a bit jovial which might have been for my benefit and as we entered the toilet and I sat on the toilet bowel in the aircraft which was a real bowel rather than a hole in the ground and I felt comfortable as my mind wandered off again thinking when all this happened I was so angry I could have burst a blood vessel and I was sure that helped me through the first breaking, now I do not have that anger and I can not seemingly able to get it, then it occurred to me that the anger might have kept me alive or have the ability to return after I was pronounced dead, so now if it goes that far maybe we will not escape and not return as we have no drive, no anger! "Are you done in there Aureus?" "Yes Sir just washing my hands Sir" and with that Niobi came through the curtain that allowed one some privacy, though it was more for those that were not naked and in chains methinks. Then Niobi picks me up and starts back up the aircraft when Master Musson spoke saying "Master Niobi Sir you may sit her over there on the long seat, but leave the blindfold on her, she looks quaint in it!"

"We are waiting for two greyhounds to take to another location so she may as well sit there for now!" Master Musson added I would know his voice anywhere I thought and then I felt a hand touch my right hand and another voice that I know to be friendly Istra, "I have missed you" then she said "I know but sometimes they will separate us especially after the last few days it all seems to be a mess, worse than what you do to Masters floors" she said and it sounded like she chuckled as I could not see if she smiled. "Istra why do we need a couple of dogs?" Istra replied "Dogs? What are you talking about?" "I just heard Master saying we was waiting for a couple of greyhounds and them is dogs" "oh I see where you is at, over here they are also buses or coaches, I imagine that at some time they must have been quick or something like that to get that name." "Silly me how stupid can I get." "No not in the least if you have not been to the USA before there are a lot of things you might not know and I know you have never been a slave before that messes Masters floors, but its not your fault and Aureus let me tell you.!" Istra's voice changed note to a serious side she rarely used except to get a point across and she said "I think we would all be amazed and think there was something wrong in your mentality if you did not make a mess on Master's floors with blood, tears and snot so you fill your boots!" I think that to mean carry on.

Istra spoke again saying "Aureus stand up as the Domestic girls want to change our tabards for the white ones" and I did gingerly as I could not see through the blindfold and did not want to land on my face.

Then I heard Master Niobi's voice saying "Master Musson Sir The transport has arrived and I have lined them up at the rear of the aircraft so that transfer can be simple." Then I heard Master Mussons voice saying "Masters Ahmed and Niobi pick up those two Masters Matt and Steven pick up the second pair and Masters Craig and Daniel pick up the third pair and lets roll."

Master Musson then added "Some of our security staff and the Domestics will join us in the second Greyhound bus, Master Robert and Lathander will bring the guests from the front section via the stairs and join us in our Greyhound bus leaving a security ground crew to monitor the safety of the aircraft!"

As with the UK trip where we got off the aircraft and had to board a bus still required our carriers to place our bare feet on the ground so that we could get into the bus in single file and like that night at Stanstead airport, UK. Though it was not cold here and again Istra then said "You better hold my hand so I can guide you to the seats at the back as the Men and the Guests will want to sit at the front." "Yes Istra I understand." "Are you alright Aureus you are trembling?" "Just scared" I replied. "Yes I know that one" Istra said.

I had no idea where we was going I knew it was daytime as I could feel the warmth of the sun coming through the windows, as I could not see I can not say if like the coaches that were used had tinted or darken windows, though from my limited experiences so far Master Musson seems to pull such clout that he seems to arrange for each country to use their security Men to act as security escorts sometimes even with the blue lights brigade or police if to be accurate. All this does all the time is to impregnate us with the realization that what has happened and is happening to me is for real. I think I know Master well enough to know even if I verbally submitted to him, his way and this life it would not be enough he needs my other self to act that out after again we shall be suffering at the hands of these guys. "Ouch!" "You ok Aureus?" Istra enquired in a quiet voice, "No stupid me just burned my crotch by dropping the chain into my lap and they slipped between my legs, the chains are hot from the sun I guess, not being able to see, I would usually let them dangle in front of my legs down there. The last time we was in a bus was late at night and in winter, and you did not warn me silly" "I am sorry Aureus I never thought about that we have never had that happen, at least none of the others have expressed it sure we have been on buses in day time and hotter countries than this, it is my fault I should have stopped you when I heard your chains come up from in front of your knees and I did hear and felt you alter your position, I never saw the consequences coming." "Hey Istra its no big thing, they used to just order me to close my eyes, has all that trust gone?" "Its probably because you would have to keep your eyes shut for so long and they figured you might slip and lose that control is the best I can come up with, whatever it is they do not want you to see is beyond me." Istra said quietly.

"Anyway it looks as though we are arriving, sorry I am not allowed saying more" Istra said quietly and squeezing my right hand at the same time. Again it flashed through my mind that Istra really does try to look after me, and when we get the chance of being closer so do the other 4 Musson slaves.

The Bus or coach has stopped methinks and am waiting for orders as if I am in the shit for faults that are not my doing, I should hate to discover what my own made incursions might be. As I can not see I dare not move for fear of hurting myself, though it felt drafty so I figured we must have open windows on the bus or coach. Then I heard Master Musson voice "Now my slaves whilst we are on our own, though I have included Master Niobi in our merry gang I have come to the conclusion that my drive in this enterprise is because you are all beautiful and thus distracting."

He paused and then said "To that end my Men and I believe that all females should be tortured and punished for the distracting you all do to us!" then Master Niobi jumps in with "you should all not be so pretty" he said. "Oh great I said quietly and I always thought I was ugly" Istra adds quietly "you are Aureus but I am uglier than you!" She said in a firm but quiet manner and I thought Ok I know where this is going. Then I heard what sounded like a lot of hob nailed boots climbing the short stairs up into the bus or coach and then Master Musson said "ok Guys each take a slave into the compound."

When we got inside the where ever place, Master Musson removed the blind fold, "You may open your eyes slave Aureus," he said as I opened my eyes to see Master in front of me and the room fairly dark, Master turns to his rear as if to communicate with troops behind him and saying "SEE! She knows to wait for orders to affect every move." Then he says quietly "does not stop what I have to do." And then he walked into the darkness. It was then I heard the jangling of my sister slave's chains as they were being placed in their positions as the musty room filled gently with the sound of background music as standard.

It was then that Niobi appeared out of the musty gloom in his traditional Arabic headdress plus his bare chest self and wearing black slacks and in a smooth action took hold of my wrists and linking chain that was in front of me as he lifted my hands and arms and as I raised my head a little I could see a motorized guy wire line descend with a climber cleat at its end. And with equal precision he connected me to the cleat and the motorized power of the overhead line raised my arms further upward as I felt my feet move the standing on the ball of each foot, but then a voice rang out "STOP!" "Back up I want her feet firmly on the ground!" I recognized Masters commanding voice and then he said jovially "we do not want a repeat of slave Aureus femoral plaster patch being stretched do we Doctor!" Then the Doctor appeared with a bandage to add support to the plaster wrapping the bandage around my waist then down through my legs and up covering the femoral plaster patch. The sounds of an auditorium just before lights went down and a sort of hurried rustling and the music got a bit louder and Master's voice breaking through "Come Doctor must she have all that there?" and the Doctor replied "err Yes Sir! If you want the patch to not come off and leak on your nice clean floor Sir! "Get out of there Doctor!" Master said in annoyed fashion. As the doctor disappeared I heard the wheels of the whip trolley approach followed by the Doctors white trolley and two handsome paramedics pushing the damn thing. I knew we had been here before even though we were in another country.

Then Master approached and said "I ordered you to rebel slave Aureus and you are not" then he added

Master Niobi Sir bring slave Istra out here! Now! At which point I responded saying "AS YOU WISH MY LORD! FUCK OFF THE REST OF YOU! Master wants to play!"

"I like it Master Niobi Sir she has hidden depths yet!" and at the same time the slave sisters began jangling their chains in protest. "QUIET! Or you'll all be strung up!" Niobi approached me and said "Lord eh? You never honor me with that, you may regret that!" I said tongue in check but you are not My Master! Niobi Sir! As he walked away I could see for some strange reason I felt sure he had been hurt by this and I was about to be hurt.

Then Master said "Wait Master Niobi Sir, lets have slave Volga out here, lets see how deep this sisterly slave affection goes!" at which time Istra Was taken off into the darkness and slave Volga appeared and taken directly opposite me with clearance enough for them to fly their whips at both without actual whip contact with another whip.

Master approached slave Volga and said "You will not mind stepping in for slave Istra. Her cell mate!" As he turned to face me Volga said "NO MY LORD!" in a good clear voice and then she smiled at me as Master then said "Ahh we have the balance back in play, slave Aureus likes Balance don't you slave Aureus!" "Yes My lord" I said not so loud and at which time and unexpected impact landed diagonally across my back and stung in a way I felt sure I did not know the operator. "Hold it Operator Sir she is not ready yet!"

Master Musson said in a loud voice and then a voice I had not heard, at least not at this pitch and level that said "Don't you dare look around slave Aureus!" where have I heard that voice before and then I wondered if that was the voice they all wanted for me not to see, hence the blind fold. At the same time Niobi appeared with a something I knew I was not going to like another of his damned electrodes. "Well at least you are bit wet slave Aureus; it will save me some of my valuable spit!" Niobi said and I said in response "must you do that Sir it makes me feel sick!" and then "oooow!" I muttered as it slipped into my vagina. "But that's not all slave Aureus "Niobi said as he made that noise to bring spit to the fore and then "oooow!" good God Man not in my arse as well "This is the negative return my dear you have not had this yet" Niobi said in a sort of gleeful happy state! I could now feel both and they felt so close together I was shit scared, I went to try to expel the anal probe but it would not move. I could see slave Volga say something, but she was too far away with the music to hear properly, though I did hear Master Musson say "If you do not keep quite you can have one too!" "Its her own fault, she not rebelling enough, if I have to slave Aureus I will have them all out here if you do not do what I commanded." And with that I shouted "YES MY LORD AND MASTER FUCK YOU!" then Master Musson spoke "see she can do it when she wants to and then I can do this!" and then "Jesus Christ what the fuck was that!" I said loudly as I pulled on the chains and lifting my legs clear off the floor, just hanging by my wrist which was also hurting as not designed for this as the overhead line is a stabilizer, but I was using it as a reaction response as the shock went from my vagina to my arse and I was sure it was all on fire. "I could hear Niobi giggling like a school girl and thought stupidly by saying it "I hear you giggling like a school girl Niobi Sir which brought on a second shock. The second shock had the same effect; my feet cleared the floor as I pulled on the overhead linkage. The Doctor then in his often worried mentality said "Sir is that overhead cable strong enough to take her full weight, I thought it was a stabilizer drop line?!" Master Musson rushed forward saying "Yes the Doctor is right Master Niobi Sir Lower a second line, lets be sure we do not have a disaster. Then the voice behind me said "surely Sir she's a slave does it matter if she falls?" then I remembered it was that posh voice I had heard before, I wonder who the hell he is, I thought "No Sir! slave Aureus is worth a least $2 million dollars as she is, you can not buy the state of mind she has, all my slaves have it and here we push it to a perfection you will not find anywhere else Sir!"

"I thought you knew that is why you have that gadget in your ears so you are not brain washed as well, but we are building all the time on their brain washed state to be the best pain slaves possible, our friend Lathander is trying to nurture them to become Masochistic Nymphomaniacs, that is why the Colonel wants them especially young Aureus there! Sir"

"Ahh now I understand Sir" the posh voice

exclaimed like he had a light bulb moment in his head when it all became clear.

"The best is to come when we use the bullwhips as well as the electrics Sir!" Master Musson said in a commanding fashion, as if God.

Then Master Musson said in his Arabic broken English "Quiet now please! Gentlemen what we are about to do is not playing games and if you feel ill or you have no stomach for it my Guards will escort you to an anti room or the medical room for which ever is your greater need!"

"Let's Go Niobi Sir!" "Yes Sir" and then it began with the first few lashes may have been to warm us up, mostly on my back and legs the occasional ones on my hips which always stung and as I twitched so I felt the burning electric and when I went to pull on the supporting links above, it seems in the confusion someone had clipped my ankles to floor linkages and so I could not react. At which point I heard Niobi laugh and then the attack from the front and a shot from inside felt like it was burning my insides out an soon I was confused as to which was more painful, then they increased the speed at which point I know I was dripping snot and leaking blood but it no longer mattered. Then suddenly the body shot bolt upright as if to stand to attention but failed. Suddenly the electrical intensity had increased dramatically without warning, it was too much for me and I must have passed out, though Ms6 tried to come into her own but failed as I saw a glimmer of the scene from a different angle but then blackness fell all about. I could hear the other girls jangling their chains in the background as I/we began to regain consciousness.

Then on my left I saw the Doctor but I could not communicate, he then looked up and I could see Master Musson come into what I now realized was the medical room and he spoke "Will she be alright Doctor?" "She got a nasty jolt from the electro device, I am not sure what happened to be sure" the Doctor exclaimed. "Some one increased the settings without authority, which means we have a traitor in our midst, better give her a shot and sleep Doctor!" "Yes Sir" replied the doctor.

I was later told by Istra what happened and Ms6 tried to stand in but it became too much then our body slumped on the chains and the Doctor stopped it. Several of the Domestics were also violently ill and a couple of his Masters guests but not sure who.

Then the Doctor appeared and said "the Master has sent for some special Doctor to check that you are not badly burned from DC arcing, so until then you must rest and I have given you Morphine to ease the discomfort slave Aureus" "Istra climb into that bed if you have permission to stay and watch her I have things to do!"

When the Doctor was out of ear shot Istra continued saying "You did well, I am sure Master Saw it too, 5 of the domestic girls started vomiting and 3 guests had to be led out, I thought I had seen everything."

"Master thinks one of the Colonels Men turned up the settings and he is not happy, furthermore because a lot of jangling went on and Master was not impressed with the rest of us. I think we will have some delayed punishments, but it will be worth it." Then the curtain swung open at the door and Istra had stopped chatting in the nick of time as Master Musson plus a guy I had never seen before came into the room followed by our Doctor. Then it seemed likely the other guy was this special Doctor whom said "Let her rest and douche her vagina with saline waters, plus continue with the pain killer, I will check back tomorrow. "The new Doctor slipped through the curtained doorway and was gone, Master Musson was slowly following and then said "Niobi Sir get me a car and a driver; also fetch my brief case from the office.

Later Master Musson appeared with both our Doctor and the one I saw earlier "She looks a lot better today Doctor" our Doctor said to the other one. Master then broke the silence with his Arabic broken English as he stood there in one of his expensive suits with his Arabic head-dress on "When can she be moved back her cell Doctor?"

Then I whispered "seems I am under the Doctor again" and Istra said "Yes but it's not your fault-though I am beginning to wonder who is at fault for us all, Master never did this before, but then the Colonel never took such an interest in any one of us, so why you?" with a croaky voice I said "Maybe that Peter that I was with is the link, Peter and the Colonel are Ham Radio buddies so they could be in it together. I know they was good old buddies" "sorry I can not speak more" and again dropped off to sleep escape thinking I must be drugged up to the eyeballs.

When I awoke again it seems another whole day had been lost to sleep, again I could feel my throat to be croaky it felt as thought I had swallowed something big then my eyes saw Istra "hi" was about all I could get out, just as a nurse came into the room and adjusted my pillows to assist me to sit up a bit then she said "The doctor wants you to sit in the chair for a while." Then she left as I croaked "water please" looking at Istra and Istra again filled the plastic glass with water, Istra looked sad or glum and so I croaked again "what's up? Sweetie, my affectionate attachment for Istra as she had primarily looked after me since I arrived, whether she influenced the Master to do that or not I was not sure, but she deserved to be treated decently as I could. Then she blurted out "you're! You're legally dead" "yeah" I croaked "and legally married to Master but I never attended the wedding, did you guys?" Istra sprung forwards and burst into tears, "hey hey what's all this" I said croakily, she "whispered again but you're dead" "but I have been there before you know that. You've been there before, we've all been there before, that's the way he likes it." "Anyway if I am legally dead the Colonel will have no further interest in me, unless he's into ghosts and all that shit, trying not to laugh as its already hurting my throat trying to console my friend and cell mate Istra.

Istra stood up again by the bed, "I – I did not think of that, maybe that is Master's plan, now I think on it maybe that is what Master had in mind all along and in front of witnesses, but then you collapsed and your body caught a metal frame that dropped from above just seconds before and it was clear you was injured."

"So what caused the mental frame to fall I wanted to know?" "I don't know, I am sure Master will investigate. "Well Ok" I croaked reaching for the water again, "what's happening here, have we all moved in or something?" "No Master has hired the whole floor so our Domestics can look after you and me, though I am here to keep you company so Master told me."

Master spoke first "we have a spy in our midst, one of the Colonels Men I believe turned up the electro punishment controls, so I want you both back in your cell as soon as possible, its easier to Guard, I do not want to start a war with the Colonel.

The Doctor here believes you will recover. However I have had to postpone the re-breaking process, but we shall in the fullness of time complete it slave Aureus!" Besides the purpose was to put the Colonel off pursuing you for his whore house and whatever else he may have had in mind. You did very well slave Aureus, I did not plan for you to be injured. Then Istra interrupted Master are you sure the spies are the Men? Could not some be the Domestic girls, we have had them do similar in the past?" Niobi then blurted in his twopenth worth "yes yes! Master Musson Sir! That makes perfect sense" Then Master said "Niobi Sir let it be known I offer fifty thousand dollars for the identity of any saboteurs or spies amongst us, lets see if greed can expose them." As you know I have to fly to Canada the day after tomorrow so Niobi Sir I want you and Ahmed to stay here and keep a close watch on the events here!" "Yes Sir Niobi" replied then Master Musson began to walk towards the doors of the medical room and stopped dead in his tracks and said "Niobi Sir!" Yes Master Musson Sir?" "The Doctor has a special project that I want done as soon as is possible on all my slaves. Now see that he gets on with it, now is the ideal time!" "Yes Master Musson Sir" With that Master Musson disappeared through the double doors out of the medical room.

I looked at Istra and she kind of looked back with a sense of vagueness.

More wondrous adventures I thought were now afoot, what with a spy in the camp and something the Doctor has to do, maybe its anti Man vaccines was about as my mind wanted to deal with more unknowns, even my humor was dying a death.

I decided to risk it and whispered to Istra, "What is it that Master wants the Doctor to do?" I asked. Then Istra reached out with her left hand from her bed seeking out my hand which I could see and so I equally held out my right hand until we were linked holding hands and our wrist chains clinked as they made contact in a gentle way. Then Istra said quietly "Master had contact with one of our competitive slavery operations and they told him they keep their slaves in a way that is so uncomfortable they stand still when straddling a pole" "sorry I do not follow" I said. Then Istra continued as she looked me in the eye and said "It seems they pierce their labia so that nails can be knocked into the poles through these holes pierced in the slaves labia, it seems to difficulties are the removing of the nails at the end of each session, and to repeat the operation we are all to have a pierced hole in each labia and a sleeper installed until it heals up." "Master is most excited by this idea!" "Shit not sure I like the sound of this" I said but there is not much I can do to avoid these new adventures Master comes up with.

Then I must have drifted off into my favorite pastime of sleep escape. When I eventually woke up I sensed pain between my legs and soon it dawned on me that during my sleep the Doctor must have performed his task, as I grew more awake I was aware that Istra was awake a looking across at me as if she wanted to say something and then she spoke quietly "The doctor thought it better to give you a shot to put you into a deeper sleep" and then she added with a sigh "he woke me up to do mine." Then Istra said "You need to rest as much as possible as Master is on his way back and he has set up a party and he wants us all in attendance, the Domestics will be in shortly to give you a wash and." brush your hair."

It was not long before the Domestic girls arrived to get me out of bed and to stand in the shower receptacle whilst they rinse me down then soap all over and then again finally rinse once more. This daily practice is a lot more simplistic than what we was used to back at the Tripoli base compound.

Then the domestic leader said quietly to anyone that

might be listening "Don't worry the Master will come to terms with the Colonel, and the Colonel knows it, we have been here before and they always resolve their differences and besides mostly all the linkages are set to take all the equipment are in place. So the chambers can be up and running within hours rather than days or weeks" she said with grin on her face.

"I expect we will be on our ways as soon as the Master gets back from Canada" I whispered "I must admit it was a place that I had got used to and knew the lie of the land." "Sit on the stool slave Aureus whilst we brush and braid your hair" "Ahh here is slave Istra and where have you been I wonder?" the domestic leader said in a belligerent way.

"Doctor was checking my piercing had settled down, do not worry I had permission!"

It was then that Niobi stuck his head in the doorway and said "have you finished with these two Domestic ladies?" "Yes Sir" the Domestic leader said and they vanished through the doorway.

"We are going back to base, more because it would take too long to re-equip a new venue, the Master believes you two are in danger of being abducted by the Colonels Men and so the best way to protect you is for us to re-break both of you so that your driving or directing mind is only directed to the Master, in this way no other Male or Man could ever re-program you back enough to re-direct your obedience. The Master instructed me to inform you of his plans so that you may prepare yourselves and his most insistent instruction is that you are not allowed to invoke standing order 4 because you are his property, Is that clear!?"

I looked at Istra with a tear in my eye and she looked back and said "out of all the girls I am glad it is you that is my team mate and no disrespects to them" and with that for the first time ever we embraced each other in a hug, in front of Master Niobi whom must have understood something and I always thought him to be evil. Then Istra uncoupled us and turned to Master Niobi and asked "Master Niobi Sir when is this to begin?" "We are all now departing for the airport so that as soon as the Masters aircraft has landed it can be refueled and stocked as we all board and get settled, you will both stay together and be double guarded night and day when we get in!" Then Niobi left us in this room and our thoughts.

It occurred to me that I had only really survived with the help and support of all the other 5 girls, if I had been alone I would never have survived. It was easy to think because we lived through it once before we could again, but I could tell by Istra's face that this one would be tougher, heavier and even more painful. In them early days when I longed for someone to come looking for us and find us, but they did not and it was clear escape was impossible because of the chains, plus being naked and in a foreign land. Then Istra whom was sitting on the floor struggled as usual to get up as we all did and she said "Aureus we have to be strong for each other!"

I could see she was as scared as I was, but I

think trying to put a brave act on for my benefit and I reciprocated as I was equally scared of what was to come. This could be like the worst punishment ever, but then it would be a lesser ordeal than what might be if the Colonel was to get his hands on us. We knew a lot of his girls go missing never to be seen again. Then Istra and I again embraced in a hug and laid down on one of the beds and we must have dropped off into sleep escape.

SEQUENCE 17

We were awoken by four giggly domestic slave girls, because they caught Istra and me in a cuddly embrace while asleep. Then Master Niobi was in close pursuit and remarked "Shut your mouths and do your works, if you lot knew what was ahead you might source a little comfort in one another. You've seen nothing and if I hear repeat of your giggly source you will pay heavily do you understand!?" "Yes Sir!" they all said together as if in a choir.

I think I was in shock as maybe Ahmed may have come to our defense, but to date Niobi never did, so I thought I shall have to think differently about him, Istra seemed stunned to but she was not talking, probably the safest thing for us both.

The Domestics gave us a quick wash and re brushed our hair to make us presentable for Master, soon we was ready and Niobi called Ahmed to come in, that too was a shock as we did not know how long he had been outside, what maybe he had seen and would he tell? As if we were in enough bother to start with, we did not need more.

The Men got themselves into their usual position so that we could place our wrist to wrist chains over their heads and they were able to pick us up in the usual way. Usual for us and I did wonder what others might think because it was seriously hard work to move anywhere in the chains, so stopped all notions of trying to run a ways. Soon the guys had us outside and it was raining, no mackintoshes for us as we was in our birthday suits I thought, but then we was in the limousines and then we was off to the airport.

When we arrived Masters Aircraft was on the apron close to what looked like workshops and hangers, fuel trucks were filling the aircraft with fuel and another truck was delivering food, fresh water and other supplies.

For the first time we had to wait for the fuel trucks to finish and pull away, not seen that before but maybe that is the way the Americans like to do things, though it was not that long and once again we was driven up into the garage part of the rear end of the aircraft.

As we was getting out of the cars the guys were securing the cars to the aircraft floor and I thought again without speaking aloud, Yeah put the cars into bondage everyone else is smiles. Ahmed lowered me into my usual flight seats and Niobi did the same with Istra and they also for the first time secured our seat belts. Again I thought they are pushing the boat out with these extra chores that we could have done for ourselves as we had before?

Then the bang of the rear garage ramp door could be heard to close and all our own ground crews started to come up the stairs and then you could hear the stairs retracting back into the aircraft then the doors were all shut and then the engines could be heard to start up in symmetric order, the fasten seat belts light came on and the Captain said "Please Gentlemen and ladies, please buckle up as we are soon to taxi for immediate lift off"

I remember these take offs as a bit scary as the aircraft seems to get to a height no so far off the ground and then it seemed to go level briefly before climbing again and them engines sure had power in them.

The Domestics soon had the porridge and milk prepared; I was ready for this on this occasion, but before I could get started. Master Musson was standing before us and then spoke "You two were caught holding each other in your cell?" "Yes Master" we both admitted together," "It was my fault Master" Istra said in a stuttered way. "Under the circumstances it's understood and your admitting it shows me your loyalty for the truth, but only in your cell not in public! Understood?" "Yes Master" we jointly responded as Master then said "What I hate most, are slaves that tell tales on other slaves, well they will now come unstuck!"

We remained silent as he walked away and began to eat our now cooling porridge as Istra turned towards me and smiled, I also smiled back though I felt sweat running down my back and I said "I thought he would throw us out the door," "so did I" said Istra and she added I have wanted to cuddle up to you since Master put us together just for a bit of human contact if that is ok" "yes its ok because I wanted to do the same as well but I was too frightened, but as the human contact understanding" "Then we think alike" Istra replied and I smiled. Though I am not sure we will be smiling for long. I just realized that was the first time I had seen Master wearing a tweed suit and a flat cap and not his head dress thing, usually he wears more expensive suits from London and always his second head dress, I think his best one is all white and the any day one is white with red something's in it.

Master Niobi approached our seating position and I thought, here we go when he said "The Master thought you two might like to rest on the beds for a couple of hours," Istra looked at me and I looked at her and shrugged my shoulders and we both said "Yes Sir" and with that we both stood up and hobbled up the aircraft isle to the Black Curtained area where Master had beds mounted to the floors so that they would stay put and one could be strapped in, though it was protocol for all passengers to be in seats on landings and takeoffs so we was told at some point. I often longed to lie down whilst on the aircraft rather than sit in them awful seats. Istra was first to climb onto the bed and she was on the left hand side of the aircraft. On her right was the side curtain and on the other side was another Isle running the length of the aircraft with a door leading into the front part of the aircraft, something we had not seen.

Then there were single seats on the Port side facing inwards so each chair was backed up to the aircraft sides, remembering that as we sat on the bed we faced towards the rear of the aircraft. The black curtain went all the way up to the ceiling and actually was like a tent within the aircraft. Master claimed that this is how his people would travel the sandy wastes of the many deserts and so I guess it was a reminder of his roots. On the corners were poles floor to ceiling and lights were attached to the poles with two more in the middle. Two large beds occupied this space and on our left was the same set up with an Isle on the outer side of the curtain on the Starboard side of the aircraft and also single seats facing inwards as well. The single seats allowed a certain protection I think. But in the middle of the aircraft on the outer side of the tent wall and facing towards the rear of the aircraft are several sofa type seats with individual seat belts to secure all those sitting in them.

With our newly acquired permission from Master to be able to cuddle up, Istra made the most of it and that distracted me from my mental scanning of Masters flying harem. It was then that Istra whispered to me about what could be ahead as she often had Masters Ear being his number one slave.

Istra whispered to me "When we get in Master will be very busy as he's been approached by the Soviets and in equal measure the Afghans as its likely a war will commence" As I was tired I was not thinking clearly until I blurted out "You mean to say Master will supply both sides!" "Yes Istra replied he does that." "No wonder he is a billionaire then, and we are in the middle" and then Istra said "what do you mean?" "Well it seems to me that we as a human race, we hate each other so much we have to attempt to annihilate each other rather than seek harmony or peace, we Master Mussons 6 slaves, all of different cultures and races and we are in harmony together, we are not trying to kill each other. You would think these Men might learn by that!"

It was then I dropped off into my sleep escape…

"Wakey! Wakey!" Said loudly by a Domestic leader whom had come into our tented area to prepare us both for the day ahead and then she added "we will be landing in an hour, Master wants everyone to be ready to disembark as soon as possible after landing and getting back to the base compound" With that I slipped out from the single cover and dropped my chained ankles and feet onto the carpeted floor of the aircraft and yawning, Two more girls came in through the curtain opening with their buckets and towels. They proceeded to give us the usual bucket bath by having us stand on a towel then rinse our bodies. Then soap all over and then re-rinse down till all the soap suds was gone, they then dabbed us dry with more towels as this was the best way not to further damage any broken skin or cuts we slaves may have. Finally they would sit both Istra and myself down on small stools, then brush and braid our long hair so it would not be damaged by any whippings.

Then Istra and I hobbled back to our designated

landing and take off seats towards the back of the aircraft.

It was not long before we heard the Captain speak again "Gentlemen and ladies please return to your designated travelling seats and fasten seat belts, please extinguish all cigarettes and naked flames, we are about to land at our base aerodrome Tripoli." Then soon after that there was that gentle bump as the back wheels touched the ground. I realized for the first time that the Captain did not name the aerodrome where we landed, but it may have been a security issue, even though the Captains would name foreign aerodromes by name if they had them.

However this was like a private aerodrome that Master stored his aircraft within plus I think the Colonel does too as he has his compound just down the road from ours. With that Niobi and Ahmed appeared from the front of the aircraft and began to get into their positions for us to place our chains over their heads so they can pick us up, Niobi with Istra and I always had Ahmed mostly, then we proceeded to the rear of the aircraft and the onboard garage to be re-united with the poor cars also in bondage as they get secured to the floor as we are secured to our own limbs.

Soon we was all in the cars and our ground crews had the ramp down and our drivers were reversing out into the bright sunlight and then getting into convoy procedure, but none moved till we was all ready to go and again today there seemed to be a jeep up front with Men with machine guns at the ready and then

I saw one join the rear of our convoy. As we passed the gate, out onto the open road the convoy picked up speed. A selective group of ground crews would see to the security of Masters DC 10 flying harem and make it secure, maybe refill with food and fuel as I know he liked to be ready for quick getaways.

I no longer bothered to make note of our surroundings though was mainly open desert type terrain and like Istra I longed to be back at base compound that had become my home too then the convoy turned into the rough road that lead up to our compound gates which opened automatically and the convoy passed through though the front armed jeep did not and I suspect they may have been the security boys that Master liked to have patrol the compound. I did not even bother to watch for the gates to close as we pulled up to the parking areas.

Niobi and Ahmed were quickly out of the limousine and again Istra and I struggled to hobble out of the car and then get ourselves into the Guys arms so we could be taken inside, I soon was aware that the others must have got back sooner as the music was once again in full swing and the lights and the air con was up and running. I was hoping breakfast would not be long as my stomach was a bit growly and soon we arrived at our cell and fresh bedding was laid out and the place seemed to be clean and tidy as the Guys put us down. Niobi spoke "the Domestics will bring your food soon as I am sure you two will be ready for that." And then both he and Ahmed left us to our own devices.

"Good to be home" Istra said quietly and added, "Come Aureus lets sit for a while as we shall need all our rest."

Before I could drop off to sleep escape the Domestic girls arrived with the usual porridge and milk breakfast. The Leader of the group said "the Master has gone to see the Colonel to hopefully get some cooperation so that we do not have to locate to a new base" "yes said Istra Master has a lot to be thinking on and so it will be for us as whatever the arrangement it will not be without cost," then the leader added "sadly it will be Aureus that get the brunt of that from what is the scuttlebutt." Istra in one of her commanding voices said slightly above normal speech levels "In that case we must all rally and support her that includes you guys as well!" I turned to get into this discussion when Istra said "Not now Aureus, this is not the time or place. Realizing I am still the new girl here and I still have lots to learn I sat back on the floor and tried to listen to the background music that was being interrupted by the discussion that would be bad if a Guard were to walk in I thought.

SEQUENCE 18

TRAINING BEGINS AGAIN

Soon after the Domestic girls had left Niobi and Ahmed re-appeared in our cell and Niobi said "Its time slave Aureus/Istra to begin the training schedule so lets go!" They both got into those positions that both Istra and I knew to place our wrist to wrist chains over their heads so they could pick us up and carry us both off the one of the training chambers.

I was aware in my mind that I was not looking forward to this as we had some gaps in the training schedule and lost the balanced 3 days a week training schedule and so it would be painful and hard going to just get back into the throws of accepted training levels. Then as we entered the chamber I could see Master Robert standing there with a bullwhip in hand. Istra whom in Niobi's grasp was slightly ahead of me and Ahmed and Istra smiled towards me as if to say "he looks ready to commence his work" Then within a few minutes the guys had put us back on the floor and was each leading us to two cleats that were dangling on a wire and they gathered up our wrist to wrist chains in the middle-is aspect and clicked the cleats into the chain eyes and when the time was right a motor began and then both wires ascended until our arms were above us, giving clear access to all of our naked bodies. I had instinctively spread my legs without being told, so I was learning.

Then the Doctor appeared in one corner and then two Guards, thus reminding me of Masters Wishes that from now on we have a full protection detail. Then it hit was the first lash of his bullwhip across my back and with his returning stroke I heard it crack across Istra's back. This time we could not see each other even though I knew she could take a hell of a lot more than I could before she would transition into MS1.

The lashes came in quick succession and then sometimes did not but then Master Robert was just whipping one of us, so as to keep us both off balance as the impacts cut deep I knew I was bleeding on Masters nice clean floor, but Master Robert just carried on. Again I looked deeply into nuts and bolts within the frame work of the beams pulleys

And anything that had bolts, in doing this and trying to mentally unscrew them was a way of blocking out the pain and passing time. Then in a glimpse I saw Master pass the doorway in his full Arabic regalia, or his traditional dress of a white or cream cape and the headdress over a western suit. Then I heard what I thought was a Rod Stewart number within the music playing in the background and I thought no I must not allow myself to start foot tapping. Master Robert was across my breasts and that made me wince and pull hard on my link to the wire, that and my hips were it really hurt me mostly and it would bring a tear to my eye and then the snot formed in my nose and I knew I was weeping in silence and eventually I must have passed out as I came too and was on my back on the floor and the training was over for today. The Guards had lifted up my body and placed it on a stretcher as I heard Masters Voice saying take them both to the medical wing. As we were being stretchered away towards the medical wing I could see the darkness through the sky lights and the day was into the night. I must have passed out again until I came too when the Doctor was plastering the smelly yellow Iodine all over the body and it was very stingy, then the Guards rolled my body over so the Doctor could coat my back in the stuff and that seemed worse pain than my front. Then they left me to do the same for Istra as I dropped off into sleep escape once again. Strangely our bodies would heal fast, it seemed the more training that we had the faster our bodies would heal so within 48 hours we was ready for the next days training so as to keep up the 3 days a week of training.

I must have drifted off into sleep escape again, my way to escape this place and this life, but sadly when we awake its there waiting for me and I secretly dread what I am about to receive. As I awoke I could hear chatter in the background of the medical roomed its not easy to fake waking up with so many eyes watching our every move and so like a lot of things its pointless to even try.

As I opened my eyes I could see Master Musson

standing in the corner talking with the Doctor and as I get my bearings Istra is tucked up in the bed to my right and I can see she is stirring too probably because of the racket that the men are creating in their Dominance over us.

Suddenly Niobi stepped into the medical room; I am guessing that he was in the corridor all the time. Then he says "We are waiting for Istra to wake as this effect you both!"

Then Istra breaks silence with her chains and so now we all know she is waking, I always tried not to make such a clatter with the chains at this time of day in case I missed something of importance as they only tell you once, no-one repeats anything so attention is paramount. "Hang on a moment please I need to wee, so if you have a bed pan please Doctor," "Yes I have some hereabouts are there they are" the Doctor replies and while he is gets them out of the cupboard and breaking into a sealed package a weary eyed Istra says "Me too please Doctor!".

Then Master Musson steps forward and begins "Now that we are all getting comfortable the Colonel will not back down, he really has a burr up his arse for you twos, and so I have to make it so you both become useless to him or anyone else for that matter. We have not ever had this happen before so we only effectively trained slaves for one break, but now I have to deepen that break into a possible 3. In the end you will only know that you are slaves of the Musson Indoctrination and will always revert back to the indoctrination or senior members of the indoctrination." Niobi jumps in with "senior members could be like Officers if we were a military operational set up!" "Yes Master Niobi Sir, that explains it better for them to understand" Master Musson added. Then Master said "as slave Aureus is new to this life, and comes from a country that do not understand this way of life, an agreement with your British government that you should never return was applied and you became a member of my family as are all 6 Musson slaves. So to be clear there is no way back!" Ok Master Niobi Sir we will begin tomorrow, today is recovery of yesterday, let them rest," "I need to speak to you in the office as soon as you are clear Master Niobi Sir!" With that they both disappeared out of the medical room as the Doctor now stepped forwards saying "I was afraid of this, that Colonel is the most evil Man alive" I knew enough to keep silent in front of the Men folk, but Istra picked up on my frustration and said "Doctor why is Aureus so special?, why not one of the others? Then the Doctor stuck his head out of the door hole as we had no doors and then returned and said "Its politics and racist. You only need to look how it is here, the Males Rule, the female are at best value as of Domestic service or for procreation in marriage. The Master had specific agreements with the head or a representative of the head of each of the country he would abduct you from, however if some evil were to befall Volga the Russian slave that could lead to all out war. Technically you are all Muslim slaves and in that females are nothing of use. The idea of equality does not exist in the Muslim ideology and I doubt that the British would go to war to save your butt Aureus" Istra jumps in with

"Doubt that Croatians would fight for me neither!"

Looking at Istra I said "I think he means we deserve this because we are of the wrong gender" "how can that be?" Istra asks and adds "if the world was all male how it procreates?" Then the Doctor pipes in with "by keeping females as slaves and locked away with a Eunuch to make sure none stray like in ancient Egyptian times!" "Oh now I see it "Istra said excitedly, "I think you is enjoying this Istra, I still do not see where I fit in" "That's easy Aureus" the Doctor said. "So tell us" Istra said, "Aureus was not so easy to crack and all the Men loved to see her hold out, even though the rest of you got her punishments, in their eye her fighting back gave a new edge to the whole process and that's why the Colonel wants her." Clear as mud I thought. "Now I have said more than I should and my tongues wagged enough go rest!" the Doctor said in a nice but irritated way. Istra "do you think that is what the Domestics were on about the other day?" "Did my holding back really hurt you guys?" "No and don't be so silly if it was not you it could have been a someone none of us liked, if they feel they need to do it all over again, they will expect you to hang back again." "God give me strength, I thought I was still trying to learn to take it all let alone hang back just so the guys can get their Jollies." With that Istra burst out laughing in a way I had not heard her do before. "What's so funny?" I enquired. "You-I would never have thought of that way to describe the

Men in action having or getting err- Jollies!" and with that I saw the funny side and we both laughed in a way unbecoming of any slave...

So again we lay quietly in separate beds in the medical room and look forward to sleep escape, though I am wishing for a heart attack or something to get me out of what Master has in mind, though it can not be as bad as what the Colonel might do.

Then again light and noise of chatter brought another day into the reality of it all, just when sleep escape was so comfortable.

As I opened my eyes "Wakey Wakey!" could be heard, that can only be the Domestics come to get us washed, brushed and ready for what comes today...

After the four Domestic slave girls wash our bodies to get all that dried up yellow Iodine off and make us smell sweeter, they brushed and braided the hair and then eventually served breakfast of the usual porridge and milk drink, but then I needed the loo (toilet) for a pooh, but in here its a pot we have to sit on in the bed just like in real hospitals, in the cells it's a hole in the ground. So because we had been bathed the Domestics had to go fetch more water and do that bit again after I managed to do the business, its better this way as we do not make a mess of the Masters floors in the varying chamber of horrors. After all that and we had a little rest, and then Ahmed and Niobi arrived for the usual job of taking us poor souls to work. My sense of trying to be jolly before the hell begins. Again the guys dip their heads so we can slip our wrist to wrist chains over their heads and they can then pick us up and carry us to whatever is next.

As we approach a particular chamber that I vaguely recall as to being a slave parking beam with a metal strip on the top for electro use for good measure, now I see the other 4 Musson slaves we are complete once more and it looks like slave parking again. I wanted to be jovial and ask where the traffic warden was but it might be too soon for wit, I seemed to see this second phase differently as not so intimidating as to be witty, as I failed to get aggressive with what I know is the reverse psychology and this I fear was the me that was goner attack them or try to.

No sooner had we all arrived, the beam was lowered so that we could all straddle the beam so that the beam was now between our legs and above the ankle to ankle chains so that when raised we all was straddling the beam and all our individual leg chains in weight would pull us down onto the metal strip. At least this was a bit better than an electrode up the vagina or even up the bum or both when they wanted to create a circuit in different way.

This time our hands had not also been set behind us or again with the chains under the beam so I wondered what now? Then a wire from one upright to the other was lowered and someone had thought to bring steps so that one Man could get up and raise all our wrist to wrist chains to the wire using a climbers cleat to connect each centre chain link to the wire, so I could see eventually our arms were going to be upwards and above.

We was spaced about a meter apart and I know why so either Master or one of the trainers could get a singletails in between us and no sooner had I thought this out as Master Robert appeared with a very long stockwhips. I know from bitter experience the short whips say 6 feet are more stingy but as they get longer they get heavier and thuddery like I was guessing this was a good 10 foot so I know it will be painful for us all but then so Master Musson and Master Niobi appeared and they too had whips Master Musson was a bullwhip fan and it looked like he had a 10 footer, where as Master Niobi's was an 8 foot snake whip. Bullwhips and stockwhips have handles where as snake whips do not and sort of have a knot end and start from that point. Then Masters Ahmed and Matt appeared with a snake whip of about 6 feet and we all knew young Master Matt was learning so a few misplonks could be expected as the wire that attached our wrist chains was raised to a point that suited us all as we all because being of different sizes meant that what was ok for the lanky slave was not so comfortable for the shortest and a balance was found but even so our bodies as usual were vulnerable targets for at least 4 Males so far though Ahmed and the Doctor plus two Guards were on security detail. It was then I felt that almost forgotten pain of a singletail cutting across my back, I had hoped I had gotten used to this by now like the others, but no it was still painful for me and I could hear as I shut my eyes that the others were getting to feel the same though in what order I could not tell. My eyes jumped open when a lash was across my breasts like a carpet burn across both nipples and as ever a state of shock as I can not seem to get used to that carpet burning type sensation.

Istra and I were at this end all depending on which side one stood though the whole thing was in the centre of the room so all operators had plenty of swinging room and we seemed to be getting it mostly from Master Musson, Master Robert and Master Niobi were up the other end with Slave Volga and Slave Zaire Slaves Arabela and slave Mista were in the middle, but just then the Men all changed their positions and then I knew when Young Matt and his 6 footer was on us because of the stinginess, thing I prefer the heavier stuff as it distracts somehow Then Ahmed seemed to acquire a whip from somewhere and he was laying in as well and it soon all swelled into a mass of pain and was no longer identifiable as single hits and that is when it all stopped and in my silly mode I thought yes tea break.

I had not noticed that someone had brought a trolley load of glasses that would have had lemonade in for the Guys to drink, no alcohol here mainly lemonade or water, plus tea and coffees of course. The Doctor had a special bowl that we was all allowed a sip or two of water from, that was his job looking after our health needs.

In the second half the electrics was on the damn strip along the top of the beam and that could burn some so it was bit like horse riding UK style where you try to jump up and down, I don't think the Americans do it the same, but no way could we just sit on it as it would build up so one had to use ones thighs to grip the beam to lift ourselves, though that was not so easy with the chains pulling down thrust and became an impossibility when the whipping begun again, one just got tired very quickly, I tried rocking from side to side, but I am not sure if I cleared it enough and some tried to lean to one side to get away from the strip, but the Masters had this one nailed so we just could not win. After a couple of hours we all had blood dripping from our bodies and I could see the Doctor wanted to get us cleaned up by trying to stop proceeding as it was only a training session prior to what was to come. The Doctor was seen talking shop to Master Musson, I suspect laying down medical jargon to bring about a halt. Whatever it was worked as the Master said "Stop Gentleman we do not want to over stretch this training that might compromise the set plans afoot." I believe it was going to be just Istra and myself that were in for the big show in Master's planning on this second breaking, I thought it was bad enough the first time and so all I could to fight back was to make light and take the piss.

So as the Men dismantled the beams and lowered our wrist and numbing arms the Doctor got to work painting the yellow stingy smelly Iodine stuff on us all and then the Domestics had brought some fresh clean wound tabards to keep the wounds clean and as I slumped to the floor out of exhaustion I guess the Doctor called to Niobi.

"Niobi Sir I think we better have them all on the

medical wing until they recover" "Yes Doctor!" Master Musson said over riding Niobi's response and then Master Musson said "Men if you can assist the Doctor to get them all to the medical wing then the others can clean up here! "Again I was placed on a stretcher and carried back to the medical wing. Some were carried in the usual ways and eventually we all arrived in the medical wing which was basically a large room or ward.

We spent the night all in there together and all had our evening food in the medical wing with the good old Doctor on hand whom was our only friend and ally although we knew from way back there was never ever any chance of escape except into sleep being naked and in cuffs and chains that was welded on. Just to move around the compound was hard enough and easy to have the metal rub against skin to the point it became inflamed so to run away was a no go and over here one would inevitably end up in another slavery operations as we understood there was a lot of them in Libya. Scuttlebutt was the Colonel had controls of most of them and a good few he owned as well.

Anyway soon it was time for sleep escape and still the music played in the background loud enough for us to hear and cover the sound of Guard footsteps but not so loud as to keep one awake, the medical wing like all hospital wards had dimmed lighting, enough for Doctors to see by and I need sleep as I was aware tomorrow is when it begins, today was a warm up to warm our bodies up a bit like athletes do.

SEQUENCE 19

BREAKING ATTEMPT
PART TWO

I was awoken to the sound of a lot of clatter and loud whispering, I was sure I heard it all before and sure enough it was the Domestics trying to do things quietly, Istra beat me too it saying "Must you guys make so much din with those buckets?" "Sorry Istra it's the new girl she seems so clumsy!" said the Domestics team leader. "The Master was a bit fresh and agitated that we should get you two up and ready for today!" "Yes and I can guess why, he wants his jollies again!" Then the whole ward of girls and Domestics burst into giggles the like I had never seen before, I was still stiff eyed with sleep not realizing what I had said, but remembering then I had said it before not thinking clearly. At that point the Doctor walked in "hush you lot Niobi is close at hand!" at which point like a hammer dropping there was silence you could hear a pin drop apart from the music in the background and the swish as Master Niobi and his squad of Guards as they thrust through the curtains. "Are these two ready yet?" Master Niobi said in a deep gruff voice.

"No Sir" the Domestics team leader said, "I had to instruct the new girl on the Masters procedures and time slipped us by, sorry Sir" Then Master Niobi said as he turned away in a lower voice as if it was hard to say "Well at least you are honest and I knew that to be true, shame I can not penalize you for that" and he slipped back through the curtained doorway as at that point Istra looked at me as did the Doctor and the Doctor said "That's new never heard him say or do that before, so all you girls best watch your step I get the feeling we are in for some more surprises. You Domestics get cracking; get Istra and Aureus ready first!"

The team leader went on to washing Istra, But the Doctor reminded us all that I like to have a wee before I get my bucket bath as he passed over the bed pan. I quickly slipped it into place and had my wee so the Domestics could get on with the bucket bath. I tended to remain quiet at this time, though there was a lot of faint whispering that could be heard until the team leader said "Shut up you lot or we will be in for punishments as well. It's training day for us all if you had not forgotten!" At that point I enquired "Training day?" The Team leader looked at me in a glare and with restraint said "Yes the Master in his wisdom likes to have a general all purpose training day to co-inside with the special event that you two are heading up" as she pointed the hair brush at me and then Istra. Then Istra jumps in "well I am sure Aureus and I had nothing to do with that!" then there's me "Now-now lets not be at each others throats I thought its the Men that set these things up around here?" "Aureus is right "Istra said none of us can be accountable for the actions around here or anywhere, at least you get paid to be here." Then one of the Domestics jumped in with "well you're all married to the son of a bitch, you must love it or him." Then realizing she had said too much at a point that Master Niobi walked in, that I realized that there are times I just refer to him as the rank and file and when he's in ear shot I seem to call him Master Niobi, so maybe I am no better than them for being disgruntled. At that point the team leader said "Sir Slaves Istra and Aureus are ready for you," Master Niobi said "thank you team leader, I will see your Master is made aware of your speedy efforts today." As he ducked down so I could pass my wrist to wrist chains over his head so he could pick me up easily I saw the team leaders face drop and that made me wonder if Master Niobi said it with some relish on his mind, thinking back to what Istra was saying About these guys get their enjoyment from hurting us or threatening us to see how we react. I do not know too much about the Domestics whom Istra once told me they were BDSM people from the USA and they like to do this for a livelihood or something on those lines. So why should the team leader worry about punishments if they like it, its not as if they get put through what they have done to me so far and that which they must have done to the other 5 before I arrived. Because my train of thought was so deep I had lost track of where we was going until I saw the magic roundabout. It was then that

Master Niobi bent forward to place my feet on the ground as he withdraw his head and I kept, my hands in a clear position so that he should not get caught up, though as this was a day of action he was bare chested, with slacks or trouser on and his head dress that they all wore even if they was not of the faith, but I think those are the less decorative ones, but I am not sure. Many of the Guards were so decked out, but then it could be a warm day here and even hotter if they get to use a whip. Ahmed wasted no time at all in leading me up onto the turntable thing, I could see Istra was directly opposite me. Did I dare to think Master was Zebedee?

Or was that living dangerously, I know from previous experience that this thing turns slowly and we can have at least three whippers on us at any one time. But for me that's my limit in breathing difficulties.

I could see that it really was going to be a festival of pain by the number of guests arriving and though my eyesight was not so good without my contacts or my glasses I had a feeling I saw the Colonel, but he was not alone. About then our wrists were being hoisted up not too far, but enough to clear our bodies to make the targets clear of obstacles then they cleated our ankles apart but I had already moved into that position so as not to be told. Legs had to be apart always around here, which took some getting used to, mainly because Moms and Dads teach their daughters to keep legs closed so as not to entice Men to think we are loose girls looking for some attention. I seem to remember something about a chain on the ankles was supposed to indicate something similar.

Soon the roundabout was rotating clockwise but slowly and it was lit up like a Christmas tree, so when it turned and I could see the guest area and where the other four Musson slaves would be in the special kneeling position where your bottom was clearly on the floor and your legs bent back so you was wide open at the front as a Master liked to get his whip into our crotches without us flinching legs shut which its impossible to do, but bloody painful to say the least.

Then it happened the Colonel was right up close to me and I could see him clearly and I am guessing his guest another Arabic looking personage whom I knew to be another political freedom fighter, but I could not recall his name, probably just as well. His other guest was typical looking middle aged Arab, pot bellied, though for some reason he had a scarf or some material covering his nose and mouth, bit like the women have.

Soon more activity lends it hand when the whip trolley appears, followed by the white medical truck with the two Paramedics behind to assist the Doctor, who was to one side of the medical trolley allowing the younger Paramedics to do all the pushing. Master Niobi appeared with Master Musson both stripped to the waist with only their headdress or tea cozy I used to call them. Then you could hear all the doors closing and the Guards would assume their positions at the doors. So I began to wonder about the Domestics where do they fit in here, normally they sit in a special position and watch but not today, though they maybe with their associate partners undergoing their training whatever that was. Ours was mainly being whipped and tortured. "Shit" I said here we go again as Master Musson walked up behind me and he stopped the roundabout right there. and lifting my braided hair and putting it over my left shoulder so it dangled across my left breast as it dropped to my waist, I could see Master Niobi doing the same to Istra's braided hair, then Master Musson said "now how are you going to get out of this one young slave Aureus?" and I/we replied in the only way we could.

"Not Master, to do so would deprive you of such excitement you'd get a headache" then he replied "Well now Master Niobi Sir! It would appear our young slave Aureus has developed a sense of humor, ask Young slave Istra if she will support this new development?" then clearly it could be heard as Master Niobi said "Young slave Istra do you support this new development that seems to have taken young slave Aureus?" "Yes Sir! Master Niobi Sir, Aureus is still new to our operations here, but she has a full head of steam that makes the rest of us look silly!" at that precise moment there was a clatter of jingling chains from the four remaining Musson slaves, even though the music playing in the background and I was not aware of any microphones, the others heard both Istra, myself and the two Men hovering like eagles on the wing. "Think we have a mutiny on our hands Master Niobi Sir! "Yes Master Musson Sir! I believe we should have sold tickets!" Then they both stepped off the now stationary magic roundabout and moved away to positions I knew what was to follow and so it did within quick succession each impact building, I judged the pain to be an 8 footer easily, could be a 10 footer, even I was becoming an export on this end, though my eyes were shut I know Istra was getting it in equal amounts from Master Niobi when I heard "do you need a hand Master Musson Sir? And I knew that was the voice of Master Robert. "What about slave Istra on the opposite axis." "I can assist Master Niobi Sirs!" realizing that Master Matt was on hand as well to make it a double double attack, I knew this takes some serious concentration as they will strike from different quarters. This means I shall have no time to think it must be spontaneous for us to get our breathing just right. I know this will in one way give him his dare I say Jollies, but he will fake being mad Master Musson in different locations and Master Robert had a similar pressure to that of Master Musson and I had to forget my friend Istra as the pain was through the roof with Master Musson on my back and Master Robert on my breasts, belly and legs front. Realizing I thought too quick as Master Musson increased to include my bottom and the backs of my legs. It then dawned on me that the roundabout was not moving and we was stationary otherwise the impacts would have an uneven variant where as Masters Musson and Robert had about the same pressure density when they applied the whips. I was lost in pain not sure where or which was worse as the worst thing happened and my eyes watered and snot gathered in my nose. Then Master Musson said loudly "Get ready back there slave Aureus has sprung a leak." Then I heard Master Niobi say loudly "slave Istra has too Master Musson Sir!" then Master Musson said loudly "OK Guys BEGIN!" then in the background you could hear more whippings to the point it was covering up the sounds of the Music. I then got the courage to say loudly "I can't hear the Music Master, How- how am I expected to concentrate with that entire racket behind me Master Sir!? Master Musson stopped in his tracks as if to think about this as more snot dripped to his nice clean floor, Master Robert stopped as well then as if following in a line of marching Men the other two stopped as well Masters Niobi and Matt. "What's up Master Musson Sir?" Master Matt was enquiring. Again I said loudly "Tea break time Master Matt Sir! Which Master Robert applied an extra stroke across my breasts with such a force the cracker fell off and the end of the whip really did cut in and create a leak. "Doctor you better get over here and attend Aureus, Master Musson said loudly and then adding I think we all needs some lemonade. Then Master Matt piped up "You are letting them win over a glass of lemonade Master Musson Sir? "No Master Matt Sir, I need a drink and slave Aureus is leaking blood, snot is one thing, blood needs the Doctor. We will soon resume they all know this no-one is stalling for time beside they are not going anywhere are you?" "No Master Musson Sir, I am just not sure of these tactics?" "Master Matt Sir You must learn to pick up off the slaves, slave Aureus is going to fight us with humor and sarcasm. So you can not have it both ways, slave aureus will not give in easily we have seen this before Master Matt Sir you are here to learn, please do!" "But Sir she is blatantly insulting you!" "Yes Master Matt Sir and I like it, because she does not give in or quit easily it makes the hunt more entertaining, you have a lot to learn about humans my boy!" Master Musson said. The Doctor was holding something to the side of my left breast waiting for the blood to clot I guess Master Ahmed was coming around with lemonade for us to drink, at this point I did not care my little game had been discovered, but at least we all know where we stand.

"OK" Master Musson said lets get back to work, "Oh so we are work now are we Master Sir?" I said. Then he turned away from me and said loudly "don't you love this kid she isn't scared of me anymore, I can see I shall have to change that notion and soon!" "Master Musson Sir!" "Is that a promise or a treat Master Sir?" I replied. Then Master Matt stood back and then added" "This is what I meant Sir she is downright rude and disobedient, she needs to be taught a lesson in manners was that not what her partner originally wanted?" I could see Master Niobi was irritated by the proceedings and it was not going well. Then Master Niobi spoke "Young Man you are new to this enterprise, if you just let us continue without interruption Master Musson will teach even you a thing or two, NOW SHUT IT!" then Master Robert had his say "If you Gentlemen had been with us since the inception you will have learned that only slave Istra had enough gumption to retaliate the other 4 were more as a part of business deals so we have not had so much fun until slave Aureus turned up, Now can we get back to it before it becomes lunchtime?" "Sorry Gentlemen I did not know" Master Matt said in a sheepish fashion. Master Musson then added "There was no need for you to know they are my slaves and that is why Istra and Aureus is together in the same cell, they are a sort of a team. They bounce off one another as you will see and Master Robert is correct it's too close to lunchtime so Guards release them all and return them to quarters, we will résumé after lunch." "If nobody has any further objections, you are all welcome to join us for lunch Gentlemen!" With that the whole room went into overdrive and the Guards released both Istra and myself from the roundabout and returned us to our cells where the Doctor and his damned Iodine were waiting and fresh clean tabards to keep our wounds clean. The other four Musson slaves were nowhere to be seen so I was at a loss there; we could not see them clearly from our position so I have no idea where they went...

The Doctor did his painting and two Domestics gently placed the tabard garments over our heads and tied the side ribbons, where I went ouch to the amazement of the Domestics. Then Istra and I sat down on the beds on the floor and was handed our bowls of lamb stew with vegetables and potatoes. Then the Doctor said "now I will tell you the secret of the world, your world, I knew this was coming and I tried to warn you guys. Istra my dear did you not know that the other four were part deals with the Armaments program in different countries a sort of human bribe if you like." "No I did not know that" Istra said a bit dejected I thought as if she had been kicked hard in the wrong place, the Doctor continued there's only three of the Musson slaves that was abducted, you two and Volga. I changed hands to hold my spoon and reached out to hold Istra left hand with my right hand and she sensed this and met me half way. "So what's next Doctor" I said disrespectfully, then thought it's not his fault and said "Sorry Doctor" "that is ok I would not to be in your shoes if you had any" and he smiled as he left our chamber.

After Istra and I had finished the lamb stew and had our metal glass of milk, we wanted to lie down and rest but there was a good chance the operational program would kick in again, so we could not relax. But then as if by magic three Guards sort of fell through the open doorway. Out of the three there had to be a leader and it was him that spoke "Master Roberts wants you both up in the guest lounge!" then two Domestic girls arrived to remove our tabards and bring us back to operational nakedness. Then the other two Guards go into the position that Istra and I know so well for us to place our wrist to wrist chains over their heads so they can pick us up and carry us to the desired location, if we had to hobble our legs would be so rubbed roar it would be too painful to do much. Then we was all off although the domestics disappeared down a different passage way, clearly they was only there to prepare us, not to attend us to wherever.

Thinking as we moved swiftly through the maze of passage ways and into a lift it occurred to me I have never seen this part of the compound and it could be where all the guests hang out.

When the lift stopped and the doors opened the guys carrying us stepped forwards into large expanse that had lots' of chairs and sofas in it all over the area. Masters Musson, Robert, Ahmed, Niobi and that Matt were all on a set of three sofas and this is where we was taken and placed with feet to the floor and released by our carriers, then Master Robert said "slaves position one" and we both stepped over our ankle to ankle chains and lowered to the floor adopting a position like in a Yoga format where ones bum is touching the floor and legs bent back so open canyon best describes a channel into which a Master can fly his singletail down there into our crotches should he wished to do so and there is nothing the slave can do to repel or block she must just accept whatever pain levels find their ways to our bodies.

"Now that Master Matt has let the cat out of the bag Master Musson Sir how do you wish to proceed" Master Robert said, "What cat have I let out of the bag?" Master Matt enquired. The purpose of today is to help save slaves Aureus and Istra from the clutches of the Colonel whom wants both for his whore houses as he thinks they could increase his wealth either as performers or might even sell to a third party and you have alerted him to the fact we had planned to rebreak Aureus and thereby put her into a deeper mental break state that she would become useless to any Male or Master that tries to command her. "You see Master Matt that is why we break our slaves to keep them, locks, chains, gates and prisons can be broken into. However it is not so easy to re-direct broken slaves mental status to another commander, even Doctors can not undo this work very well and the slaves become vegetables." Master Niobi added. "Nobody told me!" said Master Matt. You are here at the bequest of your Father. It is not important to tell all our guests the why we do anything within our operations; your father never told us about how he operates his slaves or even keeps their loyalty. Maybe you would like to divulge that piece of information; we might be able to use it to misdirect the Colonel. "No Master Musson Sir!" "My Father would not like how he operates to be banded about by all and sundry!" Well then young Master Matt I suggest you keep your big mouth shut when we have dangerous Men here like the Colonel or I will instruct to your Father the damage you have done and see if he wants to pay the $12 million dollars that Istra and Aureus are valued at!" Master Musson exclaimed in an aggressive tone. "You can not be serious Master Musson Sir! No female is worth that amount of doe!" Master Matt responded with equal aggression. Then Master Robert added "You fool I thought your Father requested we teach you to show you how we do that to make slaves worth such amounts of money, both slaves Istra and Aureus can handle somewhere in the region of 2,000 plus lashes in one training session, I am their trainer for God sake, if you think I do not know my own business on how to train these girls then you have much to learn!"

"Then I apologize Gentlemen, its an inspired operation, I, we never realized the human female could be trained to take so much so I can see why the Colonel wants to acquire them, again I apologize I do have much to learn!" Master Matt said.

"Gentlemen I think we should begin again tomorrow its getting late now and evening meal will be coming up soon. I am sure slave Aureus will long to get back to sleep escape in preparation for tomorrow. Ok Guards return then to quarters they have been very good here this afternoon!"

With that the Guards got into the position to lift us up and carry us off back to our quarters. I remained shocked to believe Master thought we were valued at about $12 million dollars but I am still learning as much as that playboy Master Matt supposedly is from his end of the whips. Soon we arrived back at our chambers and I was pooped and really just wanted to sleep but I need the food to build up my reserves.

Soon the Domestics were here with the lamb stew and our warm milky drink, even though my welts could still be felt I knew we had been here before, sometimes its easier to carry on with open wounds than to let the fully heal and then start again.

Istra you know my orders, how can you just sit there and not hate me for what I have to do tomorrow, before I was not sure if you knew Master came to me whilst he and I thought you was asleep and he told me I had to use sarcasm and innuendo to effect a retaliatory attack. "Aureus I knew it had to go that way, I've known Master longer and I knew he would find a way to get you to look like you was being rebellious and you must do it else he may force you by punishing one of the Domestics or threaten to attack me!" Istra said. "No I will not allow them to make threats on you, I will obey, but if I can not I am sorry!" I said and then Istra added, "I am ok I can handle much more than the levels you have been brought up to. In time he will bring you up to the same levels as me it's in his plan, but for now we need to stay here, not be dragged over to the Colonels whore operations and Master is right a second mental break will change how you perceive things." "It seems as though I can not win again, so He wants me to rebel so he can punish us both, hoping to cause me to crack again. Istra interrupted, "I hope you do not!" "Well that does not matter what he does to me!" Istra was saying, "but it does, it matters to me there is a risk you could be sent into barmy land, why can't these damn Men leave us alone," "worse still you might go insane yourself and be useless to both Master and the Colonel, there is something else to as slaves we have a caring nature to all other slaves, or at least those that claim to be slaves whether it be in the BDSM or real slavery so we have to back and honor all our Domestics as they claim to be slaves and those on the outside. You must remember this and abide by it!" "Yes I know I have seen it in our orders or the slave law. Probably you banging into me from the early days, anyway have you ever seen me let any

Domestics down even to save the Catricks girl, though she put my life in danger and then the other one!" "Yes I know Aureus you have done better than we expected when really you was only supposed to come here to be more respectful of the Peter guy, but Master saw something in you," "Yeah stupid bitch that's me!" ""He liked what he saw and you were lost to your old life and a sister slave to us." "No! Aureus don't cry!" Istra said.

I am not sure I can carry this off I muffled while weeping as my emotions kicked in." "I think you need sleep escape Aureus." I then crawled in my bed pit and slipped into sleep escape.

(Unbeknown to me Master came to our chamber in the middle of the night and talked with Istra. "How is she doing Istra?" "Master respectfully if there was this much danger why did you not leave her in England before we left?" "You know full well not to ask such questions of me Musson slave Istra, but I will let this slide. Simply because I want her here, she stands to have more worth than the other 3 do you realize that, so YOU! Slave Istra, slave Aureus and slave Volga are my best pain slaves, help her as much as you can and get some rest slave!"

SEQUENCE 20

I awoke to the sun glinting through the skylights way above our heads, Istra was still asleep so I tried to hobble quietly to the hole in the ground for a pee, but it was no good the damn chains seem to be against me today as they caught every which way and then "Your awake Aureus?" "I think so" "feel a bit stupid" "why?" Istra asked" "For years I have set ideas and I am ok providing I am not challenged and somewhere that femininity sneaks in an so far, but somewhere along that path, Master will say something and I get weepy like last night I lost it and got emotional, it means I can go just so far with this winding up Master and using sarcasm, but somewhere he will say or do something and I will have nowhere to go except inside me or be a sobbing mess. It means I can not really stand up to Men and if I do it only last for a very brief period and then I would say being female kicks in. In the beginning I could not believe all this was happening and the security services would be banging on the door wanting this nothing person back. Now if I was

A rich person's daughter. Then that might happen, but not with my luck!"

"Now I am scared I can not keep this charade up for long so do not blame me if it goes wrong" "No we will not because we are all like that, we are all female with femininity qualities and I cry too, but secretly or quietly like yesterday but they was watching us closely to see when we started to weep, because we handle a set amount of pain then it becomes too much. Then we all lose control, but the next time it's further away. You will see in time, Master thinks very highly of you and me. He saw that from very early on. We are his team!" "Well then maybe I am frightened to let the team down" "then best not to worry about it because you can not stop it happening anymore than I can, it is what it is Aureus! I am just as liable to let the team down. But if the Men get what they want out of it, then it must be all to the good." "Clear as Mud" I said again "Anyway Istra I would rather the Domestic girls not see me in this state, they might cheer" "No silly they are invariably scared of their own partner Masters, in case there is a problem!" "We do not need any more problems Istra!" I will try to do my best as always" yes I know you will Aureus."

Then we could clearly hear the bucket and spade brigade, clanking the bucket methinks they will attract every Goon for miles!"

"Goon?" Istra enquired, "I am just trying to slip into my part" "well done Aureus I am impressed," "so will

I be, if we do not attract more punishments because of noisy Domestics!"

Istra spoke "Where is your team leader?" "We do not have one" "so whom put you 4 together then" Istra added, "just one of the Guards we are new to this operation." One of the 4 Domestic girls said "I can imagine" Istra sad. "Then do you know your chores here today?" The one that spoke before then said "Yeah we have to wash and scrub you bitches to get you ready for your punishments!" Istra looked at me and I was equally stunned and that almost got my blood on the boil as I laid back in "You guys need to learn some manners and the racket you have made getting here would not have gone unnoticed and someone will have clocked you, if they also hear your dialogue you'll be in for punishment or the first plane home!" At that very second Master Niobi appeared through the doorway and he said "Hush slave Aureus, these girls clearly need to feel the whip for their insolence getting over here and to call the Masters pride and joy Bitches, I think not," "NOW GET THEM WASHED! Then brush and braid their hair, now get moving! I will be back in 30 minutes!!" Master Niobi said loudly which reminded me of my first days here and then he disappeared and the Domestics sheepishly got on with their work as Istra looked me straight in the face "Goons Aureus?" which she said in a low voice and I returned a smile and said quietly "well maybe not Master Niobi he's not so bad." "I think I mean there is good and bad in us all and different things can nominate that mood." Then

Istra said you're becoming institutionalized!" "That's a long word, do you really think so?" I knew the term and what it implied and basically it implies I am becoming comfortable with my situation here, I know if I was alone I never would have survived and the other Musson slaves helped me live through the first lot and even some of the Domestics. But then that thought brought home the realization that not all the Domestics were clearly all nice some were clearly aggressive.

The 30 minutes soon passed, it seemed like just a few minutes since we last saw Master Niobi and here he was again with Ahmed in tow, I chuckled to myself "backup" I could see Istra heard me, but I kept quiet as now was not the time to be sarcastic in front of this crew of horrible Domestics.

Master Niobi spoke "There is good news and bad news, the good news is you are ready in the allotted time!" "Then Istra asked "Pray tell what the bad news Master Niobi Sir is? "You missed breakfast because the wash and brush squad were too slow in their duties, they too will have to forgo there's too." Then it came out "What Mister we have to miss our food because we did not get these bitches ready for their punishments on time, I don't think so. I came here to earn some bread not be insulted by the likes of you!" then she and the other three pushed passed Masters Niobi and Ahmed as they stormed out of our chamber.

Istra was clearly in shock as I saw her face as she looked in my direction, and I was watching Master Niobi as I did not really want to cross him, there was enough aggression from the wash and brush up crew as Master Niobi put it to get his blood to boil.

Master Niobi then said "come you twos lets get to work and they came forward and presented them selves in the well known position for us both to place our wrist to wrist chains over their heads so they could pick us up and transport us to today's planned event.

We was off out of the chamber down the long corridors until we arrived at one of the open space rooms where they just have guy wires dangling down, This is where we often have training program which is just 500 lashes apiece, they can knock it off in a couple of hours and the advantage here is the singletail operators can chop and change targets at will, so once again Istra was placed on my right and she was about 10 feet apart. The nearest vertical upright is like about another 10 feet to my left and 10 feet to Istra's right so there was plenty of room for the Guys to move around us.

It was not long before the Guys started to appear like Master Robert came first followed by the Doctor, Then Master Musson appeared with that Master Matt again, not sure I like him.

Masters Ahmed and Niobi were also present plus several Guards to insure of security being maintained.

Now that once again the Guys had made sure that both Istra and myself were standing legs apart and hands lightly above our heads and the centre of the wrist to wrist chains was connected to the lowered guy wire and eyelet so they could connect our centre chain link to the eyelet with a climbers cleat, a sort or almost triangular thing with a spring-loaded arm so both eyelets could be connected together and they could then raise and lower by how much our arms were to be above our heads enabling our whole bodies to be clear targets for the whips. The testing trick was to leave our ankle to ankle chains lose to see how long it would be before we instinctively closed legs and created punishment conditions, what I call crafty maneuvers.

Then it was Master Robert that wasted no more time in getting the session underway as he landed his first Stockwhips impact down my spine sort of neck to waist and I tugged at the overhead restraining wires as I had not seen it coming, now I must get my breath control into gear so as he lands I am taking in air and as the pain builds I begin to release it and grab another gulp of air. At the same time Master Niobi is attacking slave Istra, but I realize with so many Guys about that this will not remain one on one for long as it's bound to be a multiple whipping session. Though just when I thought it could not get any worse the Guards I assume on Master Mussons orders come into the large room with two pyramid towers. These only serve one function and that is electrodes in our vaginas and the bit I dread would again soon be Master Niobi and his damn spit to lubricate the electrode so it would slip easier into my vagina. I lost all sight of Istra now as they had me facing away from her as I straddled the pyramid and the electrode had been eased in as Master Niobi spoke "Good girl you are getting better at accepting these devices into your vagina, lovely electrodes to invade the whole of your body" though I was sure he meant to say "Hole rather than Whole." Then they secured the pyramids to the floor and connected the long power cables. Then Master Musson took over and he came up close from behind and again said "Young slave Aureus how are you going to get out of this predicament?" and I said again "I am not Master! As would cause your whip arm to cramp up and then we could all take a holiday?" "Are you hearing this response Young slave Istra and what is your recommendations?" "Simple! Master takes a holiday and saves us all from a headache, Master Sir you created Musson slave Aureus and now you'll have to suffer her weird ideas as we all do as lovely as she is!"

"Master Niobi Sir this is a new development have you heard the like?" "No Master Musson Sir, maybe the Doctor can enlighten us as to the nature of the slaves thinking?" then Master Musson says "Doctor lets have your valuable medical input, well Doctor?" "It strikes me as maybe you are asking too much of a slaves brain as they are there to serve and maybe they have no positive answer Master Sirs" "Good point, so lets ask the young Master Matt what he thinks?" "Me Sir?" "Yes you Sir"

"Well Gentlemen I would say I think we are wasting good whipping times!" Then Master Musson "just like a young Bull not to weigh up the advantages, however in this instance I think he is right. Then without warning the pain of Masters bullwhip was across my breast with such force it felt like carpet burn and it could be heard another lash from a singletail as it cracked on or around slave Istra and then Master started to speed up his attack and I hated this as I had to speed up my breath control with short gasps for air and release, then I felt the two prong attack on other parts of my body so I now knew another Male was assisting Master in his attacks, but I had shut my eyes as it helped concentration. I felt sure I could not endure this for long as then Master just stopped saying "Doctor where the lemonade is?"

"Here Gentlemen is the lemonade!" "Good" said Master Musson and then adding "I have a new toy for you two to try out slave Aureus and slave Istra, I have had a special singletail made where the central core carries a metallic strand and will aid an electrical contact as it strikes the body, what do you think to that both?" "Slave Aureus first" "Dangerous Master Sir if the polarities were accidently reversed maybe Master would get a shock!" "Yes I forgot slave Aureus is an Electronics specialist" "What does slave Istra have to say?" "Master Sir Maybe it's possible for some poor slave to mentally reverse the polarities as slave Aureus suggests and we could have a holiday!" "Don't you just love this pair always thinking of a rest?" "Well maybe after we have tested this ne whip" "SWITCH ON Master Niobi Sir!" and within seconds I felt the shock from the vaginal electrode shoot through to my arse as that is where the whip landed but it was also the ideal angle for Master to pull back and reverse the whip onto slave Istra's buttocks and I could hear Istra slips out a quiet ouch. Then Master went into over drive and sped up his attack using the new whip and in some ways the electric shock was a pain on a pain and could sometimes self annihilate itself but some of the time in the most sensitive areas could be over powering painful. Then when I thought we had got a handle on it Master Niobi had such a whip too and then they both sped up until the shocks and the pain were so bad I lost it and tears swelled as did the horrid snot which we had no control over, in-between strikes I could hear slave Istra weeping as well so there was no lost honor we had fought the best we could go to endure but there comes a time when its just too much.

"Gentlemen I believe it is time to stop on this first occasion "the Doctor said loudly and then the two Men stopped and Master Niobi said "now I need Lemonade. "Doctor your patients need you!" Master Musson said loudly and the continued to talk generally "right Master Matt Sir what have you learned today then?"

"That's easy Master Musson Sir! I can now see that you do not want mindless slaves, you want them to have some positive inputs even though they know as you do that they can never win!" Then Master Niobi said "Has nothing to do with winning or losing it's about absolute control, but we allow them certain freedom to breath within that control. "Guards when the Doctor has finished painting the iodine on and the Domestic girls have put the tabards on return them to quarters as it's close to lunchtime we shall all retreat for lunch.

With that the Masters all vanished leaving us with the Doctor and the Guards, then the Doctor said "Guards help me remove these electrodes so we can clean them up!" which they did and then the Guards assumed the position for us to place our wrist to wrist chains over their heads so they could pick us up and take us back to our quarters, the Domestics seem to know to take the electrodes away for cleaning to rather than just left on the floor.

Soon we arrived back at our chamber that Istra and I shared and for a while we will have some free time, but the day is young and it's not like Master to stop for breakfast let alone lunch, so I think something is afoot.

Istra spoke quietly "when those odd Domestic girls were here, I am sure you said something just as Ahmed came in." "I did-I said here comes backup." "I do not follow" Istra said, "those so called Domestic were not acting like Domestics for us, one of them girls really tore into Master Niobi I thought he would burst a blood vessel, so I wondered if they were here for some other reason, especially when Master Niobi did not retaliate, nor did Master Ahmed!" No you are right Aureus; they both took a tongue lashing of a female worker!"

And neither of them said nothing if that had been us we would have been on bread and water for a week." Said Istra and I added "and then some!" "So it must have been for our benefit" Istra said quietly and calmly.

Then 4 Domestic girls appeared without sound other than the sounds of music playing constantly all over the compound it was difficult to hear the comings and goings of Domestics and Guards, unless of course they was making a racket like the 4 this morning. But this crew had our lamb stew lunch, some bread and a metal cup of milk presumably to keep our strength up. The team leader of the Domestics pulled Istra over to one side; I only realized when I heard Istra's ankle chains from no noise to noise as she was moving. Then the 4 left us to our solitary confinement and to munch on the a stew which was of lamb in little chunks and potatoes and some vegetables and in a light gravy substance, I rather liked it more because it was a regular as this was no posh restaurant we got only what they cooked and that was this stew.

Istra moved closer to me in a way I realized she wants to say something but on the quiet as if to whisper but that was not always possible because of the constant sounds of the music. Then when she thought she was close enough she said "the team leader thinks there is plot afoot!"

She added "the team leader whom I have known a while is usually not wrong and said we should watch our backs, something is not right around here."

After this morning I am not surprised I thought, the problem is we never know what is afoot if the Domestics do not leak the odd bit of information every now and then, some do and a lot do not, more because they fear Master Musson as we all do in a way because he has the control of the whole thing.

After Istra and I finished our lamb stew and begun to laze about as in resting because there is bound to be something on the cards, the day has had its moments and started early and its not like the Master to start early and finish early, no something is on for the afternoon and I am sure I can feel it.

Then Master Niobi appeared on his own, so I thought oh only one of us was going somewhere until he stuck his forefinger to his lips as if to indicate SSsh or be quiet. "I can not explain just now but be on your guard something is not right." "Yes Master Niobi Sir I figured that this morning with the wash and brushes up crew, people do not act like that in the normal way of things." "Oh so this is normal to you now slave Aureus!" Istra said defiantly, "Easy now slave Istra, Aureus is right people do not do strange things then try to act normal or the other way around. The Master still has the breaking program set for today and this evening, but this is because he cares enough to do it. Trying to keep you safe from a more evil predator than himself, you have to believe me, Istra knows this as well as I do, he does things for a reason." Master Niobi said.

"Now here is Master Ahmed, now SSsh!" "Are they ready Master Niobi Sir?" Then as usual the dipped their heads so we could place our wrist to wrist chains over their heads, so they could easily pick us pick us up and carry us to the next chamber of horrors.

It was not long before it was clear we was headed for the arena and likely to have a whole load of guests, its goner be a zoo. There again was the magic roundabout waiting to greet us for another attempt to send us to the depths of insanity, already the room was filling with people or bodies as they was all a blur to me if they was not right in front of me. I had Master Niobi carry me this time and that in itself was an honor I knew that Istra would not have worried, she is not like that, we are really quite simple and easy going. I had not really thought about it before but I am with people that care and we are a sort of family much like some military units seem to see themselves, though more on the term of a band of brothers and sisters if there are any women among them.

Master Niobi placed me on the platform of the roundabout thing so I would not have to hobble step up. Then he secured my ankles apart, as setting the path that I would not get to choose the path on my own, all the paths were being set for me as the owned property of Master. At the same time Istra was going through the same process with the assistance of Master Ahmed. Then again we was both connected to the cleat that dangled from above to hold our arms up thus clear our whole bodies was as naked target for the whips. When we was secure and could not move from our location without help a new development seem to be taking place as many of the guests decided to do a fly or walk past as I am guessing some kind last respects type of thing. A Domestic exclaimed "You dirty bitch I hope you get everything you got coming!" then she spat heavily all over my back.

Then Master Niobi who was acting as Guard stood within a few feet of me, called the Doctor over and saying to the Girl almost at the same time "that was uncalled for, you should know the rules is you have a grievance with any slave or party within the operation you should make the security aware of it so we can deal with it in accordance with the rules. "Fuck your rules I am here just for the bread man!" I think we both Istra and I realized it was the girl from this morning. I then said "Master Niobi Sir" and before I could say more he replied with "SSsh I know" then Master Niobi said "Musson slave Aureus shut your eyes and keep them closed that is a direct order to your destination Identity" and like lightning my eyes went shut as if on automatic and I knew he was commanding the self of me that is directly linked to Master Musson, though I can not explain it further its like a switch that switches me out and her in especially when addressed formally Musson slave Name.

I knew straight away as soon as I heard the voice that this is what is thought to be someone of presence or power with a distinctive voice that have their fingers in every pie as he spoke it that posh almost slow clearly spoken words We meet again young lady, the Master is going to let me watch while he breaks you into an obedient soul, I must admit I have longed to make this journey to see this event!" then it could be heard "That's not goner happen your lordship as I have a grenade in my hand and so do my buddies, that bitch is worth a million bucks and I mean to have it," Then Master Niobi interjected with "well she's actually worth two million bucks!" Then Master Robert interrupted with "but you'll never see it if you plan to go to the Colonel, he'll slap you in chains because he lies, he hates women that think they are Men or try to do business in this way." "Well we will have to see about that! Now release that bitch and one of my buddies will take control of her while I take charge of Mr. Lordship here. Master Niobi released my wrist to wrist chain and lowered it gently so it would not tug and then he bent down to release my ankles and I sort of swung to my left using my chains as a weapon and their weight made them fly in a way to act like a weapon and the chains caught the buddies off guard and as they collapsed I fell to the floor. The Doctor moved in on the buddies and Master Robert moved in on the girl holding the unknown lord. Compound security rushed forwards to contain the situation and calm was restored. The girl with the big mouth said "You stupid bitch I was about to get you released and free!" I replied "Don't tell lies you wanted to try to get a million dollars or what was it "Bucks" from the Colonel, I would not trust that snake any more than you," "But at least you would get what they are about to do to you!" "You want to bet on that?"

Master Niobi Sir Re-connect me please I trust them a lot more than you or that snake the Colonel!" then Master Niobi said "spoken like a true Musson slave should I am proud of you slave Aureus!" "I will second that "said Master Robert. The mouthy girl said "what's the bitch doing? Some thing you would not understand she is a broken slave and obedient to the Master here, than to any one else. It's your antics here that make you the silly bitch said the unknown Lord." Then Master Musson appeared and said "he's correct all the Musson slaves are my slaves, they know and realize they are a part of my family. I say family not property as it could be argued that, but they are not mindless articles they are slaves in my family and thus loyal to me and me only."

Master Musson then added "This may surprise you all Musson slave Aureus or slave Aureus should we continue to affect the second breaking of your self?" then one of us replies with "Yes Master!" And adds "The Unknown Lord has waited a long time and journeyed specially to see it we must not disappoint him or yourself Master, plus if I may add if. I can do anything to be assured that the snake the Colonel can not get his hands on me I will do that too. Lords, Gentlemen and Sirs!"

Compound security leader asks "Master Musson Sir what do you wish to do with this girl?" "Put her in hand cuffs for now, but hold, "Slave Aureus would you object if she watched she may learn something?" "No object at all Master Musson Sir so long as she does not make a noise or interrupt!" "We can make sure of that Master Robert added with a smile. Then the unknown Lord said Master Musson and combined Gentlemen I am overwhelmed by your professionalism and integrity and thank you for this great honor."

Then Master Musson said Gentlemen all please lets get settled time is passing and we need to make a start, what a lot of you people may not fully understand is if we let slave Aureus go, there is a very real risk that she would end up in the hands of the Colonel. That guy Peter that she was with let me buy her for £100,000 if she just returned to him I would expect he might try to sink another deal with the Colonel. So in the fullness of time she is far safer with us as our family and a friend to many of you. As you witnessed today she acted in honor and with loyalty to her Master and friends in their safety."

Then slave Istra said loudly "you're a better slave than I gave credit for but honored to be your cell mate!" then I said sheepish like "no more please you'll make me cry!" "Please Master lets go!" I said loudly and with that as in tradition Master Musson air cracked his bullwhip prior to the next stroke landing on my body, I think I was pretty well depressed and it no longer mattered where he landed them, we would just take them as I or we felt was loosing the will to live. Master was landing down the sides of my spine on both sides top, Middle and Bottom, then he would change tactics and be all over my front from, my breasts to my belly and then between my legs up and down each leg as though there was a pattern he was drawing. I / we was not really aware of being in any pain then down my legs at thigh height the attacks were so the ends of the singletails landed at the ends to create stripes, Master was not the type to effect wrap a rounds if they had no real benefit. Then I said loudly "May we have Master Robert as well before I fall asleep!" I suspect I must have had an increase of adrenaline as I needed to feel the pain for reasons I could not explain, I could see the Doctor was agitated by my request, but Master just carried on and totally ignored the Doctor and the blows were thick and fast. Strangely I was able to maintain control of my breathing. I was aware that my body was leaking either blood or sweat or both, as it ran down my body to Masters nice clean floor. Again I had just realized that the roundabout was not rotating which allowed for the two Masters to move their positions. Then Master Musson stopped, followed by Master Robert. I had not realized that Master Robert was the other singletail operator. The Doctor moved in with his medical pads. The Doctor then pressed some of the more leaky cuts and gashes. Then I heard Master Musson talk to the Compound Security Leader "You better double the Guards in the tower and add more as it gets darker, bring in more Men if needed and dogs too, I want the strip between first and second fence patrolled by three Men teams in each patrol lets not get caught with our pants down the girl would have had a meeting place to give over slave Aureus. Let's make sure we have everything covered."

Master Robert then said "do you want to stop the breaking again?" and Master replied with "No it's not fair on slave Aureus to keep halting every time the wind blows a fart besides she knows we are not out to harm her, this will strengthen the desire to remain with us and be with us today proves she has lost interest with the outside world, though I am still shocked about that which took place today. I should have seen it coming Master Robert Sir!" "I think we all should have seen today's events coming, so I feel we must be getting complacent now. It's clear we have enemies...

Then Master says out loud "I am sorry everybody I cannot continue, I am concerned for all our safety, I would prefer if all our Friends and Guests should stay the night, stay in the compound we are bringing in the reserve Guards as I speak. Guards release slave Istra and Aureus and take them to the medical wing with the Doctor. I want around the clock Guards on that area!" Then Master came up to me and said "I am sorry slave Aureus, I must make sure we are all safe and this must wait!" "Yes Master I understand we must make sure everyone is safe!" In any case I am exhausted as well as it's been a longer day than normal and I need my sleep escape. As the Guards carried Istra and myself to the medical wing I heard Master Say "take the girl to the Brigg and lock her up for tonight" A gleefully response was "Yes Sir Master Musson Sir!"

When we arrived at the medical wing and the Guards placed me on the bed in a sitting up position as we had to be covered in yellow smelly Iodine liquid, one of the paramedic guys attended slave Istra whilst the Doctor worked on me. Then three Guards appeared and the Doctor said "Guard out in the corridor if you do not mind it's a bit cramped in here, besides we are sealed here, there is no outer walls or windows!"

Then the Doctor put a clean tabard over my head and tied the waist ties and then said "Now lie back and get some rest slave Aureus and you too slave Istra when the medic is finished with you."

It was not long before the Doctor left turning down the main lights to leave night lights burning.

Soon I felt tears fill our eyes and snot fill the nostril cavity, Istra sat up asking "what's the matter Aureus?" I replied "will this become all my fault putting all these people in danger from stupid money hungry Domestics as well as that damn Colonel?" "Oh no Aureus that's not your fault and I've now understood a something I have never ever seen before, You wanted to be punished for the events of tonight and that is why you wanted Master to continue and why you handled it all so well!" "I am not so sure I could have done that, I am wondering if Master has seen it as well and that's his real reason for stopping, you make me look so small Aureus." "Sorry Istra I never meant that and I do not know why I/we wanted to continue, just seemed the right thing to do to prove the girl was wrong in her actions to put lives at risk and what for but money! and you still Master Mussons number one, if you think I have overstepped my ranking tell Master. He is sure to come to a solution, not sure I can and this failing in the girl will invariably anger the Colonel and he may then take even more risks to get what he wants. Logically I should invoke standing order 4 before I have someone's death on my conscious!" "No! This is not your fault, but it's too serious to leave to ourselves and you know I have to let him know what concerns us, now Aureus you need sleep escape you must be exhausted so go to sleep." I soon dropped off into deep sleep.

I awoke to the sound of buckets clanking and water rushing from the medical wing tap into the buckets and of course the regular beat of the constant music being played 24/7/ 365. Then I saw the Doctor with a stern scowl on his face. "What's up Doctor? I can not talk about it but you have to stay there until the Master visits." Then I look towards Istra's bed, but she still there fast asleep. "Don't look there Istra did nothing, if there is a culprit then it's yourself," as the Doctor points to a small button microphone attached to the headboard light unit. "Oh" I said as I know electronic listening devices as a something I have come across in my lines of work.

"Any chance of some water Doctor my mouth feels like sand-paper," "sure that should be Alright so long as you do not have a secret stash of Cyanide." "No Doctor I do not." And then Master Musson appears just as Istra is awakening. "Dare I say morning all? Then Master Musson says "leave us everyone!" and the Doctor plus one paramedic leave the room then Master sticks his head out the door beyond the curtain and says "its fine you can stay in the corridor!"

Istra looks at me as if to ask what's going on and Master says "your conversation last night was recorded and you're not in trouble as I know Istra would have told me anyway!" "I need to make it clear that non of that what happened yesterday and last night was your fault and I appreciate your believing that it was your fault and that you yourself took it upon yourself to allow us to punish you for a something that was beyond your control, now had I been in the room when that girl pulled her stunt I would have told everyone to stay still and do nothing, as you could have been damaged or damaged another inadvertently trying to save others, its something that has never happened before and I had not made allowances for the possibilities of such an event. In this instance standing order 4 does not enter into it and you need to forget about it slave Aureus. I am not sure that you really need to be broken again, as I think your brain is as loyal as it can be, but the Doctor feels as I do it is better to be safe than sorry, I can not allow the possibilities of that Man getting a hand hold over you as I am sure he will destroy you for his money thirsts over and above logics. So as soon as we can reset things we will continue and we are still impressed by your mental and physical actions, though I would rather you let me handle the situation next time, if there is a next time." "Slave Aureus! Slave Istra will remind you if you need her understandings."

"I sincerely believe that if we sent you back to the UK and that Peter guy was to locate you he would invariably try to resell you to the Colonel.

I believe you are safer with us, even though I had not planned to let you go. I had not planned for the Colonel to become hell bent on trying to take you and Istra. Then he smiled, I want you here." And then he left the medical wing through the forever open doorway albeit had a curtain that could be pulled across and that left us in our own silence apart from the music playing in the back ground that covered Masters shoes on the floor of the corridor.

After a few minutes Istra turned towards me and smiled, I sort of waved my right hand because of the damn microphone I was too scared to speak and then pointed up to it and then Istra whispered "its alright now that its all been explained you can not act on your own even to save Master, we are his slaves and we do as he commands, in the main you know that. Master can not foresee every problem that might occur." "Yes Istra I see that now, though I was so scared that the girl had a possible bomb so close and I was scared for the royal whom I could not see clearly anyway just reacted I guess."

"So what happens now?" I asked Istra "We go back to our chamber in the morning maybe or back into training program, you remember 3 times a week the whip and whatever gives at weekends." She said with a smile. "Yes I know Istra" I replied equally with a smile as its our life now and thinking I wish people would let us get on with it without interruption. And with that as the lights dimmed I drifted off into sleep escape.

SEQUENCE 21

TRAINING BEGINS AGAIN

I awoke to the sound of noises in the medical wing, that being the wash and brush up crews as we got to call the Domestic girls applying that job, though thinking about it they do all sorts from cooking for us all on mass and some are delegated to clean the torture chambers or the rooms of horror.

Then Istra came to an awoken state almost as if from a night mare and she sheepishly looked at me and said "I'm alright just a bad dream" That's to come I expect." "You're so very right!" said the team leader and continued "The Master wants you both to have a soak!" "God No" I said quietly and Istra backed me up saying "Your joking!" as I looked at her and I said "That has to be a punishment if I ever knew one, do we have to wash our mouths out with soap?" "No the water does that Aureus, but you are right it sounds more like a punishment than a bath!" "So when you two are ready the Guards are outside to take you" the team leader said almost as if she enjoyed the moment.

The Guard soon entered the medical wing and then

they performed the usual routine to lower their heads so we could put our wrist to wrist chains over their heads so they could pick us up and carry of off to the next torture chamber.

We soon arrived at the large holes area, or the wet rooms maybe here there are some round holes in the ground with a mechanical plug at the bottom so I am told, not seen it empty, probably just as well empty swimming pools and empty holes in the ground frighten me for some strange reason. The operation consists of an electric winch on what looks like an "I" girder high up in the lofty reaches and it travels this way and that so as to lower poor slaves into the water and one of the Guards is getting me ready for the plunge by using the famous climber cleat to lock my centre wrist to wrist chain link to the eye link at the end of the winch guy wire so that my wrists and hands are virtually level and then they motor up the winch that lifts me up and then the Guards push my body over the appropriate hole whilst I get my breathing sorted for to hold my breath. Then down we go and as frightened as I am with my eyes tight shut I know this is one of three dunks, and then to my relief we are going up again. Then the Domestic Girls soap us from head to toe with soft sponges and lots of soap, then its up and over the damned hole again to rinse off and again I have to hold my breathe and shut my eye tight shut, down we go, but this time seems longer than before and I know I am bursting in my chest to gasp more fresh air and its all water then my arms drop and I am now in a panic as I start to lose the grip to keep my mouth shut. But then like magic my arms are raised and slowly my head clears the waters surface and standing there before me is Master Musson and then he says in a very determined way "Musson Slave Aureus If you dare to do that to me again, think for yourself I will leave you down there!" to which I spluttered a reply as "Yes MASTER!" and to show he meant it the Guard lowered me down into the water and after a short period I was raised out of the pool and lowered to the safety of the floor and four Domestic girls with towels to dry my body and whilst this was being done I saw Istra going in for a rinse and wondered was she goner be told off too? and she got rinsed and was halted at the point her head was just out of the water, as then Master knelt down and told her something I could not hear and she was then brought up to another four Domestic girls with towels to dry her body as well and with that Master left the room.

After about an hour I am guessing the Domestic girls had finished drying us and using an olde-worlde looking hairdryer and then brushed and braided our hair, I think I was too terrified to speak out loud in case Master was still hovering about though I kept looking at Istra and she seemed to be trying to mouth something to me, but lip reading or mind reading is some thing I had not learned yet.

Then the Guards turned up to take us I assume to our chamber for breakfast if it was not too late, but I figured we will soon find out and again the Guards dipped their heads so we could place our wrist to wrist chains over their heads so they could pick us up and off we went away from this horrible chamber.

But no food as we passed our chamber onto the next horror chamber of the day until we ventured back into the auditorium chamber where the magic roundabout was and so then as I could see the gathering bodies, even though I could not make them out, I knew what was to come and sure enough my Guard placed me on the platform right next to Master Niobi who was waiting to link my arms above me prior to connecting my ankles apart, it all happened so slick like and even Istra was ready when I clearly was not.

The music picked up a bit in volume and the lights went down except those on me and Istra opposite me on the roundabout and then I heard Master whom I could see clearly to my right air crack his bullwhip and it looked like a really long one, must be all of 12 feet I am thinking. That's going to hurt as the body has to be thicker up the handle end to carry the weight of the length, these long whips carry a natural punch of their own without the operator inputting power. Then Master Musson comes over to me and he says in my right ear in a low voice "You know this had to happen I have to be sure you are mine, MINE! SLAVE AUREUS!"

"Master this has nothing to do with Istra please leave her out of this, it's clearly between you and me and any Masters you wish to bring in!" "Did you hear what young slave Aureus has requested Master Niobi Sir?" "Yes Master Musson Sir!" "In point of fact for once I think young Musson slave Aureus is learning to be considerate of others here" "Master Musson Sir!" I then request on behalf of Musson slave Aureus that we comply with this request for once to show we are equally considerate and cut Musson slave Istra loose." Master Musson stepped back out of my line of sight and then said "As you wish Master Niobi Sir! And of course Musson slave Aureus" "Guards release Musson slave Istra!"

Then Istra disappeared from my visual sight and then Master again air cracked his long bullwhip, which I knew was soon to follow, it did across my back to start with and then with spacing's he ventured down my back and sure enough it had to be a longer one than I have felt in a while as it cut deep straight off and it hurt like hell and I knew I would not be able to maintain my breathing at this pace and then my worst fears when Master Niobi began on my front though with maybe an 8 footer, but it was enough to bring tears and the dreaded snot was already dribbling down my front and some even got flicked of by Master Niobi's whip. It was not long before there was a lot of red in amongst sweat and snot dribbling down my front as I could not see behind me I had no idea about that side, but I sure could feel the pain like dull mallet with a thuddery sensation, shorter 6 foot whips tend to sting 8 footers have a bit more impact but less stingy 10 footers have thuddery feel but Master 12 footer was thuddery with a sensation I can only imagine a mallet of something wood like. It was then I turned my attention to the nuts and bolts that were closely visible I wanted with my mind to unscrew or undo them nuts and bolts that could be seen close above me as a distraction, I knew I was weeping quietly and the two Master's carried on relentlessly I thought I saw the Doctor where Istra was stood, I could see he was not amused, never is when the Masters are doing their thing. I knew I was beginning to lose it as I started not to feel the pain, must have been a couple hours now as in training we get to know how many lashes approximate a time factor though only the Master's count, somewhere my legs gave way and I was kind of dangling on my wrists, it felt more like my spine had collapsed and sort of bowing forward. I knew the Doctor had moved from his position and I heard in the distance, "GET AWAY DOCTOR!" "We are not finished yet and neither is she, you know it!" and then they started again though in my mind it was all jumbling into a mix of confusion until I black out completely.

Again when we came round, it was as before like my mind could see it all taking place as if another personality was in control until I recovered enough to know we was back as Musson slave Aureus and we was collapsed on the floor, we was passing in and out of consciousness this time I just wanted to sleep, then Master Musson asked "WHO ARE YOU SLAVE?" and we feebly replied with "Musson slave 6 Master" "Good she is back again" then the Doctor said "Sirs I must insist we get her back to medical I do not like this passing in and out of consciousness!" I vaguely recall hearing Master Musson saying "What do you think Master Niobi Sir?" and he replied "You know yourself Master Musson Sir that only the first break is dramatic, I think she cracked differently than what we have seen so far and again she fought it for 4 hours." Master Niobi said, But that is normal for Musson slave Aureus!" then Master Niobi replied with, "Is it, I have not seen this reaction before, we could be in uncharted conditions and the Doctors concerns maybe a warning Master Musson Sir!" "Are you weakening Master Niobi Sir?" "No Master Musson Sir! No just being cautious!"

"Gentlemen-Sirs While you are trying to evaluate her mentality she could die here and now so for fuck sake decide I do not want to be responsible for Musson slave Aureus if you two can not make up your minds what you want to do" the Doctor said angrily and most emphatically.

Then Master Niobi said well at present she is passed out so she will not feel anything anyway so you may do more harm by continuance, we can always repeat it later if its required" "Guards get a stretcher! Doctor she is in your capable hands. Do not let me down!" Master Musson said.

We awoke in the medical wing though I was still very groggy and not me as I know, but we are now in Ms6 personality, only the Doctor realizes that this was never achieved before and its another level, another deeper personality there's no knowing how long this personality could or would retain controlling our brain space or whatever the term is.

Even the Master has miss read when he asked who

we was and the response should have been Musson slave Aureus not Ms6 as this has never been recognized by the Master or anyone. Except the Doctor.

Then I/we could clearly see the Doctor but we did not speak, having been here before I knew primarily she would only communicate with the Master. It was clear the Doctor had plastered his smelly yellow iodine on and we had a tabard on to keep the many wounds clean and also had something around each leg like a leg sheaths to keep wounds clean I had not seen before. The Doctor raised the headboard part so we could sit up and it was then I saw the Domestic girls with a single bowl of food on a tray with one metal cup of milk.

Everything happened in total silence except of course for the constant playing of music through the many loudspeakers within the compound, but the Domestics too have all seen this before as the Musson slave personalities only ever communicate with the Master.

Partly why the Domestics in the main obey all commands because they can see just how far the Master will go to keep order with all of us, the other part would be not to offend their own partner Master or be flown home.

I knew something was different and changed, if we ever got to be back as ourselves we had to change with it and be closer to the Musson slave Aureus personality.

At that point Ms6 burst into tears and the Doctor seemed to be concerned. For reasons I can not explain we was crying for hours as if we could not stop. The

Doctor was clearly concerned and phoned through to the Master to get here quickly. When the Master arrived whoever we was could not look at Him, "Doctor what is happening?" Master Musson enquired

"I think she is having a nervous breakdown is the best I can tell, I think she needs to forget what she did wrong, but its not so clear in my mind, I am not sure that she did think for herself, I think she acted to save You Master Musson Sir!" "EXPLAIN DOCTOR!" "I believe she acted to save her heart beat as in you, without you there is no Musson slave Aureus, at the time I think slave Aureus had gone to Musson slave Aureus to deal with the shock of what was before her eyes, that damn Domestic girl turned rotten and I can not say when slave Aureus personality will if ever returns not knowing more about the mind and the incident your telling her off in the soak room then a training whatever directly after the soak may have helped do more damage. You also have missed when you asked Musson slave Aureus who she was, she said Ms6, now we both know you never officially claimed her that so I believe you have broken the broken slave if that is possible? I believe you forced the Musson slave whomever to go into two levels deeper, it's a wonder she is still alive and I am not a psychiatrist you know" "I believe she needs E.C.T. I have the equipment here but I need to call in a specialist to assist as I do not want to damage her further, do I have your permission Master Musson Sir?" "Yes of course Doctor and why the hostility?" "I think you have misread the situation." "I have seen it before where the subject broke the first time went to a deeper level than was realized and by the time they applied it a second time it was too much and she died because they went too far,

You may have come close to that here, I would be guessing but I believe that the body that holds all the Aureus personalities have a strong survival constitution and that has saved you from a murder charge!"

"My psychiatrist pal will better be able to explain it, but for now I must sedate slave Aureus into a deep sleep."

When I/we next awoke, I/we could see that we was still in the medical wing with a distinctive headache of a type I do not recall having before, I felt sure someone had hit our head at temple level on both sides with a hammer on each side! But I did feel calmer and my memory was something of a blur and not sure what I did this time to end up in the medical wing. Then the Doctor appeared saying "Good morning Ms6" but we did not reply as we only spoke to the Master, The Doctor did not seem bothered that we did not reply, so I/we never give it another thought. Then four Domestic girls arrived to bath and brush my hair, one was carrying my bowl of porridge and metal cup of milk, I seem to think I had a feeling I had somehow missed this but I did not understand and so let the Domestic girls do their miraculous work.

"Good morning Doctor" said Master Musson in his broken English voice as he entered the medical wing and continued "how is our patient this morning?" "Ms6 seems fine today." Then he faced us directly and asked "are you ready to rejoin slave Istra in your joint chamber Musson slave Aureus?" "Yes please Master!" and then he said "then we shall arrange it," "Doctor your plan seems to have worked, if possible it might be useful to have your psychiatrist pal on the payroll, what do you think?" "As a consultant maybe, I am not sure I want him here underfoot otherwise he might start trying to psycho analyze us all." "As you see fit then Doctor though he was very useful and I found a lot of his interpretations useful to our operations here."

"Guard sees that Musson slave Aureus gets back to her chamber with Musson slave Istra, this morning if you please!" "Yes Sir I will do it directly." Not sure what that was all about but then it is often better not to know too much.

The Guard entered the medical wing and he helped me off the bed and then lowered his head so that I could place the wrist to wrist chains over his head in order for him to pick us up, then was on our way to our chamber and then we was there and there was slave Istra standing waiting to greet us, she put her hands together as she often did like the Hindus do to greet a fellow. The Guard dropped us off and left us to ourselves.

Then Istra whispered "are you alright Aureus you have been through a lot these past few days." "Yes Istra not sure what I did to get myself back into the medical wing, I seem to be accident prone."

Istra knew it was not the "me" that she had come to

know and I was locked inside our brain and could not communicate I knew she knew.

Then Master Niobi appeared with Master Ahmed so I knew it was time for chores of whatever that might entail. The Guys did the usual thing of lowering their heads so we could slip our chains over their heads so they could pick us up. I specifically noticed that there was no slip of routines for Ms6, she obeyed just as I would, though me it would be more out of fear, I think Ms6 loves it and so we was off down the long corridors and into the usual training room for the 3 times a week singletailing I could see Master Robert waiting with 2 Guards and the good Doctor. Master Ahmed was my carrier this time and Master Niobi was Istra's carrier and we was placed in the centre of the large room about 10 feet apart, this allowed the guys to move around us without tangling with the other operators providing someone was keeping a careful eye out for a clash. The electric winches were lowered and the centre link in our wrist to wrist chains was connected to the winch guy wire eye with the climber locking cleat. Naturally by now we was used to have legs spread to a certain gap, but for good measure each link closest to each ankle was cleated to the floor eye loops so our legs remained apart as I know Master like to surprise us with a singletail up between the legs. It soon began and I had Master Robert. As always the operating Master would air crack his whip and I think he had the 10 footer that Master had the other day and then it begun, now in this mindset Ms6 just breathed normally at this point, and

I was sure she was enjoying it, something I needed to learn as there will come a time I shall slip back in there. Each bullwhip impact was like a thuddery sensation, but it had changed because of the different operators as each can apply more or less force. Ms6 did not seem to need to look for distractions she just seemed to lap it up. After an hour or so the Guys stopped for lemonade that had been brought by four Domestic girls and as it was a routine training program with no Guests it was a relaxed ordeal and we too got a drink of lemonade. But no sooner was that rest period over and the Guys was back in action, now I had Master Niobi and his 8 footer and for Ms6 that was toy, she hardly murmured and Master Niobi even speed up his attack and she was now keeping pace with her breathing which was now picking up. It was then that the surprise was when Master Niobi welcomed Masters Ahmed and that young Matt to join in. As I could not see who was behind me, I had to guess that it was Master Ahmed as I am sure we felt his attack before, though I was not really feeling it as Ms6 still had the reigns and soon after that came another stop which stop breaks help one recover a little. But not for long this was enforced captivity not a tea party when I saw those damn Pyramids again and of course the vaginal electrodes to get us off balance. Master Niobi positioned mine whilst Master Robert positioned slave Istra's, then Master Niobi get an electrode out from his right pocket and showing us like he always did and then did that awful sound men make when they want to gather an amount of spit up from the throat and as I said "yuk how disgusting." Then there was aloud bang, like a bomb going off and I lost consciousness though it became clear I could hear people shouting and what seemed to be rushing about, plus the smell of burning electrics you could smell a distinctive electrical smell. It seemed I was now forced into sleep escape.

SEQUENCE 22

SABOTAGE ATTEMPT ONE

Someone shorted out the electric shock device in such a way it exploded and caught fire and thus the training program had to be stopped.

Then Master Niobi said with a sort of joy "She's back Master Robert Sir!" "Excellent!" Master Robert added as I peered over my left shoulder I could see Istra smiling as well. Then the Doctor spoke "Someone should notify the Master as I am sure he will want to know Musson slave Aureus has recovered and she is back with the living!" "Yes!" Master Niobi said "I will do that!" he disappeared as another Guard entered the room to replace Master Niobi as I was aware that Master had specific instructions that there should be at least 8 Males present at all training programs just in case the damn Colonel appeared. This gave the guys time to discover that the feed cables to the electrodes had been shorted out and caused the electric shock device to destroy itself. In the meantime the Domestic girls served everyone with some lemonade. The shock of the explosion caused my bladder to leak all over Master's floor and I was really thirsty. Then Master Musson appeared with Master Niobi and Master came right over to me and said "hello Musson slave Aureus are you alright?" and I/we replied "Yes Master though I am very thirsty" Then the Master addressed the Domestic girls and said "Team leader give Musson slave Aureus as much lemonade as she needs!" "I hope I can do as well as Ms6 Master." "I am sure you will do your best Musson slave Aureus!" Master Musson said. Then what I feared yet, someone switched the backup electrics box on without making sure the controls were off or it was done on purpose. Then the Guards rushed over to the electrics box with fire extinguishers and killed the fire, but then another very loud bang and the electrics box burst into flames again. I sort of jumped up but my ankle linkage to the floor stopped me getting any further. I could see the Doctor having words with Master as Master picked up Master Robert's long bullwhip and then he politely asks "Master Robert Sir may I borrow your bullwhip?" and Master Robert replies "You most certainly can Master Musson Sir!"

Then Master Musson air cracks it right in front of me and I try to remain as calm as possible and then it begins and its like before with Master Musson. It feels like a thuddery effect with a mallet applying pressure so the impact is I guess stiffer, but we cope and continue to cope getting our breathing right so we in hale when it lands and the exhale as quickly as possible for the next impact and as he speeds up we try to keep pace with him, failure to do so and you lose control of ones body and whilst I am thinking is he or isn't he and he does he speeds up to a speed I have difficulty maintaining and so again the tears begin to creep out and the nose fills with the dreaded snot and then just like that he stops and says "Thank you Musson slave Aureus you and Ms6 are one just separated by personalities!" Now I suspect that was to prove to us both that nothing has changed, that he is still the Master and I/we are his slave. "Now Gentlemen we have a mission that requires us to fly so I want the Doctor to look after the slaves Istra and Aureus plus 2 Guards!"

Master Niobi asks "Master Musson Sir what do we do about The Domestic girl in the Brigg?" "Stick some chains on her legs and we will take her with us and leave her at one of the other bases," Then Master Niobi replies "Is that wise Master Musson Sir?" "If we let her go here or even at any of our other bases and if she gets out she will run back to the Colonel?" Master Niobi Sir I am not sure what you are implying but I am not in the habit of killing anyone let alone mischievous domestics or any one or any slave, now you of all people know that is not my character, maybe if we keep her with us she will have a change of heart!" The Colonel is fast becoming a headache; I do not want two of them!" "Do as I say now let's get busy!"

With that the Guards and the Doctor released us from all the equipment and the Guards picked us up and took us back to the medical wing again, I thought this was becoming my second home as the Doctor followed.

As soon as we arrived in the medical wing the

Doctor wasted no time in getting the smelly yellow iodine painted all over our bruised and bleeding bodies and then 4 Domestic Girls arrived with the clean but the white traveling tabards to cover our wounds and then we were lifted by the Guards onto a bed each to rest until we was called for, which gave me time to slip into sleep escape again. Though I am worried that this thing with the Colonel is getting out of control and I pray that Master really can handle it as I do not want, more to worry about.

Usually with Guard carriers to a waiting limousine, though with the way things is I know the compound is on high alert and a crew will remain here but remain in constant communications with Master.

I awoke hearing Istra asked the Doctor "where are we going now? You usually know as soon as the Master does because you have to make sure the aircraft have all the medical gear onboard?" "Istra you know far too much for your own good now rest and be good!" Istra looked at me and I looked at her and we both smiled as I put my forefinger to my lips and then up where the Microphones are and indicating to be quiet, I can see we both be getting in trouble because of them damn microphones in here.

"You two are likely to be strapped into the medical bay on the aircraft so be warned, the Master wants you two fit as soon as possible and I do not know more so do not ask me!" The Doctor said smiling at the end. Then a few moments later two Guards appeared and the leader said "the car is waiting so lets go and with that they lifted us both off our beds, then they lowered their heads so we could put our wrist to wrist chains over their heads so they could pick us up and carry us to the waiting car. Istra risked it and said in a jovial tone "we travel light just chains and smiled at me." As we exited the building Master Musson in his traditional Arabic costume was stood there with Master Niobi by his side with the rear nearside door swung open so the Guards could put us down just outside the car, then all we had to do was step in and hobble to the seats we usually sat in, but this time the two Guards followed us in and sat on the nearside as Istra and I had gone straight across to the offside of the left hand drive stretch limousine. It was then I realized the Guards were armed with what looked like short machine guns. Then I thought again Master likes to run things like a military operation so maybe that's a part of it. Master Musson and Master Niobi both sat on the back seat by the doors on either side. Then Master Ahmed got into the nearside front seat and the last Guy to get in was the chauffeur and then he started the engine and we pulled away and then I see that we joined a convoy and our car went into the middle and military style jeeps lead and tailed the convoy then the gates opened automatically and we all drove out onto a sand track road until we met the highway after the last vehicle cleared the gates they closed and two Guards moved in and then stood in front of them. Not much to see except a few houses or buildings in white though I was not paying too much attention to the surrounding area. I think I was still nervous at being driven in a car naked in that deserted, but public area. Istra had gotten used to all this, then as we approached the airfield the first set of gates opened and the soldiers there saluted I assumed Master, then the gates to our rear closed, then the gates to the front opened a bit like an entrapment zone with gates either end incase they wants to inspect vehicles' I guess. But soon after we passed through the second set of gates Masters giant DC 10 could be seen as we got nearer the rear ramp could be seen lowering and there was armed guards all around the aircraft, I could see a guy dressed as a pilot checking the underside of the aircraft as we mounted the ramp and drove up and into the usual spot this car would be placed in prior to its wheels being put into bondage to secure it to the floor, the thought tickled me.

Then the Guards got out of the car after Masters Musson and Niobi exited the cars from both sides, then Istra and I hobbled to the door and stepped down where the Guards lowered their heads so Istra and I could place our chains over their heads to enable them to pick us up and carry us both on into the main rear section of the aircraft and the Doctor was there ready and waiting to usher us to beds along the portside of the aircraft, effectively when in the beds we was facing one another and I was basically traveling backwards and Istra forwards, it was then I noticed through my portside window two coach loads of what I first thought was people but they was our Domestic girls and their Male partners. At that precise moment the two portside doors swung open and the auto steps could be heard whirring away as it feed out of its built in steps so both groups of people could get on board as quickly as possible back and front.

I never really took much notice of this section of the aircraft because it was screened off as the medical bay so there were just 4 beds and the Doctor made sure we was belted into the bed. We often used to use the bed on the centre section wall but just for sleeping in, here I guess the Doctor will be attending our wounds etc: Soon I heard the engines begin to start and as soon as they was all up and running the doors were shut and the auto stairs retracted back into the aircraft just under the doors the rear ramp closed with a thud and then the ground Guards came up the last remaining auto stairs on the starboard side at the very last moment, The Captain spoke "Masters, ladies and all travelers please extinguish all naked flames and be seated with all seat belts be applied as we will make a fast take off at a steeper than normal airlift for safety reasons thank you!"

Then the aircraft headed out towards a runway, then when it got there you could hear the engines revving to full power with the brakes firmly on but the aircraft wanted to lean forwards, then the brakes were off and the aircraft picked up speed very quickly and we was soon lifting off into the air even though I had no idea where Master was going.

Then Master Robert appears through the curtain, because the medical section has to be in some ways isolated and so there is a sort of isolation wall that runs along the edge of the path that runs the length of the aircraft and we are like in an elongated cubical that has 4 beds attached the side fuselage. The area from the side of the aircraft to the isolating wall that separates the medical section to the main areas of the aircraft is about 8 feet I guess so there's enough room for some seats that back up to the isolation wall between us and the rest of the aircraft at this end.

So Master Robert sat down opposite me and then he says "I have popped in to keep you twos company" "Why? We are not likely to get off" Istra says in her jovial fashion, "thought I was the comical one of the group Istra" I said to add my two pence worth to the conversation. Then I thought seriously for a moment and then I said "can I say something Master Robert Sir without offending anyone," "Yes within proper parameters slave Aureus."

"Well Master Robert Sir you are the trainer, I assume the trainer of our bodies, but what about our minds?" "I train the whole entity or body mind and soul" Master Robert said then I added "it seems to have occurred to me or us as all the personalities that make us what we are feel the Male Species must be elevated above me or us, I can not speak for Istra or the other slaves as I do not wish to offend anyone, so I am just saying for me that is what I feel!" "Sorry Istra if you are offended!" "Of course not and in fact that is the best way that you have put it because I too have felt that but I was not sure how to the interpretation of it. I did not have the guts to say it and I did not want to offend others if they do not feel the same ways!" "I am aware because I can see into Musson slave Aureus mind where she is at and Master Musson is for all of us a living entity of greater importance than us Musson slaves!" Istra said. Sorry Master Robert I added and became overwhelmed with emotions and then burst into tears. Istra said "Aureus don't cry" and promptly got out of her bed and came to my bed and tried to give a hug, At that point Master Robert left to get the Doctor whom came in promptly saying "Master Robert Sir you better advise the Master of exactly what took place," "I do not have to Doctor the camera monitor will have recorded it!" Then Master Robert left as he pointed to a camera on his way out.

I had rolled over to face the window because I was too ashamed to face anyone for some strange reason. Istra was standing by the bed and holding my left hand and stroking my head and repeating "you was so eloquent in the delivery of the statement none of us could have done better, I am so proud of you slave Aureus. Then the Doctor said "you best get back into bed Istra, the Master will be here soon." And then in his usual gruff voice "He is here now and from what I saw on the recording I am proud of Musson slave Aureus, I had never heard any slave ever apply such depth of heart in such feelings I have misjudged her, Doctor look after them both!" and left the room.

Then someone was knocking on the wood paneling, as the Doctor pulled the curtain back two Domestic Girls appeared with two bowls of hot lamb stew a portion of bread and a the metal cups of milk. Then the

Doctor jovially said Ahh just what the Doctor ordered food for my favorite patients. I had managed to calm down saying "sorry Doctor and Istra not sure what came over me." "No explanations are necessary we are what we are, come have some stew" "Thank you Istra" and slowly eat my stew.

"Am I in trouble again Doctor Sir?? "Aureus I am not a Sir, just Doctor if you please!" "No I do not think you are specifically in trouble but you will have stirred things up some." "Is that why I feel I should be whipped to death?" "Do you feel that Aureus?" "Yes Doctor ever since we mucked up with the grenade girl!" "Aureus I am going to give you a relaxant to help you rest ok?" "Yes Doctor." Soon I dropped off to sleep escape.

I awoke and there was bright light coming through the aircraft windows and as I woke further I could tell that we were not flying, so we had to be on the ground. Then the good Doctor appeared and said "how are we feeling today slave Aureus?" "Much better Doctor, where are we?" "Stanstead aerodrome refueling, stocking up on food, water." Then Master Robert appeared "how is our favorite patient on this fine morning?" "Feeling great Master Robert Sir, where are we going now?" "To America I believe, Massachusetts area somewhere hear Boston I believe and we should be taking off very soon now and as he said those magical words the fasten seat belts sign came on and the Captain said "Masters, Gentlemen and ladies please return to your travelling seats please we are about to taxi to the runway for immediate take off"

Then Master Robert said "when we are air borne the Domestic girls will serve breakfast and later the Master plans to have a small training program for a special guest we have onboard returning to the USA. So see you later Istra and Aureus."

"Oh well I figured we was not on holiday, so we would soon have to get through the mornings tasks to be ready for a training program to run for Masters special guests" "So who might that be?" Master Lathander you remember me slave Aureus!" "Yes Master Lathander Sir!"

"May I ask Master Lathander Sir do we have any special requests today," I asked "Aureus!" Istra exclaimed. "No she is ok to ask slave Istra you both are something of a topic within the community that we associate with, I suspect there will be a something later today!" "Master Musson may want to put you two through a mild training program in readiness for that and these people will be very impressed if they see you both have markings on your bodies!" Then Master Robert appeared "Have you told them Master Lathander Sir?" "Yes slave Aureus figured it out and asked me politely and I could not see any reason not to tell her and slave Istra." "Though Istra tried to stop Aureus from asking but I approved, hope Istra you are not too upset with Aureus being forward in asking?" "No Master Lathander Sir slave Aureus is very special to me and us all if "I" may say that." just then in comes Master Musson saying in his gruff voice "You may indeed say that slave Istra, slave Aureus is very special to us all we are very lucky to have her." "Right Gentlemen lets retire to the lounge and we will explain how we came by slave aureus." The Men all shuffled through the small doorway of the medical unit to the rest of the aircraft I presume ventured into the front lounge of the aircraft. The Domestic girls arrived for our Bucket baths, so we had to have a good wash to get the yellow smelly iodine off our bodies so that we can be clean for the next encounter. The Girls brushed and braided our hair and just as the girls finished with us the breakfast arrived. Then the Doctor spoke "The Master has said if you are well enough he would like you to return to the travelling seats, you can have your meal there." So we retreated to our travelling seats on the starboard side of the aircraft. As we then saw that young Master Matt enters the front lounge where all the Men were.

The following was told to us by the Doctor at a later date though it was more to update the Young Master Matt a Saudi prince in his training to be a fully fledged Master at his father's request.

Master Musson and others talked about the acquisition of slave aureus to those that did not know, like Master Matt.

Just as Master Matt entered the front lounge Master Musson said "sit down Young Master Matt you might find this interesting." Master Robert was telling the story.

"Slave aureus was offered to us by a Gentleman friend of Master Niobi I believe they were radio pals over the airwaves and this guy Peter J. C. whom Aureus was the girlfriend off." "Peter came to see us and showed us a picture and gave a rough account that for a fee he requested that we train her to be more respectful of him and in his words teach her some manners. So Master Musson agreed and then we did some research on her like we do from birth upwards and she interested Master Musson. However we tried to take her in Malta whist they were both still on holiday and she got away."

"It would have been seen to be in bad form to pursue the abduction in Malta, so we let her get home and we rescheduled for later in the week, so we set up a photo shoot as the trap and sent a car with a driver, because she thought her luck had changed and could have a better life as a photo glamour model and she did everything we figured she would, human nature. Naturally we sent one of our rigged cars just in case she had second thoughts or thought she might be in danger, in that event she would not be able to get out of the car." "When she arrived we led her into a room and then let Istra minus her chains, but naked under a long cape into the room to give her support and whilst chatting to Istra Someone offered her Champaign, but as she does not drink she was declining and we realized we would not get her with the doped Champaign so the Doctor slipped a needle into her arm and that's how we got our slave Aureus." Then Master Musson stepped in. "I could see that she was no fool and I could see that she was capable of retaliating. For the first time we would have a subject that fought all of us. So we were delighted to have a girl that would resist and she did all the way to breaking." "Then as a slave and she accepted this destiny as a slave as if she had done so in a previous life and I was took aback as she gets deeper and becomes a slave of a type I have not seen before or since she really is gold Gentlemen!" Then Master Matt says "but what about this Peter guy will he not be trouble for us?" "No Master Matt, I offered him a hundred grand for her to stay here; he nearly shook my hand off in accepting the deal." "I could not let a moron like him have such a valuable commodity." "No Master Matt Sir! You do not sell the most prized possessions; you keep them and polish them.

Unfortunately Master Niobi did not tell me that our friend Peter also knew the Colonel and somewhere along the path the Colonel came to visit and liked what he saw and had it set in his mind he wanted his cut or better still the whole slave for his whore houses so Gentlemen we seem to have a private war with the Colonel!" "Well then Master Musson Sir why can we not move to another country like Saudi Arabia, where my father rules the Kingdom!" "Because young Matt Sir we need business permits and I need authorized authority to operate my business there and store my munitions plus I need a large compound that does not draw attention to our activities. I have been trying to get licenses in other countries but is taking time so young Matt Sir you will all have to be on your toes!" "But Master Musson Sir if slave Aureus is going to cause us so much trouble as I have said before why not just get rid of her" "STOP!" "Now listen Boy your father begged me to train you in the ways of slavery, but for the élite, not the run of the mill slavery operations that are 10 a penny down the road, Your father expects you to learn something to take back so that he AND YOU, THOUGH I AM NOT SURE THAT IS WISE AS YOU ARE LIABLE TO SHOOT THE STOCK JUST SO YOU CAN STILL BE THE PLAYBOY ENTERTAINING YOUR WOMEN! ACCORDING TO YOUR FATHER. If you do not stop this rubbish I will send you back with a complaint and your father will shoot you himself you know this!" "Master Matt Sir I hope you have not had any underhand dealing with the Colonel?" "Well -well he did offer me a lot of money if I could get the Aureus girl out of the compound. But! But! I did not take him up on it," "No but you thought about it without telling security or us, what the fucks the matter with you boy?" "well she is only a girl, there are thousands of girls that could fit the bill, and we could rest easy. Damn you Boy I have had enough!" divert the plane to the nearest airport I want him off. Captain where are we," "Sir we are approaching Dublin." "Right get permission to land and say we have a flashing light," "Yes Sir we do!" "We do what Captain?" "Sir we have a flashing light somewhere in the baggage compartments I think." "You think Captain, how long has this light been flashing Captain?" "Sir I was about to bring it to your attention before we left land underneath" Then Matt stepped up and said "Sir if you please that will be the Colonels Men?" "The what! Matt!?" The Colonel wanted to put some Men on the aircraft so as to effect a hijack over the sea so his Men could take the, Aureus girl as she just a girl so the Colonel says, he-he gave me $50,000 dollars to pull it off and that you would give me another $50, 000 as she was such a burden to you! The Colonel said." "Stop boy before I throw you off the aircraft. Captain goes to full security alert, no alarms by word of mouth. "What about my money!" Niobi get him to the Brigg before I throw him into the sea. Master Robert go make sure slaves Aureus and Istra are safe, take two Guards with you! Captain tells the ground we have a fuel leak and we need to be on the ground now! "DO IT!"

"AH Yes Sir!" "Master Lathander get a gun and monitor the Garage area, do not shoot if it can be avoided I do not want the aircraft damaged, "Sir the ground are not buying it, then tell them we have a hostage hijack in progress and we are landing whether they like it or not," "Yes Sir! - Sir" "yes they say that will be ok, land as far away from the terminal building as possible." "Ok Captain! Get on with it get us on the ground a.s.a.p. Have all the Guards secure all the females onboard and the rest standby to Guard the aircraft as we check all the doors and spaces, ask the ground if they can muscle up some military police units, I will pay for everything by bank transfer.

Then Master Robert returned to the front of the aircraft on his own only to report that two of the Colonels Men have slaves Istra and Aureus in the front seats of one of the limousines in the garage demanding that we open the garage doors and ramp so they can get away. What are they using as the enforcer? Master Robert. Master Robert replies with, "it looks like another grenade from your stocks Master Musson Sir!" then Master Musson walks around in a circle and then says "I wonder, tell me exactly the situation Master Robert!" "Well Sir from the doorway into the garage it looks like Slave Istra is in the drivers seat and slave Aureus is in the passenger seat holding the grenade and sweating profusely," "Now that does not surprise me, Right lets get down there, have the security team on the outside fully armed, so they want the garage doors opened." "You are sure slave Aureus is holding the grenade?" "Yes Master Musson Sir and I am sure she is not happy about it," "scared stiff do you think Master Robert Sir?" "Yes I would say that just about sums it up," "I can not understand why the Men are not holding the grenade?" "They are only young Men they too maybe scared, maybe not used to ordinance at close quarters!" Master Robert was explaining. "Let's see if they really are scared now, because they soon damn well will be when we give them something to think about!" "Then you have a plan Master Musson Sir?" "Oh yes Master Robert Sir like putting the fear of God up their pants!" Then Master Robert stopped in his tracks and said "Sir –You don't mean?!" "Oh yes Master Robert!" "I do indeed; they will not be expecting that - lets see just how well slave Aureus is trained!" "After that last encounter with a grenade I am sure she will obey your every command Master Musson Sir! Then smiling Master Roberts says "It's inspired Master Musson Sir I bet the Colonel would not have warned them about how deep your training programs go?" "Yes that is what I am banking on!" "Still a bit of a risk though Master Musson Sir?" "No! Not really just remember we are in the business of training slaves to be obedient to the tenth degree!" "Are you ready Master Robert or do you wish to leave the aircraft?" "No Sir I am with you all the way!" "Good Man!" Then Master Musson opened the door gently between the rear passenger compartments and the garage. "Now listen to me slave Aureus, You are a good slave and I hate to lose you. PULL the pin and drop the grenade into the foot well, do it, do it NOW! I / we just said "Yes Master!" then obeyed Master Mussons command, pulled the pin and dropped the grenade between our legs into the foot well whilst moving our left hand to grab hold of Istra's right hand. The two guys sitting in the back seats were out of that car so fast only a fast motion detection camera could have recorded their action as they opened the rear doors and got out. Then the two Men approached Master Musson saying "Your more ruthless than the Colonel, he does not pay enough for me to lose my life. You must have terrified those two girls," "No more than you, they are trained to obey everything I command that is why your Colonel wants them!" Then Master Robert said "but surely the Colonel must know he can never change who is the Commander?" "Yes Master Robert Sir! He has been told on several occasions, he just will not accept that to be factual!" "Let's waste no more time and get them out of the car!" "Yes Sir! Let's do that!"

Master Musson and Master Robert approach the car, Master Robert comes to my side and opens the door and intimates for me to get out, though still terrified of the grenade below my legs in the foot well of the car I manage to get out and Master Robert lowers his head so I can place the chain over his head so he can carry me. I get a glimpse that Master Musson has Istra in his arms and we are like children in adult's arms, still shaking from the events that have just taken place. I can not remember if Master Musson or Master Robert ever carried two slaves before usually done by lesser Men. Master Musson takes Istra into the front portion of the aircraft and both are out of sight for a brief period. Master Robert takes me to the bed in the black tent in the back middle portion of the aircraft and leaves me on the bed looking into space while he uses the phone, Then I hear him talking to Master Musson saying I will spend some time with slave Aureus I think she needs some other comforts that are not streamlined for your prized possessions Master Musson Sir! And then he hangs up the phone. And then says "close your eyes Musson slave Aureus!" and I do without hesitation, I feel Master Robert tucking my legs into the bedding. Then I asked "Master Robert Sir why is it that we slaves feel like children?" Master Robert slides into the bedding and I can feel his naked body laying to my left and then he replies with "Musson slave Aureus it is part of the breaking procedure, when you go deeper you lose self-responsibility towards yourselves and its like going backwards in time and you become more obedient without evaluation of the commands or thought. Slaves then learn to do almost everything by command just like children growing up they learn as they go, and you unlearn as you go, if you can understand that." "That then explains why Master was worried when he thought we were thinking for ourselves and truthfully we were so scared I or we lost control." "Now Musson slave Aureus forget all that for now and relax." Master Robert made sure that my hands and arms were behind me when he maneuvered my body into the bed by making me step over my ankle to ankle chains prior to slipping my feet into the bed. So my body was now defenseless, this I think is an unwritten law between the Men folk here so if we are interrupted it will be clear I have no advantaged position on a Male even if on top of Him, though in this case Master Robert slid my body underneath his and lay on my body. I wondered for a moment maybe God made females to become a mattress or bed for Males to lay on. Then I said "Will I be punished for distracting the Men again Master Robert?" Master Robert said after some thought "do you feel that you should be punished?" I instinctively replied "Yes Master Robert Sir!" "Then I shall have to consult with your Master later, but for now I want you to take this into your vagina and pleasure me slave Aureus!" "Yes Master Robert Sir." Sex with Men made me groan instinctively and make noises that might draw attention and incur even more punishments, but then I began to feel that maybe that is all I am good for is to be punished by these Masters so they could get their jollies or maybe they needed it to feel better about themselves. Then I remembered way back into my teens I was told I could never have children and all I would be good for is for Men to have sex with me. Though I dismissed it and though I could still have a good relationship with Men, but then I did not know Men. Now I have to see them as a my superiors, even though I had these thoughts I was able to perform to a satisfactory position when Master Robert came and shot his load into my vagina and promptly fell asleep on my body. My wrist to wrist chains was under my body so I was trapped but that did not matter. I could now see my life has changed so dramatically that the only way I could see myself is like a glove for a Male hand to fit in or be a receptacles for Men to fit into so that I might even be an extension of them, maybe it was that part of themselves that they wanted punished where as I wanted to be punished so there was no bad feeling between us. There is nothing worse than bad feeling amongst humans, better to relieve it in some way than to let it grow into something bigger or war.

Now I had come to the realization maybe that was now my designation is life to seek to be punished and thereby alleviate the pressures Men had in life to make it better for others as strange as that might sound.

Then someone was tapping on the wall to attract attention!" Master Robert Sir I think someone wants you!" Master Robert awakes and says "Yes come in, what it is? "Please Sir Master Musson requests your presence as soon as is possible Sir!" Then Master Robert says "close your eyes Musson slave Aureus whilst I get out and up, I will send the Domestic girls to give you a wash and brush up, and that was very nice slave Aureus." Master Robert has to cover himself as we slaves are not allowed to see the Male Genitals, another rule Master Musson applied to certain Men, like the Royal Gentleman. It was not long before the Domestic girls appeared and wanted to give me a bucket bath and they used a plastic hypodermic to suck water into itself so they could squirt it up my vagina to clean out Master Roberts semen or jungle juice as I called it.

When the Domestic girls had finished with my wash and brush up I stood up so the girls could change the sheets and the duvet cover on the bed, whilst I was Waiting for them to finish I heard hobbling chains approaching the bed tent and then Istra appeared through the curtain and she hobbled in and we embraced forgetting about the two Domestic girls as was not supposed to do that in front of them but what the heck too late now.

Then when the two Domestic Girls went I said to Istra "what is happening now?" "We are grounded until the police complete their investigations about the hijackers. It seems we made the news and Master was not very happy. There is a lot more too that young Matt guy, His father does not want him back and Master does not want him involved in our operations so until something is sorted we are stuck here," Istra exclaimed. "I thought we were due in America," Yes we are but we cannot go until the police have completed their enquiries and what to do about all those Men." Istra added and then she looked at me in a worried look and said "thank God they are not now on board Master had the Irish Military Police dogs come and check the whole aircraft inside and out. Master and the Captain have been conducting an inspection to be sure the aircraft is not damaged!" "What you been up to or should I not ask? Master Robert took me," "Yes I thought that was going to happen, been on his mind a while." "Yes Master had me too just to remind us that we are slaves and we are here for them." She said smiling. "Istra I am not sure you will like what I have to say next!" "Why? "I asked Master Robert will I be punished for distracting the Men and he said he will consult Master." Then Istra said we are a right pair you and I, I said as much to Master, he said he would consult Master Robert our trainer." "It seems we think alike in a way similar to twins." "Then I said "Maybe just good slaves trying not to get complacent or create misunderstandings. After all I seem to recall that was Masters prime directives that we cause distractions as females and thus require punishment?" "Istra may I ask would it be wrong of me to want to be punished to make sure that Master was happy with my servitude." "I was thinking about asking you the same question." "How can that be you? You have been here longer I am still learning, why I have to ask you all these questions because I do not want to offend anyone by just doing what I think is right however strange that might appear, maybe I am mental to think like this." "No I do not think that, but the statement you gave the other day showed you have a better understanding of our positions." "Anything that stops Men brooding or getting steamed up about a something and then if we have to introduce that by allowing them to punish us seems ok to me!" I said. "You're a strange one too Istra said smiling!" "Thanks and I love you too, then it must my brain has got rewired somehow to think on these lines." And the Istra replied with "the amount of pain and punishments you have endured lately and you are still a novice here I am not surprised your thinking like a punishment slave than a pain slave." "So what are the difference then Istra?" "I don't know I was thinking on my feet trying to answer your questions and curiosity, but I think a punishment slave would crave to be punished all the time and a pain slave that is us, we crave the pain that Master gives with his love because its what he wants to do and then its back to his prime direction on how he operates this organization.

SEQUENCE 23

THE PRICE OF FREEDOM

As no-one has come to tell us anything and not being sure what is required Istra and I decide to lay on the bed behind the curtain and so we do. Soon it will be time for our evening meal. The Aircraft is like a travelling or flying Harem and probably the only eunuch might be the Doctor. So because we are away from base does not mean holidays, everything goes on as a standard or even a military operation. So as Istra and I lay on the bed Istra says "Aureus you know that now the Colonel has performed two attacks on Master to try to gain us and this is really hurting Master," "Yes but the Colonel wants me, so they should be my punishments." "Istra now be honest how many times did the Colonel do this to gain you before I arrived on the scene?" "None!" Istra said. "So since I arrived the Colonel has been making advances, bribing the Domestic Girls with money. Now he bribed that Master Matt. It's clear it's me he wants, am I really worth all this aggravation? And why should you be punished for my failing or whatever it is that is driving these Men nuts?" "Istra my mind is all over the place just now and I am frightened that I will draw you into something that is not your fault or your doing and you should not be punished for my faults!" "Aureus you recall that conversation about us being in this together?" "Yes Istra" "Stop worrying, we are of the same mind, we have been a team for a while now, I support you and you support me, so stop worrying.

I think seriously there is something afoot and as we do not always know what is going on till it comes through the curtains so would you mind just closing your eyes and rest there's a good slave!" "Yes ma-am" I said jovially, "Now then, there's no seniority here Aureus" Istra said. "But you were here first!" I said in response and then Istra said "Maybe but you respond better to Masters Trainings you might have something the rest of us lack" "Yes a sense of humor and I do not mean that nastily, If I could not balance some of the things we do here, I would probably end up half way around the twist!" "Twist?" Istra enquired "ok then half way around the bend or mental, might even be there now" "Oh Now Aureus do not say that, you are a great companion, the best I have felt comfortable with for years and you are right that with the humor you throw in from time to time, does lighten the mood of us all.."

Then two Guards approached and knocked on the paneling by the Curtain Istra say "You can come in Sirs!" "Your wanted ladies!" the lead Gentlemen Guard says. "Ok come on Aureus Istra says quietly" and then the Guys lower their heads so we can place our wrist to wrist chain over their heads so they can pick us up and carry us off to wherever. Its then clear that wherever that is the limousines are apart of what is afoot as we approach, then Master Niobi opens the door from the inside and steps out, then I can see Master Musson in just one of his western business suits on the other side of the back seat of the limousine. The Guards put us down and then we step into the car and make our way to the centre seats so that we are facing Masters Musson and Niobi. Master Musson spoke first saying "It seems our reputation has preceded itself to here and we have been asked to give a demonstration!" Master Niobi adds "We are not entirely sure what they specifically wants so we will have to play it by ear. Security will be on duty to prevent anything getting out of hand, if it turns sexual we shall make sure all are clean and use protection which the Doctor will supervise." Then Master Musson said "we have a midnight flight plan out of here, so when we get back to the aircraft, you can sleep on the flight. Master Matt will not be joining us, the police here have other plans for him that we can not get mixed up in." Then Master Musson added both Master Niobi and myself will whip you both as in a standard training program followed by Masters Ahmed and Robert, we can then at least claim that you will be too tired to do much else we hope and the Doctor will back that up medically." By then the limousine had arrived at what looked like a working Mans club.

First the Guards got out followed by Istra and me, then the Guards did their head lowering bit so we could slip the chain ns over their heads so they could pick us up. Then 12 more Guards got out of 2 more limousines for additional security. As we all entered this large hall type place with a bar at one end and lots of circular tables and chairs for people to sit and drink. As soon as the Men saw us two naked chained girls there was momentous whistles and cat calling noises almost to the point of blocking out their background music. Our carriers followed Masters Musson and Niobi up some stairs onto the stage and then put us down so we could stand. The guards made sure that we was steady on our feet, before they stepped back and our naked bodies were in full view of a mass of Men, then I became scared. Then there seemed to be a surging forwards of a sea of Men racing towards the stage edge, but our Guards all lined the edge of the stage to block the Men that raced forwards to the edge where our Guards stopped them. I could see Master was talking to someone from the club as I did not know him so I knew he was not one of our Men. Then that guy picked a bullhorn or megaphone saying "Gentlemen please if you do not calm down and return to your seats our Guests will leave as they have come to give you a demonstration of something you will never see again in this country, now Gentlemen please return to your seats!"

Then again with the Bullhorn "Gentlemen I give you Their Trainer Master Robert" "Good evening Gentlemen we operate a Muslim Slavery in Libya and the two girls before you are our best" then a "heckler says "they are white how can they be Muslim!?" Then Master Robert tries again "Gentlemen please and I will explain different nationalities operate captivities around the world and mainly females that fall into their traps regardless of Race Color or creed can be trained under that heading, we are all nationalities from Russian to Canadian. Now Gentlemen Musson slave Istra on the left is Croatian and Musson slave Aureus on the right is British.

Masters Musson and Niobi if you please!" both step forwards and roll out a 10 foot bullwhip apiece on the stage floor and then air crack them both towards the audience which brings a sudden hush to the room as the lights go down and the stage lights come up and both Istra and I take in deep breath as we do this in a free standing position and silence holding our weighty chains above our heads arms full stretched. The first lands and I hardly felt it, neither the second, I know I have Master Niobi and Istra has the Master. Master Niobi is striking mainly my back going down to my ankles and them back up and as he is on his way back up he pops one in-between my legs saying we must not forget in there which causes me to draw in breath as if from a deeper part of my lungs. The audience jeers with excitement as they affect a shallow laughter. Then he speeds up and I have to draw in breath faster as he approaches waist level Master Musson says "About turn slaves!" As Master did not mention a specific name we both turn to face the audience and the Masters both continue up our fronts, belly and up to under the breast and then right across both nipples and on to just below neckline and then Master Musson say "All change"

Then Masters Musson and Niobi changed slaves so now I have Master Musson and Istra has Master Niobi and straight away I had to draw in deeper breaths as I could feel Master Musson was really applying pressure to his whip and I guess he could see I was having difficulties facing him so he said again "slaves turn around" so our backs now faced our respective whippers, which made it some how easier and I could see my distractions that helped me through all the training programs, but then Master Musson must have thought I was day dreaming so he air cracked his whip to my right side as if to wake me up and then applied it even more pressures and at an increased speed. There comes a point where the pain becomes so fluid like I can not be sure if it's really paining me. Then Master Musson says loudly as the Men in the audience are kicking up a bit "Slaves Rest" with that both Masters stop and the Doctor quickly moves in with metal cups of water for us to drink. Just then there was a huge bang and it seemed as though the side wall to my right was collapsing as I seem to be flying through the air and I vaguely remembering hitting my head on the floor somewhere between the stage and the audience, though the stage must have offered some protection, I was in forced sleep escape or unconscious state.

When I next awoke I was in the first medical bed on the DC10 Aircraft, now with a tremendous headache I was either in or out of either sleep or consciousness and I was not sure which it was.

When I finally came to and awoke into a normal

state of being awake I could see out of the aircraft window we was high up in the clouds and I could not see what was below us. Then the doctor appeared and said "how you are today slave Aureus?" And I only managed a whisper holding my hand to my throat "ok I think. Why can I not speak properly Doctor?" and the Doctor replied "an explosion on your side of that place you was at, you got the full force of the explosion and you was blown across the room. The Master will tell you more lately, you need rest!" and with that I rolled back over to my left side so I could see out of the aircraft window.

Later the Domestic girls arrived to give me a bed bath, as I am thinking the Para Medics follow on in and say "slave Aureus we have to get you out of bed so the girls can wash your body and repaint it with your favorite yellow smelly stuff!" one said with a grin on his face, so they proceeded to do that and I was as stiff as a board and thinking I hope I can recover from this. Then Istra hobbled in through the curtains and quietly said "hello Aureus I am glad to see you are ok!" my response was "you must lead a charmed life you seem to be ok, standing up and all" "well no" she said and added" I fell over the left hand side of the stage and landed on someone whom cushioned my fall, you was blown clear off the stage and landed on the floor some 8 feet back, the Men all took some cuts and bruises, some of the audience were rushed to hospital we returned to the aircraft, our mobile home with our own hospital and medical team. Breakfast will soon be here so I will come back later!" Then Istra left me with 2 paramedical Guys and the 4 Domestic girls began to wash my body, then brush and braid my long hair.

Soon after they had completed all their tasks then the paramedics began painting my body in smelly Iodine lotion to heal our wounds for the next encounter, then they put a fresh clean tabard on me to protect the wounds from dirt or uncleanness." The Paramedical Guys helped me get back into bed, and then Domestic girls with my porridge breakfast and cup of ice cold milk arrived.

At least the ringing in my ears had stopped and I could hear the music all over the aircraft again, however swallowing porridge seemed difficult but I guess that must be that damn explosion as well. Just then Master Musson slipped through the curtain with the Doctor in close proximity and he spoke almost straight away "How is my number 6 slave Doctor?" he replied "Sir she is making slow progress, even the slave human body is not indestructible!" "Doctor I need to know has it set her back in the training program?" Then the Doctor replied "No Sir but I would not recommend any more explosions on any of them!" "Master Musson Sir we need to get them back into the regular training program without all the political involvement where possible." "Yes Doctor I see where you are coming from but it seems we have started something now which a lot of the people I have business dealings with like to see the slaves in action as well, so I can not promise that. Dublin was the only way we could get expediently away, was by performing for those guys, it was not planned. But they will get extra training and extra security even here there are two Guards outside!"

Then Master Musson walked back through the curtain and back to the comfortable front portion of the aircraft. Then the Doctor disappeared through the curtain and I was alone again for a while until Master Robert comes to visit me and Master Robert had his left arm in a sling so I knew he had been in the wars too. Master Robert said "I did not get my chance to whip you Musson slave Aureus. You are such a joy to whip surely the Master will let his Master Trainer have another go." "Surely Master Robert Sir would you not enjoy Istra more, she is far more experienced than I?" "I am still learning stuff" "Oh no Musson slave Aureus, in your own way you are still resisting and we all like that!" "Am I Master Robert Sir?" "I am not aware of it though I feel am losing the battle or failing even, I think I get these weird impulses to just leg go, but Master tells me in private not to as he likes the resistance as clearly You do!" as I look around to see if anyone's listening. "It's alright Musson slave Aureus we are alone, you can tell me I am the trainer for all the Musson slaves and some of the Domestic staff." "Master wants me to hold back as much as possible so with Master it's a command I have to obey as you know, now you are telling me all the Men like my resisting and so I have to try, even though we feel we want to just give way I could just collapse and let it all go, but then I would be disobeying Master!" "Oh I see now Master Musson has commanded you hold back or resist for our benefit and pleasesure, yes I understand your dilemma. Not sure I can help there either but I will think on it for you." Then he promptly left the medical section. Soon afterwards slave Istra hobbled into the medical section and sat down on the chair that backs up to the partition wall between the medical section on the port side and the back end of the aircraft. Then she said "they are getting the play area ready for play so we shall be in it again. Are you alright slave Aureus," "yes Istra just a bit stiff and low and I do not know why!" Then two Guards entered the medical section and the leader said "You are both wanted!" We both replied in unison replied with "Yes Sir we are coming!" The closest one helped me out of my bed and to my feet so I could place my wrist to wrist chains over his head and this enabled him to pick me up and carry me to wherever, which was only a short walk from the medical section to the back wall that separated the back interior of the aircraft and the garage bays where the limousines were in bondage as they was chained to the floor.

At that point Master Robert air cracked a bullwhip that seemed to sound like a loud crack, whilst the Guards were attaching my centre chain link from my wrist to wrist chains to a line loop with one of them climbers spring cleat type thing, then a motor pulled on my arms to lift my arms clear above me so now my naked body was full open target to whom was going to do the whipping. Which looked like Master Robert was going to get his wish. Whilst Istra was having her arms pulled up; Master Musson appeared from the front part of the aircraft and with a circled up bullwhip in his right hand. He was followed by Master Euan Lathander, I thought he flew on ahead, but clearly he did not.

Then it seems I had Master Euan whilst Istra had Master, I was on the right side and Istra on the left side. Master Musson came over to me and said close to my left ear "what plans do you have to get out of this one slave Aureus?" and I said "Nothing Master Sir, but would you please get on with it I have a dinner engagement at the next cloud base!" "Did you hear that Master Euan Sir?" "Yes Master Musson Sir, I think she does not want to be late for her dinner engagement date," "Slave Istra what do you have to add to this communication?" "Master Sir, I fear she must be worrying that she might miss her bus from that cloud to her dinner engagement and maybe she was thinking to re-schedule your playtime to another century!" "Now we have two disobedient slaves Master Musson Sir!" "I think we better make a start before the pilot gets to their cloud bases."

Then within seconds I could hear the whistle of the bullwhip flying and so I took a deep breath in readiness as did Istra. But then nothing happened. Then Master Musson said "Two can play that game!" "No Master Musson Sir!" "Four can play at this game, Master Niobi Sir Will you take the left flank while I take the right flank?" "Yes Master Robert Sir!" Then Master's Musson and Euan can attack from the back!"

Then Master Musson said out loud "Are we ready Gentlemen, lets begin" then within seconds again I could hear the whistle of the singletails amplified by four and as I took in a fast intake of breath it landed one on my breast and one on my bum, then the next was one on my back and the other across my front thighs and that stung, then it was my belly and he backs of my legs and the guys speeded up and I lost keeping track and was just trying to keep up until and I could not stop it I was weeping, then with a brief quick squint of my eyes so was Istra, then I knew that we had fought as hard as possible, snot was dribbling down my front and I kept blowing it out to try to clear my airways, as even then the Masters all just kept increasing speeds until I passed out and slumped on the one line that my wrists chain was connected too as I heard a muffled "Doctor! If you please and then they all stopped... Then I heard a muffled "Guards! Stretcher if you please!" When I broke consciousness I was back in the medical section but as these beds further up toward the middle of the aircraft faced away from each other, I could not see Istra. As I could not see Istra I called Istra with a croaky voice. "Istra replied I am here Aureus do not get stressed!"

"I failed again" I said as tears rolled down my checks. "No more than I did Aureus, I was weeping long before you began, I have more experience in hiding my tears and you will learn to do the same in time." Then Istra added "the Guys were really laying it on and I know you did not want to be sarcastic to Master which is why I backed you up, we are a team Aureus, you must remember that." "Time for your sleep escape sweetie" Istra said. And I must have dropped off.

When I awoke I knew instantly that the aircraft was stationary on the ground as it has a different feel to when in the air and as I looked out the window I could see we was truly on the ground and as usually in a secure area that seemed to be screened off I could see what looked like military personnel facing outward so all I could see was their backs, but without my visual aids I could never make out an details as they was too far away. The aircraft was now our mobile home if there were not any hotels or houses that Master could not or did not take over on these visits abroad. Because of the security cameras in the medical bays I knew the Doctor would have been notified that I am awake as I am his responsibility whilst in his medical section and care.

Sure enough the Doctor appeared along with 4 Domestic girls that will want to wash me down with their bucket baths procedure and apply any fresh Iodine if it's needed or just a fresh clean tabard as I we have to be ready to perform again if required. Yes I know I am now thinking like a Musson slave, though I thought to myself and grinned at that point the Doctor said "Ah now what has tickled you to grin like that slave Aureus?" "Whatever is happening to me Doctor must be working then as I found myself thinking like slave Istra does about the cause or our purpose, I guess we could be seen as Masters Support team I suppose in a weird way!" "Oh weird" What do you mean?" the Doctor enquired "Well I guess I never saw a team of naked and chained females as a support team I guess, you see businessmen like when I worked for Sky Petroleum, part of the Occidental group the boss travelled in uniformed painted cars and many girls all in their Sky Petroleum Red, white and yellow Uniforms surrounding the boss on mass, thinking back I had not long been with the company and so just in the basics uniform of a white school blouse, yellow necktie red skirt and a red waistcoat, the petrol station managers had the same but jackets instead of waistcoats but no nakedness or chains Doctor!" "I see" said the Doctor.

As the Domestic girls helped me out of bed then removing my tabard and then I felt the warm waters on my skin that seemed refreshing and as I looked down the bucket of water turned Iodine yellow as each soft sponge was rinsed in what was a dirty waters bucket, so each time the sponge released small amounts of clean water onto our skin, all this to avoid any cross contamination difficulties. Then the Doctor spoke but directed at the Domestic girls "You better do a good job girls as the Master is entertaining tonight and slave Aureus has to be looking good!" Then the domestic leader said "Doctor Sir how she can look good with all these cuts, scratches and bruises all over her body? We can not make her skin look unblemished Doctor Sir!" "You know perfectly well that all the Musson slaves look like that as if part of their uniform, it shows that the Master performs the training program to full effect, that in itself shows an element of control and his commanding position, now get on with it girls!"

Then the Doctor left the room or area as one of the domestic girls; peers through the curtain, "ok the coast is clear" then the team leader speaks "rather you than me Aureus this one is a heavy and you know what will be involved that's why the Master and the Guys laid into you specially last night to make sure you had enough welts to show off tonight before you get some more!" I replied "Oh No do not tell me, you know if they discover I have been informed I can not cover for you guys, I wish you would not tell me, and I do not want to hurt anyone, I can not lie to the Master so please do not say any more" "well tonight it will be even heavier so get plenty of rest" "Ok say No more please, no more!"

The Master wants you on the bed in the tent after we are done; breakfast will be in there and go to ablutions early before things kick off ok!" "Thanks Girls" I said, thinking not sure how this could all work with them guys, and that's why we the Musson 6 defend them when they accidently cross a line.

Then a Guard entered the room and said "I have to carry you to the tent slave Aureus!" "Yes Sir" I said and without prompting he lowered his head so I could place my wrist to wrist chains over his head so he could pick me up easily, and I remembered someone telling me its because of balance, and in that way they will not drop us. Soon we was on our way I could see the aircraft was operating on safety lights that's like every other light was on to reduce power so we do not overstretch the output of the external mobile generators I guess close to the aircraft and I think they have ways to connect to running water as it seems to work without hinder.

The Guard dropped me off at the tent and I had to hobble to the bed which as a giant king-size took up most of the space so was not too far to go and then I just initially sat on it until I decided to lay on it, then Istra hobbled in and as fast as she could and come as close as she dare and said one word "Trouble!" and I whispered "what me?" and Istra shook her head as if to say no. Then Master came into the tent and said "slave Aureus did the Domestics give you warning of tonight's event?!" "Yes and no Master" "Explain slave" "they told me a something being a heavy tonight before I could tell them to STOP I did not want to know because if you ask me I can not lie to you Master, thereby I can not cover for them." "Excellent slave you are one of mine for honesty, but there now has to be balance and someone has to pay!" "please Master then let it be me, I think they was just trying to be kind, I might have done the same if roles were reversed, I do not know how to stop them from blurting out stuff even if I am not interested. "Master respectfully I think someone who trains these guys before they come here should impress upon them this is not the way forward? Then Master said "She is one of MY Slaves!" "Excellent but they must watch and if any one of them closes their eyes, the one that does, takes the rest!" "Do you understand slave Aureus?!" "Yes Master" "Excellent work slave Istra you have trained slave Aureus well I am most impressed, plus she is correct and I must have a word with those that vet and train our inbound Domestics as it would save us all, if all obeyed the command structure! However the damage is done and such are the consequences but slave Aureus is a Musson slave no question!" and he left the tented area. I think I was in shock as Istra grabbed my right hand and said "When Master needs to address a Musson slave on an Administrative level another Musson slave has to be present, sorry if I scared you!" "No Istra I think I scared myself I was terrified." "Sadly you will be, but we will be in as close support as we can, in fact I think I am impressed even if Master was not!" Istra said now holding my right hand with both her hands, "Come onto the bed lets laze about while we can!" She said. I dropped off for a while until we was awoken by a tapping on the wall, usually by Domestics or the Guards are inclined to do that where as the Men as in Masters just waltz in, but its their domain…

Then Istra said "Ok Come in" and it was my Domestic crew from this morning and Istra was quick to say directly at the Domestic crew "say and do nothing!" "We are all in enough trouble now." Then Istra said looking at the Domestic crew "You know Aureus will take your punishment probably because she knows you will not be able to handle it, I am not sure Aureus can this time," then one of the Domestic girls began to cry, "STOP IT!" Istra said in a commanding way and added "if the Guards hear you we will be in deep shit, so why are you here?" "We wanted to say sorry!" "Officially?" Istra asked "No, but officially to ask if you wanted a cup of coffee?" Istra looked at me and turned back to the crew and said "Yes we do and bring a jug of coffee we may need more!" "Next timer obey the command structure and keep q quiet, if you can not keep your mouth shut at least own up to your failings we will support you as we always do! Now go!" Istra said in her commanding way. After they passed through the curtains I said "Coffee that's a new one!" "No Istra said we are in America they drink coffee like it was water"

Another crew of Domestic girls arrived with the jug of coffee, coffee the like I had never tasted before was delicious, no wonder the Americans drink lots of it I thought, Istra seemed to like it as well. Then Istra moved up closer and said "Aureus I have always known this could happen and you must believe me when I tell you that it matters not to me." "Hang on a mo you are talking in riddles, if it's more secrets I do not wish to know I have enough to worry about now!" "No it's not that, its ranking status." "Pardon? What the hell is that?" "Its possible Master sees you as being as good as I or even better than I!" "Rubbish Istra that can never be I am still learning through you and I do not give a hoot what anyone else thinks you are Ms1 and the leader around here!" "Istra please you will always be number one in my mental states what ever they maybe, I am the youngest fresh blood here and maybe they just want to see what I am made of or maybe I am fresh entertainment, more like fresh meat methinks so lets leave the politics to those that can do things with it, but if the Master does I will put him straight, is that plain enough!" "You probably will put him straight if I know you, you are a great cell mate!" "With you worrying about that I am beginning to wonder just what is going on around here." "The Americans are an odd lot and there's an old wives tale about Yankee women only do the mission position and so the guys come to Europe for more adventures" "Oh sure yes we are on an adventure!" I said smiling almost to the point of laughing when Master Robert entered the tent bedroom and said "Slave Aureus it would seem you are tonight's star attraction!" "Now what have I done Master Robert Sir?" "It would seem they know of you in America, probably from previous occasions and requested to have you within Masters Demonstration, but then this other business came up and further investigation have lead to the real culprit being exposed!" "What are you talking about Master Robert Sir?" Istra enquired "I am coming to that but it's complicated, The Domestic that learned about tonight's event from her partner one of the Masters private Guards!" "so its his fault then" said Istra "Yes, now calm down, The Master can not punish a Man you know that, so his girl will have to carry his punishment prior to being released back to their home in America and so we can drop them off either tonight or before we leave US airspace!" "So what's the problem?!" Istra again intervenes "If you do that again Istra I will put you across my knee!" At that point I quickly put my hand over Istra's mouth because I knew what she would say as I would for our beloved Master Trainer Robert as I wanted to say "is that a promise Master Robert, but he is trying to be serious, I know Istra likes justice and hates injustice.

"Under the slaves laws the Guards female partner a Domestic and a BDSM sub/slave can elect someone to take her place and she has nominated Musson slave Aureus." "Oh I see" Istra exclaimed angrily.

Then with a very fast action Master waltzed in through the curtain and said "Musson slave Aureus do you accept!" "Yes Master." "No! Master Sir that's not fair on Aureus" Istra said and almost about to stamp her foot on the floor until I grabbed her and said "its alright we can show the yanks a thing or two Istra calm down!" then I turned to Master again and said "Yes Master I will accept as one of the Musson slaves!" then Master turned to Master Robert saying don't you just love this woman!" and left the tent room almost as fast as he entered. Then Master Robert said "best get you ready then!" and he moved to the end by the curtain entry and lifted the phone and said "I want 8 Domestics to the wash room now and fetch the early meal for Musson slave Aureus plus one carrier Guard for Musson slave Istra!" and then he hung up the phone and turned back to me and lowered his head for me to place my chain over his head and then he carried me off to the wash station area where 8 domestics were gathering some holding towels and some with fresh White tabards and then Master Robert placed me down and supervised the girls doing the bucket bath while another got ready with towels and another ready to brush and braid my hair. Then Istra arrived and the other 4 started to work on her. Then I said "Master Robert Sir may I have a word in your ear Sir" "Yes of course slave Aureus" so he maneuvered himself to just close enough for me to speak into his ear and then said "Back off Girls for a minute" "yes Sir" the team leader said and they all stepped back. Because of the music I was fairly sure Istra would not hear me, as I said "Master Robert Sir can you plead with Master that I will accept any punishments for Istra's outburst earlier!" Master Robert replied "Yes I will!" Then Master Niobi appeared into our area as if been summoned by Master Robert, however Master Robert did then say "ah Master Niobi Sir can you keep an eye on this lot as I have a special mission to complete!" "Yes Master Robert Sir I will" "come along girls hurry up Musson slave Aureus needs to eat soon, you all know the drill it's all timed to the very second!" "Yes Sir" said the two team leaders in almost uniformed responses.

Then Master Niobi said "Guard carry Musson slave Aureus back to the tent room for her meal!" "Yes Sir!" the Guard said and turned to me lowering his head at the same time so I could place the chain over his head, then he picked me up and carried me back to the tent room where two more Domestic girls were waiting with my lamb stew and a mug of what looked like coffee. The Guard placed me by the bed so I could just turn and sit so the girls could give me the tray and have my last supper I thought.

Then I drop of to sleep for a while until called for and like as in sleep mode that comes faster than we humans like is a tapping at the door on the wall as usual, but not usual. For Master and Master Robert attending, it looks like Master Robert will be my carrier Guard. Master then speaks to the domestic girls that follow on in "remove the Tabard and have a fresh one prepared for later" then they do as Master commanded. Master Robert moves forwards and lowers his head and I place my wrist to wrist chains over his head so he can pick me up, So he does and then we are off Master is in front and a whole load of our Male Guards and all the Masters Niobi Ahmed, Phillips, Lathander and even a couple Arabic dressed Gentlemen but they are too far back for me to see as we leave the aircraft and head across the apron to a building just where the apron area finishes. Now there are two lines of Soldiers I guess on either flank and seem to be all armed as if we were at war. Then as we enter a building and going down corridors to some double doors just like at base and some Men either side open the doors as we and the long line of Men behind us flow into a huge hanger I would think that has been decked out to form a stage and a seated area and as we get close all the other 5 Musson slaves stand up in position one legs apart hands behind. That must be for Masters benefit not mine and then Master Niobi and Ahmed move into Masters position as he peels out and off to the right somewhere now that we are at the front of the stage but moving to the right as there are no stairs up to the stage, however there are some on the right-hand side of this stage.

Master Robert slowly but carefully steps up the stairs and along to the centre where he places my feet carefully on the stage flooring which is lined with plastic sheeting, how original I thought save someone from cleaning up the mess I am about to make and with the steps up to the stage my sister slaves will not be able to come to my aid, someone has planed all this I am thinking. As I turn to face the end wall that the stage is built up against I can hear that subdued murmur that you get in theatres that are waiting for the show to begin. Then to my right Master had crept up and took a hold of my wrist to wrist chains and located the middle ring and connect it to the wire and hook at about my breast level and then he indicates to someone to wind it up as I can not hear any electric motors I am not sure if its electric or manual and soon its just loose enough, but tight if I need to pull on it. And then Music in the background is coming up but stopped at a certain level. Then Master Musson spoke to the huge audience.

Gentlemen we had planned to give you a demonstration of International Muslim slavery, then we discovered someone had breached security and let on to one of my slaves about the event to have been scheduled. Further investigations revealed it was this Gentleman here, one of my personal Guards. I am not allowed to punish the Man or any Male as the Muslim slavery is for females only, so we elected to punish his slave partner, but she got wise and under the same law nominated a more experienced slave to take her punishment that being Musson slave Aureus behind me who is one of my 6 very best slaves. Many of you know of her from previous encounters when we have been on

US soil to give such demonstrations and Musson slave Aureus is the youngest of my 6."

"Now Gentlemen under the same law the original perpetuator this young man here will have to watch and the moment he looks away or closes his eyes, either his slave takes over or he get shot. But we are not in Libya so we have to honor USA Laws, but he will have a gun pointed at him so as to stop him running off. Your own Mps will stop him getting far and bring him back. So Gentlemen are you ready, if so please stand for a very special Guest."

"I command Close eyes all Musson slaves, do it now!"

So I close my eyes and assume the others have done so too and the there is a thunderous applause, for who that special Guest might be its not for our eyes and when near silence returns, the auditorium lights go down.

"Master says loudly Musson slaves open eyes!"

Then Master comes up to me and whispers in my right ear and says "I know you can do this see you later."
"Yes Master Musson Sir!"

Then Master moves to my right hand side, but in effect its the left part of the stage facing the audience and he then says "First pair of trainers please come forward, just then I notice the Doctors bright white coat in the bright ultra violet black light to my left of the stage where he is learning up against the wall then I see the two paramedics and the medical trolley, but clunking in the background I can hear the whips trolley that has its own distinctive sounds with two Trainers that I have not seen for months Master Phillips and Master Mackie and I was not keen on them then let alone now, but I guess this is it.

Then two pin spots come on me from both sides way back into the auditorium and I wait for the first or both whistles to give me a clue as someone raised the music volume and then just as I was drawing breathes one lash lands on my lower back and one on my higher shoulders area and then they start on down together until the get to my ankles and then its back up to my neck and I am drawing breath at the point of impact and then let it go as I breath out the pain goes with it an soon one gets into a rhythm, Drawing breath in as the impacts land and then let it go as we breath out, I think to myself I bet the whole lot of my sister slaves are doing it in unison as well and I hear Master Musson say loudly Musson slave Aureus Turn! So I turn to face the audience but the lights are in my eyes and so I have to shut them tight and then he requests can you lower the spot lamps please. I think that is a first I never heard Master say please before and then within a few moments the light were lower down probably on my breasts as the Masters were running down my belly which is all very stingy as its less protected and I have to get my breathing just so. Then Master Musson says loudly "REST!"

Master Robert brought a metal cup of water for me to drink and whispered how are you holding up, I think we are hanging in, but that light catches my eyes, I am determined to get through it to show our brothers in arms what we can do," "Good girl!" Master Robert said and left the stage exiting to my right.

Then Master Musson calls for Masters Niobi and Ahmed and then says loudly "Musson slave Aureus Turn!"

So we do and turn back towards the wall and then soon the first impact lands and I have not drew breath so am caught out trying to catch our breath Master Niobi realizes that and holds back and then I nods my head and they start again and this time I am on the ball must have got adrenaline infusion from the body as I can now get on top of the pain and so they start by going down my back and then back up again after about 30 minutes Master Niobi says loudly "Halt" and he hands his bullwhip to Master Ahmed saying "Hold this Master Ahmed Sir" she needs some support and he walks off the stage to the right passing Master and the comes back with a pyramid and if my guess is correct there will be an electrode in his pocket as he steps up on the stage he indicates to a Guard to come forwards with a box. The Guard removes an electronic item from within the box and plugs it into the extension lead on the floor that I had not seen, while Master Niobi places the pyramid between my legs and does his awful regurgitation of spit thing that turns my stomach and uses it as a lube. He then comes round to my front with smile on his face and lifts my body up and then the Guard guides the electrode into my vagina. Then they clamp the pyramid to the stage floor with my ankle chains running loosely around the outside of the pyramid so I can turn on the electrode. Then Master Niobi said "are you sitting comfortably?" "Yes Master Niobi Sir!" Then Master explains to the audience what they have done and then he asks the Audience "would you like to see Musson slave Aureus get some electrical shocks while the teams are whipping her? Hands up please so we can get a count. Then Master says "Master Phillips please we need you to control the electrics" as he approaches and he says "Yes Master Musson Sir I would be happy to assist"

Then it begins again and this time the whips are landing one after the other and the electrics are making my body jump and so when I have breath control I lose it to the electrics and then the other Musson slaves begin to rattle their chains, Master lets it go for a bit but then explains to the audience that its their sister slave and that they indicating their displeasure, but we are about to fix that. "Master Mackie Sir would you like to assist," "Yes Master Musson Sir what would you like me to do, Sir?" "Take this microphone to Musson slave Aureus and ask her what she wants?" and so he approaches and says quietly "only you can stop them!" "Yes Master Mackie Sir and then I say Sister slaves please stop the noise they only increase the voltage the more noise you make, please desist!" "Very Good Musson slave Aureus" said Master Mackie. And they stopped. But the whippers begun again and the electric was pulsating very low levels and slowly. Now the guys are increasing speed and that means I have to concentrate to get my breathing in time to the whips landing and block out the electrics, might that even be for the audience rather than me when the music is right I almost be dancing but seriously I must not get out of step, the pain that I have had to put up with in the last few days seems to be creating adrenaline or something that is easing or clouding the pains and just when I am thinking I am getting on top of this. Master says loudly "Musson slave Aureus turn," which is not so easy with the electrode in my vagina.

The guys are attacking my belly my breast and when they catch the nipples I feel someone's run a carpet over them and then again the guys begin to speed up but I can see something is going on in the auditorium possible with that Guard that broke all the rules but my eyesight is not that good without glasses and the Master says "REST!"

Again Master Robert comes with the cup of water and says "Drink Musson slave Aureus how are you doing?" getting tired Master Robert Sir" "Master Musson will be on next and myself and Master Niobi will be the commentator!" Master Robert added.

"Begin Masters Niobi and Ahmed!" and again the lashes started to fall and I have to admit I am losing my mind, I can now barely feel them, but I must hold on for Master and Master Robert and then Master Niobi said "Halt!"

I could see Master to my left with the Doctor talking to him and now Master Robert was on my right then Master said "Musson slave Aureus Turn!" and we struggled to turn but managed to get around so now facing the wall again as I heard Master say loudly "BEGIN" and they did and I was trying to keep up but I was losing it and then passed out, I vaguely felt impacts all over the body but in any event now as I could not feel anything, just warm and then a darkness fell.

Suddenly I could see the ceiling and lots of faces especially the Doctor talking but I could not hear and found myself trying to get up but could not, thinking I hope they have not used that bloody drug again as I keep trying to get up. I vaguely remember saying sorry Master I failed again and passed out again. The next time I became coherent or semi dazed I could see I was in bed again in the medical wing of the aircraft as I had the sun bleeding in through the drop down blind but it did not last long as I either dropped off or passed out again. Then the next time I could see a drip was connected to my arm through I think is a special needle that connects to a blood vessel, but again I could not just stay awake.

When I eventually awoke to see the Doctor standing before me as I lay in the bed grinning and he said "Ahh good you has come back, I had to put you into a deep sleep coma" then turning to the doorway "Guard let the Master know Musson slave Aureus is awake!" "The Domestic girls will be along soon to freshen you up and we'll change the bed and I expect you could eat something!" just then Master and Musson slave Istra appeared at the doorway, Istra being carried by the Guard that went to inform Master I was awake I think.

Then Master spoke "how is she Doctor?" "She will

live for another occasion!" "Doctor I know you do not approve of what we do here, but that is why you are being paid a lot to be here plus that the girls like you and that works for me, their health is your responsibility Doctor!" "Please keep a civil tongue when you speak to me Doctor!" "I think you just got told off Doctor Join the club, it happens to us a lot!" "No slave Aureus he is just fencing, it's the Doctor in Doctors we swore to save life not put it at risk, and he knows that!" Then the Domestic girls arrived and with Musson slave Istra too hobbling along. The Domestic girls team leader spoke to the Doctor "Doctor Sir the Master wants Musson slave Aureus to rest in the centre Black tent today, you can supervise easily, but I think he wants her to get back into normal rhythm as soon as possible" "Yes I had got that message earlier team leader, you best get on with your work then" the Doctor said hesitantly.

In fighting again I thought best keep quiet, and then Istra asked "Are you alright now Aureus," "I don't know how do I look" "you look better than you did we was all very worried about you, but Master would not let us come sit with you" "I can see I have missed some more of the training program!" as I point to Istra's marks all over her body once again" "Normal routine you know the drill slave Aureus "Istra said curtly with a smile. "Anyway you took a beating yourself the other day, a lot more than we do in training; one of the girls was counting but lost her place after 3,000 lashes, so you impressed us all, even Master I think, but you know he gives little away." "I thought I failed again!" "You did!

Musson slave Aureus" was Master Roberts voice as he entered the medical room, "Sorry Master Robert Sir I lost control passed out" "It has to be nature hitting the safety valve when the body passes out" the Doctor said "You are ok Musson slave Aureus and Istra, we are not all on duty all of the time, I come to see slave Aureus because she collapsed just as I was getting started for my turn and it all had to stop, that has happened before, so she is with me in the black tent when you lot have finished." "Yes Sir" the team leader said "I will see you later Musson slave Aureus and I will leave you in the capable hands of these ladies and Istra of course bye" With that Master Robert disappeared through the open curtained doorway to wherever possibly for his breakfast. "Now what have I done, that happened before in the Irish place I just remembered so does that mean a private session in the tent?" "No Aureus that's not allowed in there he going to bed you," "You mean fuck Istra, we are adults you know you can say it!"

SEQUENCE 24

THE SUB PLOT

"These simple terms so we all know what the plan is." I said smiling "You're getting better Aureus, your humor is back!" Istra said smiling. Just then an aircraft steward that walks the aircraft prior to landings and take offs to make sure all is secure. And he said "Ladies please make yourself secure where you can we are about to take off!" "Yes Sir!" Istra says then she adds "where is the Doctor?" "I am up here in my office what is up we are about to take off the flight steward just told us to all secure ourselves!" "I will just strap Aureus into bed and then be in my office ok!" the Doctor said and as usual and because we was on the port side of the aircraft you could hear the auto steps coming up and the doors closing with a bit of a shudder specially as the rear ramp is closed I think that can all be done from the pilots at the front of the aircraft and then all the lights flicker on as the engines start. I can see one of the domestic girls seems scared, "what's the matter I asked?" "I do not like to fly how often is this thing is checked?" she asks "Oh Master is very good its checked every flight like its serviced every flight no expense spared because its our flying home when he is travelling we all go as well, else we might loose out on the training, you'll see!" Istra said with a smile and then you could feel that gentle lurching forwards after the brakes are released and headed along a taxi way to a runway suitable for our size of aircraft. "The pilots are all very good as well they do not bat an eye to see us all naked and in chains and Master has at least 3 sets of pilots and crew, you are quite safe with us, but we do not know your partner or Master now that might be where you need to worry!" I said with a smile.

"Where are we going now I would like to know, but I guess I am waiting on Master Robert to make the next move, I presume he will come for me? "Yes I will and I am here to collect young Musson slave Aureus, Guards if you would do the honors and carry Musson slaves Aureus and Istra to the black tent please!" With that the team leader of the Domestic girls said "yes and we have chores to do come along ladies!" Istra was asking "You want my presence as well to Master Robert Sir? "The guard removed my bed strap used when taking off and landing is in effect for safety of bed patients, I would think air ambulances have a similar thing.

"You are Musson slave Istra and your name is Istra!" Master Robert said in a defiant way with a smile for good measure "Yes of course I want you!"

We arrived in the black tent. Master was there with the traitor Guard and his submissive slave girl. Master said towards the Guard "put Musson slave Aureus on the bed Guard thank you!" and as Istra arrived "Please place Musson slave Istra on the bed also Guard thank you!" and then the two Guards left and then befell silence until Master said "These two have requested to remain with us rather than be discharged. They both swear nothing like their betrayal will ever happen again, I am inclined to give them the benefit of the doubt because it will save me the problem to find replacements, but its really Musson slave Aureus choice as she paid for their crimes!" then I said "Master I prefer for you to make the choice as you are my Master and I trust your wisdom over mine!" then thought I made an error "sorry Istra I did not mean singularly, Master is our Master I maybe should have said!" "Its understood I am proud the way you said it." Istra said, and added "It proves to me and Master that you know your place with us here!" Master then said "what do you think Master Robert Sir some of these candidates were of your choosing and I respect your position as a Commander here?" "As you say Master Musson Sir it would negate the need to find replacements, if Musson slave Aureus is happy to leave the decision with yourself I will go along with that, though I would think a formal apology would be in order in front of the whole organization so there are no misunderstandings!" "Good point!" Master said "Then that is how it shall be, providing our domestic friends are happy with that?" "Yes Sir we wish to make whatever amends we can, my partner is not very good with pain she is more of a bondage model and became scared as I have already indicated Master Musson Sir!" I could see the girl was terrified probably as much as me when I was brought into this world, but I hold no grudges or malice as I am still learning, maybe I should have "L" plates back and front of my body. Istra had grabbed a hold of my left hand with her right hand as if for comfort though I feared she was more displaced than me. Master then said then I will leave you Master Robert with these two and return our domestic friends to duty though I have to broadcast a basic announcement as I do not want any reprisal." Then Master left the black tent with the two Domestic helpers one Guard and his lady.

Then Master Robert said "do you wish to stay Musson slave Istra?" and she replied with "Whatever is your command wish Master Robert Sir!" "I had planned to bed Musson slave Aureus!" and we both burst into laughter and then Istra said "Sorry Master Robert Sir I suggested that was your intention when you requested Aureus to be here with you and Aureus insisted you meant to fuck her and suggesting we should be adults and not try to hide intentions Sir!" "Yes but I was being a Gentleman in front of many ladies at the time, but I understand you girls would see thing's from a different perspective than the Gentlemen around here, not to worry no harm done, so are you staying Musson slave Istra?" No Master Robert Sir the Master asked me to do some chores for him and I must go!" Then Istra hobbles out of the black tent.

"Alone at last!" "And with my favorite pupil!" "Thank you Master Robert Sir I am honored" "You should be the way you handled that administrative

Punishment for something that was not your fault or doing!" "It would seem that the young lady that set this path alight must know something about old Muslim slave laws to pull that stunt and sadly you were caught in a position where the better part of valor was at hand and you took it on to save the Master embarrassment!"

"well Master Robert Sir I did not feel I really had a choice after the statement I made a while back and she may have been aware of that and when this thing hit, I did not want to let anyone down least of all myself or even appear as my body and soul had greater worth than that of Master, if that makes any sense!" Then Master Robert stood up abruptly and said quite loud "It does to me, but does it to everyone else that can be sucked in by a clever clogs" "Master Robert Sir you must be careful you will get into trouble!" "No I will not Young Musson slave Aureus I am third in Command here and my input is of great value to the consortium!" I believe the Doctor was equally aware that you were set up by either a cunning pair or one of them, they might be working for another enterprise which is the real reason they are staying not to further insult you as we shall be monitoring. Everywhere has now been wired for sound and vision the home base all aircraft and all the new back up locations but this is our secret. The Master is aware you and Istra will be knowledgeable in this because you have shown loyalty second to none." "Now my dear back to the salt mines and into bed with you" as he lifts up the bed covers and I slip in and close my eyes as I do not need any more problems I am thinking.

I must have been ready for Master Robert as my juices were well in hand and he slipped in, because I have not had any babies I can still seeming get tight, not sure why, however now the Doctor has us all on the pill, sometimes I think I make too much noise with sex some of it is breathing some because its pure heaven and if I know Master Robert he will deny me an orgasm and I can not just fall into it have to stay out of the cascade and then "Don't you dare orgasm Musson slave Aureus," "Yes Sir –No Sir" as I am thinking obedience is a virtue, normally I would have needed a lot of pain to get turned on but Master Robert has a way of doing sex and now I discover he is third in command and I thought he was just a trainer, but it makes sense because he's been here since forever and he knows all about the whips, how to make them cracker things and how to clean them after each girl that have touched, just thinking of those whips touching my body is enough to ooh gosh nearly lost it "Ms6 No!" "Yes Sir – No Sir" probably wants me to just have one not my usual half dozen, not allowed to have more orgasms than the Masters and the Men folk, then he says "get ready slave" "Yes Master Robert Sir" "Now! Slave Now! As he thrusts his penis in so hard I expect it to come up my throat from down there, like most of the guys here, they have a force unlike a guy romancing a female but this life is so much different to the ways of normal vanilla life here they stand on the ankle to ankle chain so they use a thrusting force. "Excellent Musson slave Aureus!" "Slave Aureus you might not understand Men, the more you orgasm maybe good for you but I lose grip and the moment or the timing you did great, I will send in the Domestics to freshen you up as he disappeared through the black tent door way. Ahh I am thinking so the wetter I get the more they lose grip, I would never have known that had Master Robert not said and could have gone on to making more mistakes and getting more punishments for someone. It was not long before the Domestic pair of girls arrived to give me a usual bucket bath after sex with the Men around here. Then soon after they finished drying me and just refreshing and braiding my hair Istra popped her head through the curtain at the entrance saying "Ahh all gone then?" "Yes Istra just me and these girls just cleaning up the mess" I said smiling. "Come relax on the bed Aureus" Istra said in a calm but confident way usually when she wanted to make something clear.

Then Istra laid back with her head on the pillow and indicated for me to do the same, then as I did she moved closer and whispered to me "Master wants you and me to play a part in a setup to try to expose either those Domestics that set you up or who their handler could be!" Then I responded with whispering back "how do we do that?" "Only one way I can think of" Istra said "And?" I said. Then Istra held my right hand with her left very tightly and said we make our cuddling up more public, so we are reported!" "Oh yeah and that will get us the thingamajig (FGM) are you mad? You know what Master said we could do it in private but do not get caught!" "Yes I know and he told me that it would be dangerous but he will try to control the whole thing himself and for us to trust him!" "What if he can not control it?" "well I can not think like that I trust him and so must you" Istra was saying and I added "I do l trust him, it's the others I am not so sure about" and I added "Well if you are sure Istra I trust you more than anyone so if you want I will support you in this as I always do" I said smiling. Then I asked "If we are not dropping them two off where are we flying to now then Istra?" "To home base!" Istra replied and then added "Master has to go to some other places in about 3 weeks so for now its home and back to routine!" "You mean basic training again Istra" "yes I suppose I do, but the more you get the better you are able to get through it as you will discover!" "Thanks" I said with a smirk. "These little trips away from Master's chambers of horrors even though I am used to them, there is an element of fear that the wrong person will use them and it could prove costly or even deadly Istra!"

Soon the aircraft lands in the Tripoli private airport that we and the Colonel use only, but it's just down the highways to our home base and wee arrived on a very warm afternoon.

It did not take long for all of us from our aircraft were on a our way to home base and within an hour Istra and I were in our cell and resting from jetlag and just about every other lag that comes into the category.

When Master comes sailing in like he does when he's on a mission and he comes right up close and then I see Master Robert at the doorway keeping watch, suddenly this has become like a spooks anon novel. Then Master says "Well Istra?" "Yes Master we will do it" as Istra again grabs my right hand with her left hand and Master can clearly see us hand in hand, then I remember Master Robert telling me that the aircraft was wired for sound and I say interrupting "Master!" and he looks at me directly and sort of nods his head "Master Robert told me the aircraft was wired so we will have given the game away?" "No" Master said and continued "yes the aircraft is wired as is this place now, but I switched of that section of the aircraft so Istra had enough time to see if you was up for this bad move, but we do not have any other choices, if we have traitors within I need to know whom and how many, now this is important because what you will be doing is breaking an old slavery law that I alone may not be able to control all the elements of the punishments and maybe compelled to follow through and apply with vigor and reality or the game will be bust are you sure you want to try this Istra-Aureus?" "Yes Master!" As we both said jointly together. "It be just another on the job training session Master!" I said happily as Istra looks at me with wide staring eyes.

So I look back and use my wit humor and say quietly "well we had nothing else planned for today or were you going shopping Istra" and Istra replied with a big smile.

Master stood up and beckoned Master Robert to come forwards and then he said quietly "Master Robert Sir you and I both know these two are not serious practicing lesbians are they?" "No Master Musson Sir

I can certainly vouch for slave Aureus as to being totally heterosexual. No Sir they are not that way inclined No Sir!"

"Good we have to remember that if things get too far out of control Master Robert Sir.

Then Master said Istra maybe you could just before evening meal that ought to set the ball rolling" "Yes Master" Istra said and the two men left our cell and I could just about hear the guards returning slightly above an instrumental playing on the compound music system.

So Istra "what are we doing?" "Firstly we will hold hands in front of the Domestics, then the other 4 Musson slaves tomorrow and somewhere along the ways I shall do this" and she grabbed me from the front and pulled me in as much as her chains pulled across my stomach and slapped a kiss full on, I'd never been kissed by a girl before, then she pulled back and said "You supposed to be enjoying it," "I can see you did" I said to Istra in a jovial manner, "I never done this before give me chance," "Aureus to pull this off like Master we also have to make out that its for real otherwise these guys will see it's a ploy of some kind and dig in!" then we will never get to the bottom of it." "Ok but do not accuse me if I muck it up and then we tried a joint embrace just as two Domestic Girls arrived making "Tut-tut" noises. "You two know that is forbidden here, you should be more careful someone might report you; some of us do not trust the last lot of replacements and hope some of the old crew return after their vacations." Then two more domestic girls arrive with the lamb stew which I had got to love and look forward to every evening, just enough to fill us without waste. As soon as we was alone and I got as close to Istra as I dare, I said "lets take it slow and see what tomorrow brings" as I grabbed her left hand and held it tight, when Istra turned and said to me "Aureus you are trembling!" "Am I? I know I am fucking scared stiff. Does that count?" "Come along slave Aureus you need some sleep escape lets coddle up while we can and enjoy the night together" Istra said like a confident elder sister and so we cuddled up with Istra behind me and that image of "Babes in the wood" came to mind as I slipped into my sleep escape from yet another chaotic day.

As we awoke to the sunlight through the sky lights high above us in the overall warehouse roof and realizing that morning was approaching and soon will be time to be getting ready for more adventures best left to the horror films peoples. I began to realize Istra was up and awake over by the glory hole, alighting herself of some other waste and useless substances and as there was just the one glory hole I had to wait. Then Istra boldly says "Morning Aureus, did you sleep well?" "Yes Istra my love it's the awakening that is the night mare yet to unfold!" "That's sweet of you Aureus my love, I think we have an understanding we can work to!" Istra said smiling a mile wide. "But still slowly please Istra my love, let's please not be charging in where angels might fear to tread!" "As you wish slave Aureus my love." Just then as if like gate crashers 4 of the new Domestic girls crashed through the doorway to our cell. Istra stood up defiantly and said" don't you girls know to knock before entering a cell or room!" "Sorry their team leader said" adding "with no doors what would be the point?" "The point being a mark of respect for others!" Istra defiantly remarked, so I thought I better step in "Istra my love these poor Domestic guys are new to our ways of life and need time to adjust!" I said smiling at Istra. Then the team leader said again "yes you are damn right we rank respect too!" So I again stepped in and said loudly "Oh no you do not respect around here its earned, not bought and sold at the flea market wait till one of you guys screws up and we have to bail you out!" "That's not likely to happen in here, you twos need to worry about that!" Then Master Robert walked in and said "So will you as you are breaking the silence rules that apply to Domestics as well as more notable slaves!" as he glared at Istra and myself as if to say belt up slaves!

Then the team leader of the Domestics said "Yes Sir-Sorry Sir we are new replacements and just learning the routines, Sorry Sir!" and left us with Istra and I holding hands and Master Robert mouthing something at us. Then as if this was Piccadilly Circus the two Domestics with the porridge for us both. I am thinking this is in the wrong order are we not supposed to be washed before breakfast and I whispered my concern to Istra and she nods in response. Then Master Robert says "The Master is in an early meeting and has changed the dynamics of the training protocol, so do not worry, yet!"

So we had our porridge and milk as usual, then the

Domestic wash and brush up crew arrived and they got underway with bathing us plus brushing and braiding the long hair, which one of the girls noticed that mine needed coloring blonde again or at least the roots, as they do this from time to time as do women all over the world. I am sure they can color the roots to match the rest of my hair with out becoming a major operation. Then two Guards arrived to take us to training, as usual the guys lowered their heads so we could slip our chains over their heads so they could pick us up and they did and we was off. The Guards now as carriers were walking briskly down all the corridors to the singletail training room or space where I could see two dangling lines and hooks, plus to the right was the other 4 Musson slaves each holding hands with their cell mates. I was thinking have they come to support us or join us.

Then the Guards drop us off in the two central positions below each line hanging down from the gantries high above with all manner of engineering up there to even lift a girl slave clear off the ground., Then a Guard connected my middle link of my wrist to wrist chains to the climbers cleat looking like device and I was connected to the line, I was hoping this would be just singletail training but no, we have to have electrics too as Niobi brings in two pyramids and I bet he has two electrodes in his trouser pockets and soon the pyramid is between my legs just waiting for Niobi to and he does not make that awful noise in his throat to bring up spit when the Doctor says "Master Niobi Sir here use this its proper medical electrical connecting gel and makes for better electrical contact than your filthy stuff." Plus it's nicer but colder as they lower my vagina on to the electrode, thinking soon I shall be roast dinner once again. Then I see them do the same to Istra and I am thinking two roast dinners coming up. Then Master appears and slips by the whip wagon picking up his favorite kangaroo Bullwhip and as if all in one stroke he air cracks and it seemed louder today than usual and I am thinking heads up the boss is here and he wastes no time at all and lays into me and slave Istra. At this point we are so used to his opening attack and so it is easy to let some slip by but now they are beginning to dig in and I have to get with it and come to an alert status in my breathing to control the building pain as Master Musson is an expert to whip at a ferocious pace and I am hanging on by my finger tips as he increases speed, I can not see what is happening to Istra as I have my eyes shut as its easier to mind control the impacts now, so maybe I have evolved. Then Master Stops and Master Robert come with a metal cup of water and he says "Musson slave Aureus open your eyes and drink the water!" I hear the same from over to my left "Musson slave Istra! Drink the water!" and as there is no repeat I am sure she is drinking as I am.

Then Master Musson says "When you are done pampering your favorite pupil and my slave Master Robert Sir I still have a hungry whip that wants to attack some flesh!" "Master Musson Sir if you need a break yourself I would be more than happy to take over for you?" said Master Robert with a certain glee that I detected I am sure everyone else did too. "I will continue with Musson slave Istra Master Robert Sir, make sure you use the same whip I am using, we do not want them getting off lightly!" Master said and with that I could see Master Robert searching the Whip truck for the correct whip which did not take too long, but long enough for Master to say "Come along Master Robert Sir! Musson slave Aureus will get cold while you are pissing about over there!" "No Master Musson Sir! She will not have to wait any longer I have the correct size and weight I shall enjoy warming Musson slave Aureus up" "Oh yes I seem to recall you saying something about missed opportunities because fate intervened, Master Robert Sir? And stepped over to my position

With that I felt Master Robert land his first outside of training right down the right side of my spine and I really had to grit my teeth as he caught me unaware because Master Musson was talking and the rule is to listen deeply when Master is communicating as he does not give commands twice and we have to be on the alert for them.

Now was not the time to get thoughtful, but to get on track and try to keep up with Master Robert and not get out of step with him but he was not slowing to my pace, then I let slip "please Master Robert Sir! I can not catch my breath!" "Then you must try harder Musson slave Aureus" "Yes Thank you Master Robert Sir" Then Master Robert cracked his whip as a sign he was about to continue and did at the same time someone started to administer electrics to the electrodes which was enough to wake up the dead and me too. Then Istra let out an unexpected yelp, so I knew she too was getting the shocks as well, I thought to myself that its about time I had gotten use to electric shocks in my vagina, but then I remember the Doctor gave Niobi some medical electrical contact lubrication that for the first time seem to make it more painful than before. Now I began to realize why Istra yelped, this was new for both of us but because I was wilting it just woke me up.

Then Master Musson said "Master Niobi Sir would you like a turn?" "Yes Master Musson Sir I do believe I would indeed like to leave my mark on these two and show my displeasure in their breaking the rules!" At which point I looked left at Istra and she did the same looking right at me and I am sure this is what Master meant by his not being able to contain the punishment reprisals.

Now wondering who was on the electrical controls as they seemed to be out of synchronization to the whipping which when Niobi was whipping he was always heavier as if he really hated us, then Master Musson said "Ok Gentlemen time to switch recipients!" and so I now had Master Niobi thinking maybe I should have kept my brain shut and quiet. Slave Istra had Master Robert whom was fair, he would apply enough pressure to produce grazes and light cuts whereto as Master Niobi liked to apply enough pressure to actual cause cuts that would leak.

Again they both increased in tempo speed and I again had to really concentrate my breathing to keep up and be prepared for them shocks, so again I started to look for things in the make up of the joists like bolts that I could try to convince my brain to undo, This was just enough distraction plus pulling now on my single wire link to the winch and ceiling as I pulled on it to try to lift myself up a bit as the electrode felt like it was burning as a burning pain is very distinctive and then I started weeping again as this was way out of my control, I was busy trying to survive I had not noticed that Istra was a few steps ahead and for the first time I actually saw she was dripping snot on Masters nice clean floor just like me. At that point I had to blow my nose by in haling orally and then shut my mouth and try to just blow out of my nose. Obviously someone had noticed and everything stopped.

I had not noticed but the other 4 Musson slaves were jangling their chains quite hard and making quite a din, though Master was ignoring them as he come over to Istra and me and he glared at us both and said loudly" Sticks and Stones will break your bones, but name's will never hurt you, BUT MY FUCKING BULLWHIP WILL for this mess on my floor slaves Istra and Aureus. So we shall continue!"

"Doctor gives them some water while I go source my heavier bullwhip!"

The Doctor was feeling Istra arms, and then he come across to me and felt mine although I just had pins and needles sensation which was pretty common for me. Then the Doctor says loudly "Master Musson Sir these slaves need at least 20 minute breaks to recoup the lost blood in the arms!" "Ok Doctor but only 20 minutes, Guards lower the slave's arms and let them rest for 20 minutes!"

Whilst the Doctor was giving Istra water he started to whisper, "come closer Aureus, I hate to tell you this, but it looks bad for you two. Myself and my paramedical guys think Master Niobi, the Masters life long friend is the traitor and is the cause of all the problems around here, because he is insisting this violation of the Muslim slavery law violates it to the point he wants the full weight of the law to fall on you two's!" Then Istra interrupted "You mean he wants FGM Doctor?" "Err Yes I'm afraid he does!", "What's FGM prey tell me someone?" I said. Then Istra said "Female Genital Mutilation" "Shit" I said. I have heard of that and the Doctor again interrupted "The Master is trying to buy him off with giving you two the worst punishments that this place can deal out, so this could take days and you could be in my medical wing for months afterwards so the Master plan has back fired on you twos!"

The Doctor continued "I have tried to appeal to Mrs. Musson because she does carry some weight politically, but it will take time, as Istra knows as slaves you have more power than his wife, but not in this and so there is no instant fix and you will both have to survive the best way you can!" Istra interrupted the Doctor and said "Aureus this is my fault I should have seen the danger when Master approached us about it and I feel as I urged you into his sub plot to discover the traitor!" "No don't be silly, if anything maybe I should have seen this coming as I knew that the Colonel and Peter used to talk on the radio after work in the evenings and another who's name I never discovered, I feel even more stupid and foolish not to realize what that Peter had in his mind because its clear to me now that he really wanted to possess me, but under some control. I might even lay odds that he may have been here in disguise as a visitor and seen what I can now do and may have a hand in all this, so Istra my dear it may all be my fault!" "Yes!" said the Doctor. Then went on to say "the Colonel brought in an unknown guest of his that was never really investigated and you could be right, but Aureus and Istra this is not either of your doing. You can not be blamed for this as the Men control the organization, I must try and get Master Robert on board!" and the Doctor were interrupted with Masters Voice.

"TIMES UP! Doctor" "I have found the one I want, for a change I shall whip both of My Musson slaves. Master Robert Sir I want you to stand in front of Musson slave Aureus about 3 feet apart and watch Aureus, Master Niobi Sir you can do the same for Musson slave Istra and watch Istra for me, Take a whip with you in case I command a frontal attack as well. Master Philips Sir I want you on the electrics box!" "Guards raise the slaves hands if you please," "Yes Sir!" the Guard said and pressed a button and both our arms were raised to about the same position as before so our feet were still flat on the floor.

And so it begun again but with renewed viciousness as he has chosen a very heavy 10 foot whip, the belly of the whip has to be built so as to carry the length of the whip, which also of an extra plait thickness, a specialized one Master must have had made to order as I never felt this before and one of these lashes has the pain value of 10 and so I am now not sure either one of us will survive, Master lays into me for I am guessing about 10 lashes and then switches direction to Istra, while I get my breath back and uncontrolled, I can see out of the corner of my eye that he can get around Istra's front as well, so this might be Masters way to show me what is to come. So I thought I was ready for him, but the first one took my breath right out of me like it did the first time I ever felt to be bullwhipped, I thought I had learned enough to handle this without crying, but I fear that will not take long, I was already aware that floor run a bright red color from the first endurance whipping which far exceeded training levels. Again like when I first came to this place I dreamed of a heart attack or some natural intervention that was not forthcoming and I wondered just how much my body could really take and then when he landed a wrap around right on my nipples and for me the tears were forming as was the snot in my nose just as Master spoke "Gentlemen in front tell me which one leaks a mess on my floor first and the other will get the punishment for making more of a MESS, than there was on MY FLOOR!" With that I tried to clear my nose by turning my head as far left as possible and wiping my nose on my upper arm very near the shoulder, then shook my head to remove the tears from my eyes. As I felt a renewed state of resistance, just as Master Robert said "nearly Master Musson Sir, I think she is resisting again!" Then he turned to Istra to try his hand over there, as he laid into Istra I could feel a sense of vibration through some connecting either the floor or our hoist wire or maybe just the air pressure as he is thrusting the whip back and forth.

For the first time I had seen Istra struggling with the pain as I was and so for the first time, I no longer felt like the novice here and that gave me a bit more of something to fight with, not sure what but it sure did help as I then smiled at Master Robert, but that might have been a stupid move as we hear "Master Musson Sir, Your slave Musson slave Aureus is smiling at me, are you tiring Sir would it help if I took over for a spell?"

"It would seem you are right then Master Robert Sir She is RESISTING AGAIN! But can see I shall have to try harder as I believe you told Musson slave Aureus to do earlier Master Robert Sir?!"

"Yes Master Musson Sir I did" and then I felt Master on my back again catching my damn spine, and then my hip bones then my breast on the top and to really show off he clipped the undersides of both breasts and to really show me he could get to me, between my legs when he shouted "MASTER PHILIPS SIR if you please, and with that the electrics came on with such force my body shot up, but not far as the chains had been connected to the floor and I had not noticed who done them as they was free when the Doctor talked to us at the break. Now I had to wonder if I had passed out at some point or had someone sneaked up from behind and connected them while my mind was otherwise preoccupied. But not for long as Master was really laying in now and something strange come over me and for a reason I can never explain I again smiled at Master Robert, then we hear "Master Musson Sir are you sure that you are not tiring?" "Why do you ask this of me again Master Robert Sir?" "Because Musson slave Aureus is smiling at me, even now Master Musson Sir!" then Master Niobi added "he is correct Master Musson Sir!" with that Master stopped. The Doctor hurried over and waved his hand over our face, I think to see if we blinked then the Doctor said "Musson slave Aureus has either dropped into another personality... or gone deeper to possibly another personality Master Musson Sir!, I must check her over Sir?" "Ok Doctor you have 30 minutes only, Guards release the two slaves for the Doctor to check here!"

Master Robert stepped forwards and said to the Doctor "Why does she keep smiling at me, and that just makes the Master more angry, but she does not take that onboard why Doctor?" "Master Robert Sir I think the Master has unknowingly found a way to break her again and again and the breaks are either making already set personalities deeper or creating unknown unnamed personalities and there will come a time where she is lost to all reality completely!" "So what is the treatment Doctor?" "Someone has to stop this madness; soon she will be better off with the Colonel!" "Yes of course I should have realized from what she stated in that statement it matters not what the Master does to her she holds him as her Master and free to waste or kill her if it pleases him!" Master Robert said then Istra interrupted, "You are not serious Master Robert Sir; she does not know what she is doing that much is clear, Master Robert Sir you must talk to the Master. At this rate and I said it once before she is the perfect slave to Master, but is He not seeing or understanding this?!" "Please Doctor and Master Robert Sir you must talk to him." Istra exclaimed emphatically. Master Niobi closed in saying "Gentlemen this is my fault! Doctor you first must explain to the Master first, then You Master Robert Sir and then I will try to explain I was jealous that Musson slave Aureus seem to take a dislike to me, unlike she has with the rest of the Masters here!" "but that's not true Master Niobi Sir" Istra declared and added "When she arrived you did not really give her a chance to like you, I felt, no we all felt that you did not like her, she seemed to me to be easy going considering how she came to us, that awful Peter Man did this to her!" "Doctor I suggest you go and talk to the Master while your paramedics paint the girls with the smelly yellow stuff, Master Robert and I will back you up Doctor!" "Paramedics please attend the Musson slaves with the yellow stuff!" Master Niobi said and the leader of the two Paramedics said "But Master Niobi Sir if the Master wishes to do more he will not want them coated in the iodine?" and Master Niobi replied with "just do as I tell you, I will take full responsibility. However if they die we will hold you responsible now get on with it and stop them bleeding all over the damn floor!"

But you better leave them here and use the medical trolley for your supplies, get the Guards to put Musson slave Aureus on a stretcher I am sure the damn floor is not helping!"

Then Master Musson returned with the Doctor, "Doctor attend your patients and get the Guards to stretcher Musson slave Aureus to the medical wing. OK Master Niobi my friend what's it all about?" "Sorry Master I knew her Peter C., he was bisexual and she was not, when she discovered his preferred choices, she only stayed with him as a job or career move and Peter wanted to find a way to force her to change her mind about him. So I was surprised when he took your money, but then Peter wanted to know what you saw in her and he asked the Colonel to investigate. Then on an occasion when the Colonel was an invited Guest he disguised Peter C. to look like some Arabic Gentleman and when Peter saw at first hand what you had done with his Marie, not only did he want her back but so did the Colonel and that's where it got complicated as I did not know who was the better ally, and then I saw Istra and Aureus cuddled up at night and I thought that it would not take long before they became bisexual and then I got jealous about why Aureus could be bisexual to Istra and not her Peter and I lost the plot. I am sorry Master I will leave, if you wish it!" "So are you supporting the Colonel in his game?" Master said. "No Master No way would I support that dirty bastard No Way on my Mothers Life I swear to you I have no dealing with the Colonel!" Master Niobi said. Ok Master Niobi Sir, I accept your involvement as a misadventure between fellow Libyans, just promise me, if you want to go overboard again you will tell me first and now we are in confessional mode I have to tell you I set up the sub plot to smoke you out or the Colonels traitors and for our long friendship I am sorry!" the Master said. Master Niobi said "you mean to tell me that Musson slaves Istra and Aureus are not bisexual!" "NO! They just cuddle up at night and I approved it providing they did not do it publically, I am sorry but who told you they was bisexual?" Master replied, and then Niobi said "one of the Domestics came to me obviously because they must have thought I was approachable because I was unfriendly towards your slave Aureus and that made me the ideal contact for them, I guess." "Master Musson Sir pray tells me how to fix this mess as I am responsible for forcing you to punish Musson slaves Istra and Aureus whom I may have destroyed mentally because of my jealousy?"

Then Master Musson suggested, "look for now just carry on as you are, because I have to know whom is fronting for the Colonel in our compound, I will explain all this to Istra and if I get the chance I will explain this to my slave Aureus, twice now I have misunderstood the situation in front of my eyes and twice let her down! Now my old friend Niobi you better not make up to Istra and Aureus yet as those we seek will regroup and go deeper, maybe its about time you bedded Musson slave Aureus, you are the only one that has not, but give it a few days. I better go and see the Doctor!"

I was on a stretcher close by whilst Master Niobi

tried to explain his actions to his best friend the Master and just listening to him subconsciously I realized it was not all Niobi's fault, it seems to still run back to that damn Peter trying to possess us is my best guess, it sounds like he has involved the Colonel to try to regain us or make more money from someone, because I know that shit Peter and the things he got up to make a quick buck. Then the Guards came to collect me just as the Master was headed that way and he asks the Guard "Why is Musson slave Aureus still here?" "Sorry Sir Istra collapsed and the Doctor was pre-occupied with Musson slave Istra, the Doctor needed all of us and the paramedics to get Istra onto a bed!" "Is Musson slave Istra alright?" "Yes Sir Now, the Doctor will explain if you please Master Musson Sir!"

Then we arrive at the medical wing again, I can see Istra in a haze all covered in the Doctors favorite smelly iodine stuff, but I fade out again, though I can hear but not see. "Doctor what is going on, what is Istra's condition!?" "I think she had a Transient Ischemic Attack!" "What is that Doctor!?" "Simply for you it's a miniature stroke which could lead to a full blown attack, now let me get on with my tests. Istra will be out of it for a while Happy Master Musson Sir?"

"Doctor as soon as one or both are conscious, I want to be informed and Doctor drop the hostility it does not suit you and you are not very good at it, I appreciate you care for the girls and that suits my purpose!" then he pulls the Doctor in close then whispers to him, Master Niobi has confessed and that part is understood, but as the other part is not we have to carry on, I may have to carry on with just Musson slave Aureus or the game will be up, now keep it to yourself or we will all be in danger!" "Master Musson Sir you do realize they both each lost about a half a pint of blood on to your floors in this last session which lasted for about 4,600 odd lashes, now I am not been here long enough to know what you are capable of but the human body will only go so far, then you have to level off or slow down, I am a Doctor not a mortician please remember that Sir!" "How do you know the count so well Doctor?" "Sir my paramedics and I count so as to keep a tally for research purposes!" the Doctor said. "Excellent Doctor that may become valuable information I am impressed Doctor!"

Then there was just Istra and myself, we were lost in some world or other with one Doctor and two paramedics and I must have dropped off into sleep escape.

Eventually I awoke some days later, realizing there was a thing in the top of my left hand feeding me liquids by drip I think they call it, and even though all taped and bandaged in place felt awkward as I tried to pull myself up, my instinct was to look to my right to see my friend Istra lying motionless with a drip in the same place.

Then the Doctor came around the corner from where his base office was the layout was similar on the aircraft I seemed to recall. Musson slave Aureus you have come back to us. "I am-am not sure what happened Doctor, I remember hearing people and the music, but I could not see anything it was all a bit hazy. Looks like I have failed again to end up here instead of our cell, why is Istra here Doctor, I can not believe she failed to win through as well!" "I do not think either of you failed anything it came to a stop, I know the Master will explain it all to you later, I will arrange for the Domestics to come and bath you, etc and lay on some breakfast as you have been out for 3 days my girl!"

The Doctor moved to the telephone on the wall and picked up the receiver and said "patch me through to the Master please. Then it's the Doctor here Sir! Musson slave Aureus has awoken and seems to be back with us, Ok Sir" then he hung up and said "Your Master will be right down" "I have to get a runner to organize the Domestics, be right back" The Doctor slipped through the curtain and disappeared briefly but then re-appeared and said the "the phone line to the Domestics is out of order"

It was not long before the Domestic girls arrived with their bucket and brush brigade and as usual they split into two teams of two and got to work washing the yellow stain of the iodine off my body, probably so the Master could do it all again even though I had not completely healed, laying in bed is not best suited to recovery as exercise also helps.

Then when they had washed a dried my face the hair brush girls both with a hair brush apiece brushed and braided my hair. As soon as they finished the food trolley arrived with the hot porridge that I had missed for 3 days was here plus my metal cup of milk.

After all the Domestic girls had gone Master and Master Robert plus Master Niobi appeared through the doorway. Master Niobi dismissed the Guard, suggesting he go get a cup of tea. Then Master explained to me how the miss understanding all came about, but before he could get into too deep with the details I said "Master please you do not have to explain I was conscious hearing wise at least when Master Niobi explained himself, and maybe I have not been too charitable towards Master Niobi mainly because of his lubricating notions positive make me feel ill, weak in the stomach as I am in the head I guess. I do not blame anyone really, well that's a lie, and maybe that Peter J. C. has a lot to answer for!" Then Master spoke "I am afraid we shall have to continue on in the same vein as we still have not discovered whom these traitors are that are trying to destroy my operation here and Master Niobi will have act up to the same standard as he was before the collapse. So I am hoping that you will be able to cope!" Yes Master just so longs as we use the Doctors lubrications rather than Master Niobi's!" Master Niobi smiled from the doorway as he was keeping watch. Then Master Robert added his thoughts saying "I am sure you will do fine Musson slave Aureus!"

Then Master said "Musson slave Aureus I need you to rest as much as possible as we have a function at the weekend and you will be performing in that and this other business will have to follow as and when we can, now this is not an order but a request, Master Niobi and I grew up together and I know him like a brother, so if you could become friends with him but very discreetly it would be a great favor to me!" "Yes Master I understand!" "I too would like that to happen as well Musson slave Aureus, I have known Master Niobi a great many years and the Master and Master Niobi are extremely close, he deserves a second chance with you!" "Yes Master Robert Sir I will obey and comply!"

When the Doctor returned I asked him "Doctor Will Istra comes back to us?" "Yes she should do most people that have a T.I.A. do not collapse into a mild coma and further investigation showed a blocked blood vessel and she required a stent. She should be right as rain in a few days" "Then it looks like I shall be on my own this weekend." Then a Guard arrived at the medical wing to take me back to our cell and as usual the Guard lowered his head o I could place my wrist to wrist chains over his head so he could easily pick me up and carry me to the cell. It did not take long and the Guard dropped me off, all on my own and all I could think to do was lie down on my mattress and as I was pretty tired still and still healing from my last encounter I felt that bed rest might be a good idea as my body was still pretty much covered in scratches' cuts and bruises; some were still weeping tiny amount s of blood like capillary bleeds and so I decide to get some sleep and sleep escape and so I lay down alone.

Some hours later the Domestic girls woke me up in order to serve the evening meal which is the usual lamb stew that has lamb meat in chunks, potatoes and green cabbage looking vegetable and I do look forward to this specific meal of the day as it's a favorite that I have come to enjoy, plus a metal cup of warm milk.

Then about an hour later a Guard taps the wall by the doorway and says "You have been requested" and he comes in and as usual lowers his head so I can place my chain over his head and he then picks me up and carries me off to some unknown destination. We pass our of the ware house where we slaves all live amongst the ordinance stock piles at one end and us at the other with the torture and whipping rooms in the middle. Then the Guard turns Sharpe right into a darkened room and I can smell incense sticks burning and some candles scattered all around and a large bed in the middle of the room with the headboard against a wall. The bedding looks like satin duvets pillow cases and sheet all in black on the outside and where the duvet is pulled back on one side the bottom sheet is a pinkish color, so I know instantly that we are in the private quarters of maybe a Master or Trainer. The Guard places me on the bed which has been opened and so I sit on the pink sheet, then the Guard says "now step over your wrist chains so your hands are behind you!" "Yes Sir" I replied. Then he lifts and spins my legs round, at the same time lifts the duvet and places my legs plus ankle chains into the bed and lowers the duvet, and then he says lay back and rest with your eyes closed. "Yes Sir!" I reply.

Then I felt the sensation of someone getting into the bed on my left side and I sense its Master Niobi when he says "Musson slave Aureus, I would like us to be friends." "Yes Master Niobi Sir!" "Respectfully Master Niobi Sir I had become acclimatized to the idea that we was all family of a kind here, I always thought you did not like me or I had insulted you in some way." No slave it is I that misunderstood your relationship with Peter C. whom I have known as a radio ham personage, though only met when he came here to see if we could train you, but then the Master saw something in you that he wanted for himself I felt that was dishonoring a friend. However at that time I had not realized how ruthless that Peter C. can be seeking money and then trying to arrange to steal you back so he could re-sell you to the Colonel, I fear we have not heard the last of him!" "No Master Niobi Sir I fear that too, he will not give up so easily, I know him to be a thief and into other things I wanted to get away from him so very badly, though I never saw this life coming, but I am happy to be here and of service to the Master. Then I felt Master Niobi slide across in between my already spread legs so he was laying in between my legs below and on top of me above the waist and whilst we was chatting he was playing with my clitoral area. So I was already wet and he slipped his penis into my vagina with ease without any of his horrible spit. I could see he was trying to make amends. With my eyes still closed it was not long before I got into the rhythms of his penetrations. Then Master Niobi said "You may orgasm slave; it will not effect my enjoyment of you, "as you wish Master Niobi Sir and I had several vaginal orgasms and what I think was the deep one, though unlike the others he just thrust harder and it was catching my breath in a way I had never experienced before so I had to control my breathing and was aware of moaning in tandem with his thrusting, I was sure it would extend through my body as if it felt like it was growing in size inside me. Then Master Niobi said "Orgasm slave I demand it!" I did and he thrust even harder and it seemed to turn him on all the more. With his weight and now he was standing on my ankle chains to lock himself in the position, I felt like he was Dominating his control with his body, where as normally its with a whip and I secretly now wanted him to whip our body as the thought turned me on as well and this was a torture of a type I had not experienced before. Then he stopped and I was climbing the walls in my mind and he said "keep your eyes closed Musson slave Aureus, I had come to recognize when they use our formal names in that way it was an order or command that had to be obeyed, then he pushed my legs up and stuck his head through my ankle chains so the chains now rested on his back as his penis entered my anus, something I found most uncomfortable, but it's a something Peter liked to do and revelled in the notions that it was a Greek and Arabic preferred way to have sex, but at this time I was turned on by pain and endorphins and with my hands behind me and the discomfort of my wrist to wrist chains digging into my lower back, I/we was trapped with a heavily built Master on top seemed to add to this torturous technique that I had not experience before and I began to realize the chains also served a purpose to help them control us, because they could stand on them to add thrust when vaginally fucking and to lock our hands behind us and the whole situation left my body completely vulnerable and open to his sexual attacks, that it felt as though he was forcing my being to be submissive to his sexual attacks, which had a similar feel when under the whip of these guys and there was no other choice, this was our life now and forever. Master Niobi eventually came with such a flood it seemed to be everywhere, though I was not able to orgasm more after he took me anally as it was not my preferred sexual interest. Master Niobi climbed out of the bed and telephoned for the Domestic girls to come and clean me up as I suspect Master Niobi went for a bath or shower, the domestic girls gave me a standard bucket bath and they used a large syringe to squirt water up my vagina then placing the waste water bucket between my legs to catch any returning waste though always seemed to me that more water went than came out but would dribble out later, so when I eventually got back to my cell my mattress had been covered with a plastic sheet and then a normal Egyptian cotton sheet on top of that. Though now I felt like that bandy leg status that we girls feel when we have been fucked by a Man with a large penis, I am sure I am not the only one to suggest that's how it feels. Now I was tired again and crawled onto my mattress and pulled my sheet covering up and drifted of into sleep escape.

I slept soundly all night till the morning arrived and the Domestic girls were there ready to give my morning bucket bath and to brush and braid my hair. That followed with the usual porridge and milk breakfast and then I laid back on my now changed bedding as I was still recovering from events earlier in the week and last night with Master Niobi and again I drifted of into sleep escape for most of the day until the evening meal arrived, but I think that was Master plan all along. Again after the evening meal I slipped onto my mattress and again drifted off into my favorite sleep escape until the next morning which of course was the Saturday of the function Master spoke of earlier in the week. The Domestic wash and hairbrush girls were there early to get me ready for the day, followed by the food trolley crew with the porridge and milk. Then I had some free time to allow for digestion and to settle into a relaxed mood.

Then Master appeared through the doorway and said "how do you feel Musson slave Aureus!" "I am happy Master, though I Miss Musson slave Istra's company, how is she now Master?" "She is awake and maybe in the observation lounge with the good Doctor and a couple of Guards!" "I just hope I have not over stepped my status position!" "No indeed you have not and if you had Musson slave Istra would be equally happy for you as you both serve me, even if you equal Musson slave Istra which I believe is close, it will not matter to her or should not matter to you as you both serve Me! Do you understand Musson slave Aureus!" "Yes Master, Sorry I just do not want to upset of offend anyone!" "In your case that's understood as you are unique, this is why everyone wants to see you perform and that's good for business Musson slave Aureus!"

Then Master Niobi and Master Ahmed arrived and Master Ahmed came over to me and stooped so that I could place my chain over his head so he could lift me up and carry me to the auditorium and we all went together with Masters Musson and Niobi leading the way, Now two Men I had a love and a respect for. I overheard Master Musson say to Master Niobi "I want you Master Niobi Sir to supervise the Guards surrounding Musson slave Aureus and at any time please do not leave her on her own!" "No my friend Sir I will not let anything happen to her other than the demonstrations!" then Master Musson stopped and turned to me and Master Ahmed and said "Musson slave Aureus from now on Master Niobi is your personal body Guard, do you understand?" "Yes Master Musson Sir!" "Master Niobi Sir!" and Master Niobi said "Yes Master Musson Sir with Pleasure!" "Excellent now we have a team I can trust!" Master Musson said and the little gathering continued towards the auditorium and the two more Guards opened the double doors to the auditorium. I could see the place was packed to the gunnels, I had never seen so many people in this hall space before, several Men stood up for us as we passed them, something I did not understand as I was just Master's slave not the Queen.

Master Ahmed took me over to the mini stage that was there and placed my feet on the wooden stage floor that I automatically spread as now like my standard operating system and Master Niobi connected my middle chains link to the dangling wire hook and then indicated for the Man controlling to winch motor to raise it till Master Niobi said halt.

Master Musson went over to the whip trolley to pick his bullwhip and then returned to centre stage and introduced me as his youngest slave and the one that had become known as the perfect slave and to prove it this was the demonstration that they all came to witness, I whispered to Master Niobi "no electrics today Sir?" and Master Niobi replied "why would you like the electrics to be applied?" Sir it might add to be a better demonstration with them?" "Yes I agree, I will ask the Master!" I could see that Master Musson nod his head and Master Niobi went via the store room and returned with a pyramid and an electrode and the Guards that surrounded me fitted the pyramid to the stage floor and my chain links, and Master Niobi had some of the Doctors lubrication in his pocket and smeared it on the electrode and placed it on the pyramid then he came to me a lifted me up while a Guard guided my body onto the electrode, the Guards busied themselves with running to cable to the portable shock box and Master Musson explained to the audience that he allowed a slave to request the electrics to give a better demonstration, thus suggesting that only perfect slaves would concern themselves with the reputations of her Masters!" and then he walked over to the position that he wanted to throw his bullwhip from, then the lights went down other than the stage lights plus the music went up in volume and he was soon underway. For the first hundred lashes or so I/we did not feel much pain, but then it started to bite, but no so dramatically that the audience would not be realizing it, so we started to create distraction and used our breathing techniques for killing pain, even though much of it was a turn on for us, but we have to be careful with that because once we recognize it as a turn on we want more.

After about an hour at Masters pace we must have been up to training lash counts as Master called a rest for his usual lemonade break and I looked forward to that. But then there seemed to be some sort of commotion within the audience, and the Guards around me went to assist other Guards to calm the situation down when a familiar face was right in front of me saying "when I get you home I will be doing all this, I should have bit my tongue and not sold you so cheaply." At that point Master Niobi had come up behind this Man that seemed familiar with his gun pointed at his head and then Master Musson stepped up as well and asked "How the hell did you get passed our security Sir" "I have come to take back that which is mine, she belongs at my home not yours." then I interrupted saying "This is my home Sir and I have no intention of leaving my home for any others!" then Master said "Guard call the Military Police, tell them we have an intruder trespassing on our property and they can take that Man over there at the same time, better known as the Colonel!" Master Niobi was releasing me from the restraints and lifted me off the pyramid. Then the familiar Man said again "she is mine and I want her back!" Then Master Musson said "she happens to be married to me along with 5 others and its all legal so you have not legal right to another Mans wives or slaves and in this country they are legal commodities and are Mine, we would be within our rights to shoot you for trespassing on private property disguised as a Muslim Libyan Gentleman. Now Sir you may remember signing a Document that stated you was handing over a young lady for the sum of £100 thousand pounds as slavery here is perfectly legal and you can not have it both ways. If you want my slave Aureus, her current value is about $4 million US dollars. And in reality I am not interested in selling her for any amount of Money. Then Master Philips spoke, "Excuse me Gentlemen the Military Police are here and they wish to speak to the owner." "Master Philips and Master Ahmed escort this gentleman to the Brigg and then we see what the Military Police have in mind as he has trespassed onto a license property.

"Licensed?" "Licensed for what?" "We have ordinance stored here under licensed conditions and that puts this establishment squarely within the military domain of Libya. So we shall see what the Military Police want to do!"

With that, the familiar looking Gentleman went with Masters Philips and Ahmed to the Brigg while Master went to talk to the Military Police. Then Master Niobi told me that the Gentleman was in fact Peter J. C. still trying to get me back, so I said "If that is true why did he let me be abducted by Master Mussons methodical operation rather than just strike up a Gentleman's agreement and stand by it?" "Master Niobi Sir, he can not just now take me, can he?" "No! Musson slave Aureus, you are owned by Master Musson under international slave laws and specifically the Muslim slave laws and secondary to that you are married to him for which he has the licenses. But he can be prosecuted for being unlawfully on Military licensed property without authority or invitation!" "Good then maybe he will leave me alone and let me live with my new family!" Master Niobi Sir has the function been stopped or what is happening? "Master Musson put it on hold for 3 hours. The Master suggested the guests should take a walk and get some air, then return!"

"Maybe someone should hitch up Peter and whip him so that he knows what its like, and what its like to have it stopped so that he goes cold like me!" "Why are you cold Musson slave Aureus?" "No Master Niobi Sir, I mean I was in my stride when the interruption stopped the demonstration and like dancers, one has to warm up and stay warm during the performance!" "Yes I see and I understand now Musson slave Aureus and maybe some one else should be punished the disruption!" "In any event it's not your fault!" "That Man is going to be the death of me!" I said in depressed state of thinking. "Not while I am your personal body Guard young Musson slave Aureus, the Master will want Peter to sign a document to demand that he does not bother us more!"

"The military police will have their own agenda and they will want their piece of the cake to, even if only to dissuade others from acting so stupid like!" "This is Libya, not England; Men might be able to act stupid like there, but not here. We take life more seriously and like the Japanese People Men come first here, women come second!" I then added "and slaves don't come at all!" "Now Musson slave Aureus that is not true and you know it from my experiences of today!" Master Niobi said, with a smile.

Then Istra came to the door way of the room that Master Niobi and I was in, while the disruption and those involved gets sorted. Musson slave Istra spoke "permission to join you both Master Niobi Sir!" "Yes most definitely Musson slave Istra and you are most welcome!" "Has the Doctor signed you off medical Musson slave Istra? "Yes Master Niobi Sir, Master Musson suggested I join you both as I think Master was concerned for Musson slave Aureus mental state!" "Then pull up a chair!" "If I may say Master Niobi Sir its nice to see you and Musson slave Aureus getting along at last!" "Yes Musson slave Istra, I was stupidly drawn in to a Man thing that, Mr. Peter J. C. was a Gentleman who made up a story that was a lie in his favor and made it look like Musson slave Aureus was nothing more than a jealous nasty piece of work. However Peter has clearly showed us all his true selfishness. I believe he has the old syndrome known as "Me, Myself and I" His manipulating of anyone that might be able to strengthen his cause with his lies and deceit is so strong.

I am truly saddened that I upset the Master who I grew up with and of course the harshness I laid on

Musson slave Aureus when it was not required!" "I hope Musson slave Aureus can forgive me!" "There is nothing to forgive, that's Peters way to draw people in to see everything from his point of view and everyone else is wrong or at fault. I believed that is what happened to the German people when Hitler came into power that he made them see what he wanted them to see and not the real ways of the world. Sorry I am rambling!" "Actually slave Aureus you make perfect sense!" Istra said.

Then Master Niobi said "It's going to be hard for me to act like Master Nasty for the benefit of those traitors the Master is trying to expose. Now if I act any differently outside of this room the game will be up, so how ever nasty I now appear its for a purpose and a reality that we must put into operation to keep us all out of danger!" "We understand Master Niobi Sir and I swear to you I wish you no ill will. We are family!"

Then Master Musson walked into the room and said" Master Niobi Sir, I would like you plus a Guard or a Trainer of your choosing to assist you in body guarding these two, Musson slaves Istra and Aureus. This Peter C. guy got past our Guards and Security and into this event, if he can do it once; there is no telling how many more times he might try it!"

"Musson slave Aureus is ok to try it again and I would like Musson slave Istra and you to hold hands as a double act as it might create a response, but it might calm the situation down, just do not start cuddling, are you both happy to give it a go?" "Yes Master" we said together in unison. "Master Niobi Sir you have explained everything to Musson slave Aureus?" "Yes Master Musson Sir!" "Though if it was me I am not so sure I would be so fore-giving if someone wronged me in the same way!" Then the Master replied "Now my friend you are beginning to understand her true value as a slave, she is so easy going, yet she gives us that extra when her body resists our attacks that as you know all the Men like, I am beginning to see why the Colonel could well be interested in her, But I can not let that happen as they will both die in one of his hell holes!"

"I will send in two Guards to carry you both to the auditorium as if we are to continue we must start soon." Master Musson said in a gentle fashion and Istra replied "Yes Master Musson Sir we are alright, but I think Musson slave Aureus needs to get back on the horse as soon as possible Master Sir as they say then Aureus will be fine!" "Thank you Musson slaves Istra and Aureus." Then the Master left and soon two Guards entered the room and Master Niobi indicated for them to carry us to the auditorium and to stay with us until he returned. Then Master Niobi left and the Guards went to lower their heads, when I asked "Gentlemen may I have a wee first?" "A wee?" enquired and Istra said "Musson slave Aureus needs to go to the toilet, it would be better now than later and if you Gentlemen do not mind I would like to go as well." "Ok sure ladies carry on I am sure the call of nature will be approved!" the team leader said.

.

Then Master Niobi and Master Ahmed entered

the room and Master Niobi asked "what is the delay Gentlemen?" the team leader replied with "The ladies needed the toilet Sir, I assumed it would be better now than to stop the proceedings later Sir." "Yes good thinking, but we need to get moving!" then I said "Thank you Gentlemen and Master Niobi Sir, its my fault I needed to go and Musson slave Istra then felt the need to go as well," Then Istra left the adjoining toilet room with this room and the Guards again lowered their heads so we could place our wrist to wrist chains over their heads so they could pick us up and they did and then we was off to the auditorium with Masters Niobi and Ahmed following.

Then we arrived and the Guards placed us both on the stage where we both opened our legs almost in synchronization, as its not something you can do whilst being carried, for this action we did not have our arms raised, to start with we faced the wall with Istra on my right and I was on her left and for this our hands were in front of us, although we knew that we would hold hands and eventually turn to face each other, then change hands and turn to face the audience was the plan. I suspect that Master also had something else up his sleeve as this action might draw out those that are effectively our enemies.

Then as usual the audience appeared and so did the Doctor plus his paramedics with the white trolley that was followed by the whip trolley.

Hopefully we will not be interrupted again. It was not long before the Masters all were behind us getting ready with each their chosen whips. Then Istra reached out with her left hand and whispered "Aureus lets do it!" So I connected with her and we started this notion, though for our amusement as well

It was then that two whips air cracked simultaneously, a clear sign its about to start, then the whips fell on our backs and until then I was not sure of the tactical as to whether we each had a whipper or was it to be one at a time. However now we know and I got Master Niobi. The lashes fell in patterns usually down one side of my back then the other not actually aiming for the spine, then down one leg and up the other then we get the command to "Turn Slaves" as commanded by Master Musson operating on Istra to my right, our adrenaline must have been up or we was both up for it though I know that it will become too much in the end, my weakened areas are always my front so I dreaded that. But for now we faced each other and now we held both hands between each other and strangely the other four Musson slaves clapped in approval I guess now thee strikes were across the spine but only the whip body not the end and the lashes were catching my left shoulder area and below to my feet and on Istra they were catching her right shoulder and all the way down to her feet and the guys seemed to be in good close unison order, then again "Turn Slaves" and now we faced the audience and it was now the frontal attack starting from the neck down. "Shit" I mouthed under my breath as Master Niobi hit my nipples in quick order having to grit my teeth for a second and grip between

Istra and myself now my left hand holding her right hand intensified by us both and I knew why. Then the whips got lower and then Master Musson commanded "Stop! Refreshment for all" that meant we got the water while the Masters got Master's favorite lemonade. Then Master said "Masters Robert and Ahmed prepare!"

Then again there was two air cracking of whips as a signal it was about to start, then in quick succession it all began again.

Then Masters Robert and Master Ahmed who were a bit more soft on us when they could get away with it, but not at events where Master Musson was commanding the performance. I had Master Ahmed and Istra had Master Robert and they repeated the same pattern as the previous two Masters had done and again Master commanded "Turn Slaves" and we did again facing each other though I could see Istra was just like me beginning to feel the effects as there was a glint of tears forming and as I figured these two were laying in to show they had no favorites. Then within the same amount of time we hear Master call "Turn Slaves" again we are facing the audience and now its harder than before, but we ought to be toughened up to this as its not our first time, but still remains my weak side as my nose fills with the dreaded snot and my eyes swell with tears and now I am more scared because its in full view of the audience, even with the lights down at the back it must be clear we are struggling, though as fast as these two Masters were going it was not long before they reached our feet and Master said "Stop Slaves Rest!" "Masters Lathander and Philips prepare!"

Then I am thinking into the final leg as Master Robert handed me a metal cup of water and he whispered "hang on both" then there was that air cracking again and soon we was underway starting again facing the wall and again these two Masters were very proficient at their art and I could hear Istra now breathing quick and deep as I was struggling to keep up with their pace, I tried to amuse my thoughts thinking they have had practice, but it fell on deaf ears as it was in my head. Master Lathander is second in command so I guess he has to show an element of established ability, though Master Phillips was a new trainer probably to replace that awful Matt. Then Master commands "Turn slaves" and we do now facing each other and I can see Istra is weeping as I am silently though are both messing Masters nice clean floor with snot and probably some of the red stuff as I can see now that Istra is bleeding by trickles. Thinking about it we have never been this close before so I never seen another slave in action and I imagine Istra feels the same as we have both had the same number of impacts and you can be sure they was full on. The Master command "Turn Slaves" and we do now facing the audience and almost the whippers though they are slightly off to one side so the audience can get a clear view. Then "Shit" again and I had not realized I had Master Lathander and he caught both my nipples with one shot as it were, but I was scared my outburst was heard. Istra instantly looked my way because I pulled on her right hand with my left as I reacted as well and the four Musson slaves in the front of the audience jangled their chains, but not for long, again it was not long before Master Lathander reached my feet and I assume was the same for Istra, it was not a good thing to look, we are always supposed to look straight ahead as we might get a head shot if not following the trained guideline. Then we again hear Master command "Stop!" Doctor and Medics to the stage please!"

At the same time it seemed some of the audience were clapping, but as they was in the dark I could not see that far back to know if it was all or some, but in any event I was exhausted and not having a something to swing on or lean on seem to tire me even faster. Then the Doctor said "Guards stretchers please!" and then he turned to Master Musson and said "Permission to remove them to the medical wing Master Musson Sir?" "Excellent Doctor carries on!" and as soon as the stretcher arrived I felt the need to collapse to my knees and the Guards helped my body onto the stretcher and I passed out.

When I came to, I was on one of the beds in the medical wing as Istra was on the next bed to my right and she seemed be asleep, so I let myself drift a bit as there's no point being awake on your own. However it was not for long as Master Musson appeared through the curtains into the medical wing, though I was just dozing and when he spoke "Doctor how my two slaves are?" "They are recovering as usual; the iodine will do its work, with regular changes of tabards Master

Musson Sir" "Why?" the Doctor asks. "We have been invited to an opposition operation in Germany, it would seem all this business with our enemies is not limited to just my operation. I suspect we shall have to put on a demonstration as I do not think they are like us, but I want my best girls to be as fit as they can! Doctor" and then he left without saying hello, but I was tired anyway and needed my sleep escape.

SEQUENCE 25

INVITE TO OPPOSITION CAPTIVITY

I awoke to what looked like a bright morning as the light was beaming down through the roof skylights high up above us, the Doctor was doing his paperwork as usual until, he realized I was waking and came out of his cubical office to see if we was both awake" Doctor I need the pan please?" "I have it here in readiness and one for Istra when she wakes" "I am not asleep Doctor just keeping my eyes closed as I feel low!" "You mean as in depressed Musson slave Istra!?" "Yes Doctor now that you ask formally yes" "Now why would that be?" "Not sure I should say" Istra said then the Doctor responded with "well I can not help you if I do not know the cause" "Its Masters plan, I over heard him tell you, you have not been there Doctor! We shall need eyes in the backs of our heads and plenty of Guards, if we think the Colonel is bad, wait till they see how we have improved, and then you will understand!" "Istra how do you mean improved?" I enquired "Well" Istra began, and then the Doctor added "Well nothing! Istra means you Musson slave Aureus to be blunt!" "I have heard rumors of this lot for years now, another group that do not spend the extra to have medical on board! Is the bottom line, but do not worry my loyalty is with us, if there's any extra needed my paramedical assistants can handle it. So put to bed your depression before the Master sees it!"

"Istra Master assures me no-one can take me out of here and Master will not sell me of give me up at any price, so where is the problem, I know last night was heavy going but we are supposed to be the best according to Masters Niobi and Lathander, so I guess it has to show that way in the state of being heavy" "Aureus you have such a way of putting words together, that make my concerns look feeble" "No You know more about this than I, I am still learning and I have the L plates somewhere to prove it, seem to have lost them just now, I bet someone pinched them!" and with that Istra smiled with a little laughter. "So what is on the menu today then Doctor?" "You two have to rest as the Master want you both to be in fine fettle for Germany" the Doctor said cautiously and Istra went "Oh I get it another demonstration, Aureus just think how rich we would be if we got paid for these demonstrations?!" "Well maybe we are if this was our work and we got free bed plus board, plus food!" "Yeah and a good whipping to put us to sleep at night thank you Aureus" Istra said with a smiles, "you forgot the free transport to work Aureus!"

"Complaining about the service Musson slave

Istra!?" Master Musson said as he came in through the curtained entrance to the medical wing. "No Master, I woke up feeling low and the good Doctor and Aureus were trying to raise my spirits" "You little liar Istra, but you are forgiven, I know you girls better than you know yourselves isn't that so Doctor" "Yes Master Musson Sir, these young ones have not lived yet and they do not know what we know Sir!"

"They are sending one of their representatives to travel back with us and guide one of our Men to drive the coach I have hired from the US Air force base, Germany. As we are friends of the US Air force they are allowing us to land there and park in a secure location. So Doctor make sure you have plenty of medical supplies aboard, we have encountered problems there in the past." "So I have heard Master Musson Sir!" "Who from May I ask?" Master said. "From my predecessor, we medicals never lose touch; it helps smooth the transition between medical staff for the benefit of the girls of course!" "Yes of course it does thank you Doctor

"And Master then left as both Istra and myself was cowering beneath the sheet. "Thank you Doctor!" "No problem I can not have anyone upset my patients in my domain, especially if he wants you two in fine form for Germany!"

Then Master Robert appeared through them magic curtains, as the medical wing can be dead boring and he said "How are you two today?" "We are recovering Master Robert, but you look happy?" "Yes I got to finish what I started on Musson slave Aureus; it seems things kept getting in my way so as not to complete!" "So Master Robert is a happy bunny Sir" I slipped in. "So why so glum in here, you two are usually whispering 10 to the dozen between one-another?" "Istra is worried by the planned trip to Germany Master Robert Sir." "No need now that Master Niobi is fully on board he is acting as Musson slave Aureus's personal body Guard and he will keep an eye on you too as you Istra is The Masters number one Musson slave, neither of you should have anything to worry about and we will all double up and be eagle eyed over our prey not theirs!" "Plus of course another demonstration so you may get yet another chance Master Robert Sir at one of us!" smiles

"Don't worry if its not here then it will be there and if not there it will here, I am not going anywhere and neither are you Musson slave Aureus!" he said smiling and left us too it, twiddling our thumbs with boredom. Laying in the bed completely naked except for the chains, I rolled over to my left side almost losing the chain outside of the bed, trying to complete gravity in motion and for some reason it made me think of how we got here because of what Master Robert said.

Soon the Domestic girls arrived with their bucket and brushes brigade and jolted me from dozing, "Come along Istra get a wiggle on the porridge will be here soon and you should be washed and brushed by then." "I need a wee before I do anything else!" Istra said. "You two are getting more like a matched pair," the Domestics team leader said. "There's no rush on today is there Team leader?" I said, "No but we need to wash you down and remove the yellow shit and put clean fresh tabards on you both." "Ok start with me." "Then whilst Istra is having her wee at least one of us will be ready!"

Its nice to have a nice clean body once again, though marked up though I can only see what I can see, but then I just look at the others and assume my body looks the same, so that will put paid to any glamour photo modeling I might fantasized about unless its for the ghost train.

Then Back to bed with nice clean sheets and the doctor to keep us amused, "No!" said the Doctor, then he added "The special envoy from the opposition slavery operation will be here at 20:00 (8pm) and a full on dinner is forecast though slaves will sit on the floor and Domestics on cushions and only Masters will sit in chairs!" "What will the guards sit on?" "They will not, they will be standing on guard!" Then the Domestics team leader said "Yup a regular fiasco, pinch me someone I want to get off the planet!" "There goes another worried soul!" Istra piped up with. "Well then bed rest till He gets here then!?" "Yes good idea at least keep you out of trouble till then!" the Doctor said. "Thanks Doctor with friends like you who needs enemies?" I said and climbed into my lowered bed as then did Istra, my best mate and friend as I rolled over to get to sleep escape.

Then suddenly we are awoken and it's the Doctor, "Time to go the Guards are on the way to take you two, come along, I have to remove your tabards, all slaves must be naked according to Masters Instructions!" "But that is normal for us Doctor!" Istra said. "I am in the dark as much as you, we shall have to learn as wee go on, do you need to use the toilet?" "Yes please we both said at the same time!" "Then make it snappy!" I managed to throw some water from the sink onto my face to help wake me up and then I changed places with Istra and she rinsed her hands and also threw some water on her face, the trouble with training and demonstrations is they build up and we get very tired. Now we are ready and the guards are her to, and they are lowering their heads so we can place our chains over their heads so they can carry us to the place of doom.

The Guards were heading for the main building where all the Masters quarters are located like Master Niobi's the other day when he bedded me, but we went on to an area similar to our auditorium where there was clear space for at least 6 Musson slaves to sit and the Guards putt us down at the end of the line, now really Istra should be at the front and I at the back, but it seemed ranking was not a concern. Master Niobi was on hand to receive us in all his traditional Arab dress and head dress all in cream or off white, I was not sure which and then he said "slaves kneel position 1!" which was to step over our wrist to wrist chains so our hands were now behind us and then we sort of splade our legs out so our bottoms were touching the floor and this was a close resemblance to a yoga position I knew something about having done Yoga. Our legs locked us open between our legs so a Master could get a bullwhip end right in there and our locked position means we can not flinch or lessen the attack and one has to bite the bullet and accept such a pain.

Most of the Domestic girls also naked but not wearing any chains just stainless steel cuffs and anklets the same as us. All the Males were dressed in their Sunday best or evening wear and for once we did look like a civilized communality maybe for a nudist colony as the tools of torture were not on display.

Then Master approached with this guy next to him in a normal business suit, dark hair and slim possibly late 30's going on 40, but what do I know. Then Master brought the Gentleman over to our area and said "these are my 6 precious slaves, this is Musson slave Istra she was my first and so she teaches the new comers, Then next to her is Musson slave Aureus my youngest and the newcomer, which is why they are quartered together however they have become the ideal team. They are evenly matched in temperament and abilities!" "Yes Sir we have heard of your slave Aureus, as you may know good news travels far and wide, but is she not the cause of the trouble we all find ourselves in? "NO Sir! In point of fact she was almost as trapped by a nasty piece of work in a Male as you will ever come across, that is not her fault she was trying to escape him when she fell into my hands and we all love her dearly all the Masters here and all her slave sisters, even I have learned a few things about myself in having her within my harem and that is where she will stay!" Then we have Musson slave

Volga from Russia, she is the third of my Masochistic Nymphomaniac trio. Then we have Musson slave Arabela from Saudi Arabia, her father wanted me to take her on rather than marry into a family that would not have suited his purpose. Then we have Musson slave Zaire of Africa, again she was [part of a deal I had with a Chief in that part of the country and finally we have Musson slave Mista from Canada and again she is part of a deal I had with her father as the wrong sort of Men kept bothering her. They can all handle themselves well, but only my first 3 are the heavy front runners of the Musson Slavery Organization!"

"Come Master Frank Sir lets go to dinner." and they went to a large table in the corner for a sit down meal, I assume the same as what we get in our bowls the lamb stew which I now love, seems to be a good balanced diet for me.

Then I whispered to Istra "what happens now?" "Us if we are not careful Sssh!"

With that I shut my eyes and tried to block out feeling uncomfortable in this position, it felt as my bones was locking. Just hope I can stand when ordered to do so.

"Istra my legs go" Aureus passes out and falls forward.

Then I come around and again I seem to be in the medical wing again, "what happened Doctor?" "As far as I can ascertain you have a trapped nerve, possibly from when you was blasted off the stage back in Dublin, you can stand and you can lay but it seems you cannot sit or kneel in that position for long, as you did and you must have been aware of unusual pain?" "Yes Doctor but I did not know what to do?" "Just call me", "But we was in that dinner thing and I could not move and Istra hinted for me to Sssh. As in be quiet and I did not have my flare gun with me Doctor!"

"Yes I know I am only funning with you, these things happen and the Master is aware of them happening to humans." "So I am in trouble again?" "No I do not think so; we just have to plan for you." Then the Master breezed into the medical wing. "Sorry Master I do not know what happened; I was in pain then lost the feeling in my leg and then forced sleep escape."

"The doctor thinks you have a trapped nerve after the explosion that shot your whole body off that Irish stage and that is how you was injured, it only showed up because of your position, normally you are either standing or laying if not on apparatus' like beams, so we will have to learn from it and hope it does not impede you too much." Then he left.

"Again that incident was not your fault it was that Matt and the Colonels doing!" "Now you must rest!" The doctor said and the he added "I am giving you a relaxant to help you sleep!" then the Doctor inserted the hypodermic needle and within moments I could feel forced sleep escape coming on.

When I woke I felt much better with the world, though still in the medical wing I seem to have a magnetic pull to this place. Then the good Doctor arrived and said "I assume you need the bed pan for a wee Musson slave Aureus," "Yes please Doctor." "There you are, better not hang about the Domestic girls are on the way over here, it's all go today!" "You mean wee are all off to that place in Germany?" "Yes the Master feels it's too unsafe to leave you here as I have to go to be on hand, so you will be my patient, my responsibility, so get moving!" "Yes Doctor." Then the Domestic girls arrived for my bucket bath and the wasted no time in getting me all wet and then dried. Another girl brushed and braided my long hair and in quick time I was ready. Then within minutes two Guards came to take me to the car I guess, but why two I thought, then one drooped his head so I could place my wrist to wrist chains over his head so he could pick me up and then did so, as we turned to leave the medical wing I saw the Doctor pick up his brief case and follow us out turning off the lights as he left. As we moved through the various passages and corridors the Guards stopped, then Master Niobi appeared at that doorway and said "Let's go Gentlemen and Master Niobi followed behind my Guard carrier and I smiled at Master Niobi realizing that he is also my personal body Guard as instructed by Master Musson. Soon we reached the car garage where all the cars were kept under cover of the relentless sun and the Guard carrier placed my feet by the rear offside door so I could release my chain from him and the turn and step into the car at that same time master Niobi stepped in on the nearside rear door so that he was always in close contact with myself. Then Master and another Guard carrying Musson slave Istra appeared and he placed her feet at the same rear door I got into the car at and she released her chain from his neck and stepped in smiling at me and sat to my right. Then Master stepped in and sat on the back seat directly opposite Istra as Master Niobi was directly opposite me. Our chauffeur got into the front drivers seat and Master Ahmed as usual got into the front passenger seat and as we pulled away I heard a loud click as it would seem the locks were applied, never did that before. Master spoke "Are you feeling better today Musson slave Aureus?" "Yes Master, I wish it never happened, made me feel silly and scared!" "Scared of what Musson slave Aureus?" The atmosphere was electric because we had that guest here with us and I know you do not like unknowns to happen Master!" "Are you requesting to be punished for one of nature's responses to an accident?" "I don't believe it Master Musson Sir!" Master Niobi said, "I do Master Niobi Sir she is a Musson slave, now tell me why? Musson slave Aureus." "I believe it would set a president for our guest to realize even unknowns are punishable to maintain a strict regimented and stable operation such as yours Master!" "I can not fault your explanation, its what I expect from my top Musson slaves and you do agree Musson slave Istra," "Yes Master, I know Musson slave Aureus is concerned for all our safety as a family and we would want other operations and outsiders to know why the MSO is the best and not to be crossed or interfered with, respectfully I trained her to honor Master and his family!" "You see Master Niobi Sir another one loyal to the core and my friend now you realize why I want you to be Musson slave Aureus personal body Guard!" "Yes Master Musson Sir and it's a great honor to serve you in this way and assist to the protection of the family as a whole." At that point we entered the Giant DC 10 aircraft.

"Just a minute before anyone leaves the car, can you hear me up front Master Ahmed and the chauffeur. The car is sound proofed, Musson slave Aureus is perfectly correct and we can not afford to show any weakness as I do not know what these people want, but I did hear the envoy believe all our troubles are Musson slave Aureus's fault and we should just hand her over, just like Master Matt was stating. Be assured Gentlemen it is NOT and I say again NOT Musson slave Aureus's fault that all this has kicked off, that Peter has a lot to answer for as does the Colonel." "Please Master to prove our point you need to hurt me in this punishment otherwise they may see straight through it!" "Yes I know and it bleeds me to even have to think about it let alone do it!" Istra I need you to prepare your sister slave Musson slave Aureus. Master Niobi Sir does not leave her side and Master Ahmed I want you to support Master Niobi is that clear everyone!" "YES SIR!" all say together. "Right lets go!"

We all get out of the car and Master Niobi lowers his head so I can place the chain over his head so he can pick me up and Master Ahmed becomes Musson slave Istra's carrier so that Master can enter the aircraft unhindered.

Upon entering the aircraft from the garage portal

the Captain meets with Master and they go to the front of the aircraft and Master Niobi and Master Ahmed carrying Musson slave Istra both go to the black tent bedroom so I can continue to rest and Istra can keep me company as we usually bunk together.

The two Masters secure the special belts across the bed so that we bare safe for take off when the crew are ready and Masters Niobi and Ahmed pull out some wall attached chairs to secure themselves as well as we hear the rear ramp close. Master Niobi picks up a phone and dials a number and then says "Captain we are all securing in the rear portion of the aircraft" then he hangs up the phone. Then the auto stairs comes up as the engines start and the light flicker from standby to flight mode, then we hear the no. 2 engine start which is the one on the back end of the aircraft, so its kind of closer and as the DC 10 is or was a cargo converted plane to specific specifications there is not a lot of sound proofing. However it is decked out like a Bedouin caravan on travels.

Then we started to roll gently forwards to a nominal taxing speed and then you feel the aircraft turning left onto the runway where we halted at the foot and after a few moment I imaging the Captain is checking with air traffic control where ever they are then came the revving of the engines which wanted to lerch forwards but with the brakes hard on unto the brakes were released and we powered down the runway until you could feel the aircraft lifting, it always seemed to me as we got to a certain height the engines seem to go quiet but then we seemed to go higher as if in a lift. Then the seatbelt sign went out usually meant we could move around the aircraft though mostly this end for us, only the men could go forwards, though as now Master Niobi was my bodyguard he was staying close. Now that I knew him better and we are in a better relationship, but that is clearly that Peters doing, as is a lot of this aggravation.

Then Master Robert appeared through the connecting door from the front to the back of the aircraft our domain and he sat on the edge of the bed up towards the starboard side so he could talk to Masters Ahmed and Niobi, Master Robert said "The microphones have been turned off here so you can update me on what goes on as I can tell Master is very worried about this whole deal?" Then the Guys went into a sort of huddle bit like a rugby scrum and whispered. Then Master Robert said "The only change of plan I was told by the aircraft captain is the no-one lease the aircraft when we land in Germany as Master will tell the envoy to tell his people to come to the aircraft, using some detail about we do not all have visas to leave the aircraft as the aircraft is our home away from home, but is representing Libya!" Master Niobi then said "That works even better for us, at least it is safer and it is not as if we have not done anything aboard the aircraft if its warranted!" he means as to us doing demonstrations I whispered to Istra. The Istra turned to me and said "Yes that is a good idea, I had a bad feeling about this and I have half a mind to request to Master if we could throw in having to go to another country on business!" "Yes Istra, I too have a bad feeling about all this, why I suggested that I take a punishment for collapsing as we can not allow them to think we are some soft operation, if its true and the MSO is the best because its based on the Muslim faith then I would expect nothing less.

Soon thee domestic girls came with the porridge and milk breakfast, with all the worrying I nearly forgot how hungry I was getting, Masters Robert and Niobi went off to the front of the aircraft leaving Master Ahmed as back up bodyguard, I always did get along with Master Ahmed as he is a bit of a softy like the Doctor but more when we are alone. Then the domestic girls re-appeared followed by Master. The Domestics removed the empty bowls and cups and left us with Master and Master Ahmed. Then Master spoke "Musson slave Aureus are you fit enough to take a punishment?" and I replied "Master you do not normally ask me, but as you have I think so, and if it's to strengthen our position I insist upon it. Then the Doctor walked in with Master Niobi. "Doctor is Musson slave Aureus fit to undergo a punishment?" and the Doctor replied "If it has to be yes, but I can not say what her endurance levels might be, she really needs more rest. However if I call a halt to it then you must STOP! Master Musson Sir!"

"Alright Doctor I hear you, but this is important to all our safety Master whispered into the Doctors right ear.

"Doctor look after her he while we set things up, Master Niobi is Musson slave Aureus bodyguard he will watch over, Master Ahmed and Master Roberts prepare the whipping arena at the back of the aircraft!" "I will explain to our friend that Musson slaves are not allowed to pass out without permission!"

"Master Niobi Sir can you ask the Master if I could do this freestanding and can we have the music a bit louder, you could ask in Arabic for these things and our friend will not know I asked for this request?"

"Yes Musson slave Aureus if you think you can pull it off I am sure it can be arranged." "Are you sure you can do this Aureus?" Istra enquired, "No but I am goner give it my best shot, you see Istra I think the Colonel is behind it somehow, I do not know why but my guts tells me there's trouble afoot. You know me I do not want to hurt or get anyone hurt for the sake of my feeble body." "Don't be silly your body is fine and so is your mind, I do not want you ended up as a vegetable as our Masters know what they are doing and when they do not the good Doctor tells them off!" "No Musson slave Istra, I am sure they will not heed my words all the time, but we must not let on about that!" the Doctor exclaimed.

Then Master Robert stuck his head through the end curtain and said "They are ready!" Then I said "So who is going to carry me to my Doom?" Master Niobi said "I will do the honors if no-one objects!" and then Master Ahmed said "Then I shall bring Musson slave Istra!" and so we all trooped out of the black tent following Master Robert and with Master Ahmed behind with slave Istra and the good old Doctor bring up the rear.

Master Niobi took me to the rear wall of the aircraft, the wall divider between the garage and the slaves domain, Master Niobi placed me down on my feet and then withdraws to a safe distance but within eye sight of me so I knew he was there. Master came over to me and whispered in my right ear "Musson slave Aureus, just for this I will appear very nasty towards you for passing out without permission, we will start on your back with your hands in front then when I command turn you know to step over your ankle chains before making the turn so you hands are then behind you! Understood slave?" "Yes Master with pleasure!"

Then Master Musson says "Raise the music volume please!" and then he air cracks his favorite bullwhip and its goner is the 10 footer. Then Master Musson says loudly "Musson slave Aureus you know full well you are not allowed making any movements when we are in the auditorium or the Masters lounge in the main building without permission, "Yes Master!" "You know the punishment?" "Yes Master!" "Then do not do it again!" "No Master!" and he air cracked the whip again and then it landed to the right of my spine, then to the left and then to the right and then back to the left all the way to my bottom, then a sides ways slash at top of my bottom cheeks and then one below in the opposite direction, then all the ways down my left leg first then down the right leg. Then Master said out loud "Turn you miserable slave!" so I bent down and stepped over my ankle to ankle chains and the turned so now my hands and arms were behind me and I faced the gathered crew of the aircraft plus the Beta flight crew (off duty), all the Domestics and their Guard partners, plus the other

5 Musson slaves and all the Masters with their special guest, the only missing peoples was the flight crew Alpha flying the aircraft.

Them Master began again, this time doing a side slash across my breasts catching my nipples which is like a carpet burn, then the other way so as to be equal and then moving on down by trunk almost trying to do Tic Tac Toe on my belly and then he slips the whip between my legs and carries on down my legs, I am breathing quick and fast trying to keep up and sweating like a pig as the tears begin to fill the eyes and the snot in my nose because my front is my weakened area. Then something I had not planned on Master spoke "Master Robert Sir! Take Musson slave Istra over there, she trains the slaves of MINE!" This he does and places slave Istra next to me. "Now you two I want you to face each other and place your wrist to wrist chains over each other so you can not escape and then I shall begin AGAIN!" then I whispered "I am sorry!" Istra just shook her head. Then Master Air cracked his whip twice once behind Istra and once behind me and the it began again this time he was doing parallels across our backs, Istra first then mine From top to toe, then he commands

"Now unchain each other and then turn back to back, then step over your wrist to wrist chains so you both have a dangling chain stopping the other from escape!" "Can you assist Master Niobi Sir please?" Master Niobi whispered "t will not be long now!" and the he walked away.

Then again Master air cracked his bullwhip in front of Istra and then in front of me and again starting with Musson slave Istra he land across her breast then mine then again and me again and the starts on down both our fronts and when he gets to just above our ankle shackles he stops.

"Release them Master Niobi Sir and Master Ahmed Sir, Doctor Check your patients please Master Musson said loudly!"

Then to everyone astonishment the Envoy a Master Frank says "can I have a go at that Master Musson Sir!" Then Master Robert approaches and says" Have you used a singletail before Sir?" "No Sir we mainly use floggers why?" "Master Robert says" it's a different tool Sir and if you damage a slave in the process, they may loose their value!" "Why does that matter after all they are just slaves, not worth the shit on my shoe?"

"Then Master Musson interrupts, Sit if you wish I will give you a singletail and you can play with it and one of your own slaves to your hearts content!" "No Sir you do not understand! I want to beat the crap out of that stupid bitch that has cost us the lives of two of our slaves to that infernal Colonel, Now give me a whip!" Then Master Niobi stands before him and says "if you lay a hand on that slave I will throw you off the aircraft without a parachute Sir!" Then Master Lathander turned up and said "Master Frank Sir we have been polite to you and honored this meeting, but as you can see our slaves are so much more superior they get punished even when nature intervenes so you do not want to take on the MSO Consortium. The colonel could quite easily train his own whores to be slaves, but he too fucking lazy, so if you are fronting for him or trying cause trouble on his behalf, you will only put your own organization at risk, Do I make myself clear? Sir!" "Yes Sir!" "Come let's retire to the front lounge for some refreshments!" Master Lathander said and they all departed to the forward compartment.

Then Master Niobi returned to me and lowered his head so I could put my chains over his head and he then picked me up and carried me to the medical wing on the aircraft and placed me on one of the beds, Master Ahmed carrying Istra were right behind and Master Ahmed placed Istra on the other bed. Then Master Niobi said "Doctor they are now your patients Master Ahmed and I will take turns keeping an eye on the medical wing and there are two Guards out here. Then they both left I assume to go to the front compartment whilst everyone else returned to what ever they was doing, whilst the one Paramedic Gentleman and the Doctor attended both Istra and myself by being coated in the smelly yellow iodine paint.

Both Istra and myself were I believe in a state of mild shock, but better it all came to a head here than in their establishment. Then the domestic girls arrived with some hot sweet tea to help calm us down as again my body was leaking the red stuff, but with training and week events its doing that back at base. Then I said to Istra "where do we go now, back to base or on to somewhere else? Istra replied with "we have to drop this Master Frank off in Germany I would guess, but there seems little point doing anything else there, though the last time Master visited these people it kept the Doctor busy and used up all the travelling first aid supplies." "Istra what is a flogger?" "Oh it's like a cat of nine tails like sailors used to use back in olden times, usually a heavy thuddy whip that if used wrongly can break bones, damage kidneys. Master does not like them he only likes the singletail, much more elegant and because it takes some practice to target it also requires them to train apart from on us, where as some simpler weapons any one can use, no experience required!" "They then sound like they could be a dangerous lot then if they only use floggers?" Then the Doctor said "yes and if we was to go there, it would be polite to allow them to have a go at you lot while our Masters try them out, I have enough to do with our own operations without mixing it with other operations!"

Whilst Istra and I were sipping this hot sweet tea, Master Robert appeared and asked "How id Musson slave Aureus Doctor?" "Doctor I should say exhausted and needs more rest, but I suspect you Gentlemen have some other ulterior motive to ask such a question?!" "In that case Doctor you are in luck as soon as we have dropped that Master Frank off in Germany we are going to stay at that house in the UK that we was in about 3 months ago, so that all the slaves can have some rest but the training program maybe reduced to 2 a week instead of 3.

"However that does not exclude whatever mischief the Master can muster for the weekends!"

"Master Robert Sir so what is happening about Master Frank and the proposed plan to visit our opposition slavery organization?" "We will land at the US air force base as planned, but we will all stay on the aircraft. The organization head has agreed to meet with Master Musson on the aircraft for whatever the proposed meeting was originally about, but as we all witnessed Master frank got the idea that Musson slave Aureus is some kind of whipping post for these Guys to vent their anger, I see this as an internal form of Domestic Violence that has no place here and Both Masters Lathander and Niobi faced up to this Master Frank insisting that was not going to happen.

If the Colonel is now widening his field of acting like a Predator in stealing or manipulating people either into his whore houses or his operations, it does affect us all, but Musson slave Aureus did not start him off on this quest and he needs to understand that! Does that answer your question Musson slave Aureus?" "Only in it seems to be politics and a lot of Men-folk seem to be singling me out to vent their anger on, so no I am petrified now to be alone." Then Master Musson appears through those curtains and says "You will never be alone Musson slave Aureus, Musson slave Istra will always be with you. Master Niobi is your personal Body Guard and he will watch over you, it might seem as though he is not there but I assure you He will be, Master Ahmed has offered to act in tandem for when

Master Niobi needs rest. Then the whole organization will protect you. It seems to me that this got out of hand because I took a liking to your spirit in resisting our attempts to force you to submit to my command, so if anyone is the blame it is me. The man you knew as Peter was a known thief in the Middle East as I believe he thought A.M. for the UK's Air Ministry stood for "All Mine" consequently he must have fallen in with local criminals and of course the Colonel. When I offered Peter One Hundred thousand pounds for you he accepted possibly a bit too quick and signed documents supposedly as your legal guardian. Then in some radio chatter with the Colonel after one of my demonstration parties one weekend where the Colonel was a guest. Peter discovered that you could be broken and trained and then of course he wanted both his cut and you back in his control. But that will not happen because you are legally one of my slave wives under Muslim slave laws and Libyan slave laws. Sadly I do not think that Peter will stop pursuing you, but it is a something we shall have to live with!"

"Soon we shall be landing in Germany and Master Franks people will meet the aircraft, although they will not be allowed on the US Air Force base grounds, so Master Lathander will meet them at the gate and escort them to the aircraft where we shall have this meeting under Guard, but I do not intend to stay as their operation conflicts with Mine and it is better that we do not mix with theirs. Then we shall fly to UK Stanstead. The aircraft will have a service while we are at this UK

Base, we will board 3 of my special coaches to take us to the House that we stayed at some three months ago. Since then I have purchased said House and Grounds, it's been converted into a holiday home for our BDSM brotherhood worldwide to bring their subs or slaves for training and rest. So far it seems to be doing well; all our own Guards and partners venture here under a special deal when they want to be away from us!"

Then there was a tannoy announcement for all to get secured for landing and Master left us in the medical wing feeling dazed.

The aircraft had that little bump as we touched down and then slowly came to a halt as the Captain had to wait for clearance to cross another runway. As I looked out of the window on the port side I saw what had to be some kind of airport control vehicle with lots of flashing lights, then when it turned around I could just make out a illuminated sign saying "FOLLOW ME" and then we motioned forwards and to the left over to a secluded parking area and as soon as we stopped the auto stairs went into action to lower the stairs, though our rear section stairs remained silent and within the aircraft as the engines powered down the standby lights illuminated as the main lighting went out.

I lay back in my comfortable bed, well other than hospital beds have a plastic mattress cover and it can get a bit uncomfortable after a while, but just now it was very comfy and then I dropped off into my usual happy place of sleep escape.

I awoke some hours later and I could see through the

window it was now night time and my first thought was I hope I have not missed my lamb stew favorite meal of the day when the Doctor looked in and said "You timed that just right the domestic girls are bringing the evening meal!" As they appeared through the curtained doorway Istra started to wake as well. Then yawning she said "all this lazing the day away and then evening meal in bed, what more could a girl want?" "A win on the lotto, a new body, I can think of lots of things but I am not so sure what I would do with them if I had all that as probably then just want to be back here!" Then Istra said "if we are doing the wishing well bit again, I just want peace with our neighbors like the Colonel not trying to wreck our homely lifestyle and mental stability!" "Oh please Istra do not remind me, if I had known or had the powers of sight into the future, I would have killed myself rather than bring all this shit onto others!" "Yes Aureus that is your nature! You have so many qualities that would get wasted because of the greed of other!" Then Master Musson slipped through the curtained doorway, and then he spoke "Good evening my slaves how are you both tonight?" "Master Sir, I wish you would ask the Doctor he is more qualified than I "Istra said and so he did "Doctor how are my slaves tonight?" and the Doctor said "Resting as indeed you should be too Master Musson Sir!"

Then the Doctor said "I presume that we shall be off soon for our next assignment if you have completed your discussions with those people we came to see Master Musson Sir?" "Yes Doctor I do not plan to waste more time here than is required as I can not see that it benefits my future plans. But if you are digging for information, you may have it as its no secret. They were seeking an alliance with our organization and I suspect a cash injection is probably behind everything. To be perfectly honest with all our people, like many I was disgusted with that outburst of his yesterday assuming that just by giving up Musson slave Aureus to the Colonel that it would stop further incursions by the Colonel. They clearly do not know the Man; you can not just give in to him and hope he will keep his word. As you know Doctor we have a form of purity because my operation has the Muslim faith slant to it which makes us the best operation in the world, the cruelest by some people's standard and the worst by others!" "Respectfully Master I disagree, ok in the beginning I might have felt that what you do here to be evil and cruel, but I see it differently as we get food and a good Doctor to take care of our health needs and to aid bodily repair, I seem to have grown accustomed to be a Musson slave if that is not offensive to anyone?" I said. "Thank you Musson slave Aureus, there are reasons why you feel that way is as Master Robert explained to you a while back that you have been broken to obey my command and your brain has been reprogrammed to see life now as a Musson slave under my command. But for reasons I will not go into. In the beginning I had set the operation up to be as close to being as humane as possible so we have a Doctor and two Paramedics on the payroll, Domestics to look after the daily needs of the whole operation on the payroll they not only look after your daily needs but all the Guards and the Masters as well. I want you all to be alive and as fit as possible to serve my command in the way I have set it up to be, now this operation they have here they do not have Doctors only first aiders and most of the inmates have to do the chores as well as serve their commander. Unfortunately for them Master Frank's out-burst showed me they care little for their slaves and I can not have their ideology or that loss of respect for the slaves that serve their command possibly infect our operations here. So I will give them only the respect of being an oppositional captivity even though I disapprove of how they run it. We take off in the morning for the new operational business venture in the UK. A sort of holiday venue for our brothers and sisters that like to reciprocate at a lesser level form of Masters and slaves on a consensual level, the Americans have been calling it BDSM, though I believe they have some more extreme followers as well and some might like to join our operation when some of our Domestics decide they have had enough. You do not have that luxury as you are mine!" Master said smiling at the end as he turned and left the medical wing on the aircraft.

Then the Domestic girls arrived with the nightly hot milk drink that we all had of a night time, either to help our wounds heal or sleep better I never really knew which, but it was welcomed, but sometimes in these metal mugs with no handle they could transmit the heat to the sides and so often had to grip it with the paper napkin as supplied. I personally was looking forward to going back to UK tomorrow, even though its not really for my benefit and I will not be allowed to go sight seeing like a tourist, certainly not naked and in chains, so whatever the desire to be there, it was unknown to me. I knew from the past that even my parents would not welcome me home, because I was the black sheep of the family. Even if I had done well, my parents would be more worried about explaining it to their neighbors. So I thought best forget all that too and look forward to my favorite pastime of sleep escape.

SEQUENCE 26

REST AND RECOUPREATION MAYBE

I awoke with a start to the sound of banging and crashing that turned out to be the rear ramp and garage doors closing for flight, then the flight steward stuck his head into the medical wing and said "Doctor please make sure all your patients are strapped in for take off!" the Doctor replied "Yes Sir thank you!" I then very quickly said "Doctor I need the pan thing for a wee!" Yes I know and here it is please being quick as I am not sure how long we have?" As I was bursting for a wee most mornings it did not take me long to ease my bladder and then the Doctor took the full pan away and soon returned, then immediately applied the 3 way strap that came over my shoulders a joined two at waist level and all connected together. As the bed was specially clipped into the superstructure it became part of the structure and then the Doctor did the same for Istra before returning to his office cubical and applying his seat belt there, at that moment Master Niobi joined us and sat in the seat to the right of my bed and to the left of the curtained doorway into the medical wing. Master Niobi's seat was also secured to the superstructure and as I recall actually was back to back with another seat just outside the medical wing for the Guard to sit in with a structural wall between the Guard and Master Niobi. I think the only place no-one was allowed to be in landings and take offs was the toilet. However I was pleased that we was getting under way, Istra had a bad feeling about coming here and I am pleased we are leaving, as if there was a hell I believe those poor buggers are in it and I would much rather be in Master Mussons slavery than the German one what ever they call that and hope I never have to return here. Then the auto steps mainly at the front as the ones covering the rear section were never lowered for security, could be heard returning to their space below the doors on the aircraft and then the engines starting with the first one on the port wing engaged and then the second one above and on the tail fin I think its called fired up and finally the third one of the starboard wing and the cabin lights flicked on and the standby lights went off until needed again. Then we had that gentle lerch forward s as the brakes were released and the aircraft went forwards and gently taxied to the end of the runway. As much as I should be used to this by now it still gave me butterflies in the stomach. Then when we came to a halt at the end of the runway and I guess the Captain was awaiting final clearance and soon afterwards the engines revved up and you could feel the strain against the brakes until I guess the correct speed of the engines was achieved so that we could comfortable take of without effort and then we moved forwards and soon gathered speed enough to feel that sensation as the aircraft left the ground. At that point Musson slave Istra said "Its alright Musson slave Aureus we are in the air you can relax and stop bending the bed bars!" she said with a giggle. "Yes slave Aureus you can relax now we are on the way "Master Niobi said supporting slave Istra's assurance as I am nervous about flying as its bad enough sitting down but laying down with ones legs apart can be frightening I thought, then it dawned on me that we do have our legs apart doing just about everything and it took me ages to feel comfortable doing that, now its instinct so as not to incur any punishments.

As soon as we was in level flight and the seat belt and harness's could be let loose the Domestic girl arrived for bucket bath and hair brushing and that was always refreshing as they also changed the bed sheets and that was followed by another set of Domestic girls with the breakfast of porridge and a metal cup of milk. I am not sure why after all this time I was thinking about these things, but its clear we was not allowed to have anything that could be used as a weapon like a china cup or a knife and fort it was always a spoon and metal cups that bounce and do not break. The Domestic girls brush our hair, color our roots when required to maintain a blonde appearance and then shave our pubic area of hair that we are not allowed to have, even the Domestic girls are not allowed that as well so it has to be a slave thing, not just us. I did discover that when transferring from aircraft to busses or coaches the Domestics were issued with flip flops for their feet so they can walk over to the alternative vehicle on their own, but then they do not have these chains that we six Musson slaves have wrist to wrist and ankle to ankle. Strangely I have grown accustomed to having the chains as a comfort or security possibly, because each link is the size of my forefinger they are quite thick and therefore heavy as well, so not so easy to hobble around in or I have become institutionalized though the Doctor assured me that it takes longer for that to happen than a couple of months. So again I find myself dozing in daytime on Masters Flying Harem Dungeon.

I awoke suddenly to the sound of the air steward touring the aircraft requesting that travelers secure their seat belts and restraints and then my humor got to me again as I was thinking maybe if he shouted "Bondage time everyone" Then the silence was broken with the aircraft Captain speaking "Gentlemen and Ladies we are approaching United Kingdom airspace please be seated and seat belts secure and extinguish all naked flames Thank You!"

Soon we was circling and waiting for our commands to land at UK Stanstead. Uk's longest runway airport, then I could feel the aircraft gradually losing height and I am thinking here wee go again as Istra comments "Slave Aureus good at taking Masters bullwhip and scared of a little bit of aircraft landing, bless her!" Then comes that gentle bump you know the aircraft has at least some wheels on the ground, now it's a question of stopping and we do and we taxi over to a building that is where the aircraft gets a scheduled service, so it will be on holidays' as we will be supposedly, if you believe that then you believe anything as I know Master and his idea of holidays, must be for the Master to have a holiday from all that arm swinging keeping us poor slaves in order, having my humorous moments again.

Its not long before 3 black coaches appear at the rear of the aircraft as the auto steps are going down and the men-folk are opening fuselage doors although I know from previous times we go by way of the rear ramp in the arms of our carriers. Those able to walk go down the stairs to awaiting coaches along the port side even though from our position we can see most of the aerodrome I wonder if anyone can see all these naked slaves going down the stairs. Then Master Niobi arrives and helps me out of my bed and then we have the ceremony where he lowers his head so I can place my wrist to wrist chain over his head so he can pick me up and we are balanced that way as we have chains behind him as well as in front on our ankles and off we go with Master Ahmed and Istra following being carried by Master Niobi. As we go passed the limos that are also being moved out as the aircraft has to be free encumbrances during a service, so the chauffeurs will drive the cars to the venue in case Master needs to use them, but we are all in the coaches that have blacked out windows, I am not sure for whom, whether for us to see where wee are going or if the general population can clock us naked ladies on holidays, kind of tickled my sense of humor again.

We was at the door of the coach and Master Niobi lowered me to the cold floor and I had to hobble my way onto the coach step and then gradually haul myself up the steps into the coach and was guided by one of the Guards to a seat about 6 back as all the Masters will be taking up front seats as security, even Master Musson had the front seat behind the driver. Most people would have thought the Master; the head of our operational unit would have gone by the limousine, but no Master like to be with his slaves us lot.

Soon the coach was full and the door at the front closed and we waited for the other 3 coaches to be ready so we could all go in convoy, but that was not long and we was off leaving Stanstead aerodrome by a gate which had security guys in their uniform again saluting either the coaches or Master I know it was not for me and soon we was going along a main road for a bit then what looked like narrow country lanes but as I could not see so well without my glasses or my contacts I could not be sure and it really did not matter as I was not planning to hobble away. Then we turned into a wide entrance way and what looked like a gatehouse with electronic gates attached that automatically opened when the coach got close. Then we travelled up a long one vehicle lane to the car park that we had all been to before even though it now looked different and there was a lot of cars in the car park, but an area marked as reserved private seemed to be where the coach driver pulled into and the other two coaches pulled in on our right side. Then Master stood up and said "We are here Gentlemen and slaves, we have our own wing and so not interfere with the other residents although they will get to see us in action, but we have security in place and we shall watch for any interference, enjoy everyone!"

Then the door opened and the Masters all stepped out and the Guards ushered the 6 Musson slaves to leave the seats in order and I was last as I am Musson slave six and as I exited the coach Master Niobi was there waiting for me and he wasted no time in getting me into his arms as it was a bit chilly and I could see he was concerned for me getting cold, but we soon entered what look like a main entrance and there was a queue of people checking in that seemed to be dazed to see 6 naked slave girls being carried in and bypassing the main check in desk and behind us followed the 30 odd Domestic girls also all naked but with their stainless steel cuffs on walking under their own steam following Master Niobi and me in pairs and behind them was all their Male Guard partners bring up the rear. There seemed to be some Men I had never seen before that must be the staff that held a wall between us and the general residents queuing to the check in desk and for reason I can not explain the hairs on the back of my neck seem to stand on end as if it was a special moment or something. Soon Istra and myself were in a room to ourselves much like a cell back at base with mattresses on the floor, no bed like as it was before when wee was here but then I think wee was in a different part of the building. Besides I was now used to sleeping on a mattress on the floor, less chance to fall out of bed, however someone had planned this as the mattress was a double so Istra and I could cuddle up at night, like we always done for humane comfort and I did not need a reason or a pain to be the urge of need for sleep escape.

Sadly morning arrived far to quickly as the daylight glinted around the venetian blinds and curtains that covered our large windows, mainly because this was a house and base was really a ware house mainly where Master also stored his munitions and ordinance, but then I think he considered us as explosive as well and that is why we needed to be tamed and controlled to his way of liking. Then with a crash and bang the Domestics girls arrived and the leader said "Sorry we are not used to doors" and Istra replied "Yes I had not thought about it we have doors!" then I said "yes but some have wedges!" picking one up that was supposed to wedge our door open. Then the leader went on to tell more "we have to share the kitchens with the guests, the paying guests!" Then Istra enquires "what paying guests?" then the leader responds with "its been set up like we have back at base, The Male Dominants are running the show on a similar line but as its BDSM and consensual they can stop at any time, where as we as Domestics for Master Musson operation wee get paid to do it, but the slaves here have to pay to bee here if you see what I mean!" then Istra adds "Do they know of Masters operation and our setup?" and thee leader replies with "well if they do not when they see one of you six they are going get a nasty shock as they think that's what they might get for punishments.!" So I then add, "I think I know what she means is if they see our bodies or our action they, may thinks that this is the punishment end of the establishment where in point of fact its our daily life!" "Yes that about sums it up the leader added as she removed Istra's tabard.

Then one of the other girls came to me and removed mine ready for our bucket bath, even though we noticed this place had showers in most of the rooms, but we have to stick with our protocol. Then the leader says as she often does "come on get a wiggle on the Master has plans for all of you!" "Yes probably a demonstration not to fall into the hands of a slave driver!" I said and Istra promptly added "Musson slave Aureus you have not lost your sense of humor, but do not repeat that in front of Master he may not see the funny side as we do!" "Yes Istra, I know, helps me not get depressed and why that should be I do not know." Istra then adds "You have been put through a lot, a great deal that was not your fault or doing, or that from any of us, just that there are lot of nasty people in this life that see us as common rubbish, Now you know Master will defend that on our behalf." "Yes and maybe if we get the day going maybe it will take my mind of distractions." Then Masters Niobi and Ahmed appeared through the now wedged open doorway and asked "Are they both ready yet Domestic Leader?" And she replied "Just finishing braiding slave Aureus hair and they will then both be ready Sir!" Then they both got into those attuned positions so we could both slip our chains over their heads and picked us up in the usual way, this time I had Master Niobi as my carrier and is my designated body guard too. The only down side with Master Niobi now is when he takes us to bed, its bandy legged time for some hours after as typical Arabic gentlemen they do not hold back you know you've been fucked to put it bluntly. Anyway must concentrate otherwise I shall incur more punishments as we arrive at what id known as the breakfast hall with enough floor space to sit a good hundred slaves if needs be, so this place must be bigger than I first thought and here we six are sat in a circle as we often do back at base when all together and straight away there was a lot of stares from the holiday makers all naked female slaves and presumably the Guards were their partners, though the Guards intermixed overall, not just Guarding their partner so must be in the rules I am thinking they may have to put up with non partner interrelationships or something on those lines.

All those BDSM female slaves ranging young to older are all wearing stainless steel anklets and wrist cuffs, just as we do. But no chains in between so I can understand a certain shock when they saw us being carried in. and they all seem to be in circles of six as well. Then our usual porridge and metal cup of milk arrives. Now its just dawned on me that wee are in Musson slave position one where the others are in whatever sitting position they can get into, the younger ones are obviously remember school days where one sat cross legged.

Then Istra asked "Aureus have you never seen these BDSM types in England?" "You're joking No! I was scared stiff at school to be late and get sent to the head for a slap on the back of the legs, I stayed out of trouble and managed to get through without such experiences!" Istra then said now look at you, you're a Musson slave and can handle a bullwhipping almost as well as the rest of us!" "Yes I am still learning my way into this pain management!" But I can not understand, no that is wrong I could not understand people enjoying it, but as we get turned on by it I suppose they must as well, though it can still get too much for me and then I drop down into one of the other personalities that somehow seems to handle it and you know like us all we are terrified to even think or suggest the S.T.O.P. word to a Master and the consequences there after!" "Sssh! Do not go there Aureus in case you is over heard!" Istra said most emphatically!

Soon our carriers all came in for us and we were ordered to stand and would do so altogether like in Military unison. Then it was off to see what kind or torturous gadgets they had dreamed up for us, but unlike back at base they were lots of rooms all different sizes with doors. Then we came to a room that had a Guard on the door and he opened it and inside was a huge wheel with all sorts of straps attached and I could see Istra was a bit nervous at the wheel behind as well so they were on opposing walls, so it was clear we was each going to be placed on one of the wheels, butt I suspect Istra had done this before and there is something she does not like about it, not sure I am exactly thrilled to bits either. Then The two Master put us both down in front of each wheel that looked as those secured to the wall and must have been 8 or 9 feet in diameter and I could see a guy wire hanging down and soon realized that we had to be winched up into the centre of each wheel and spread eagled fashion as far as our one metre chains would allow and we was secured facing outward although there was a head hole so that one could be facing inwards exposing all ones back. But today it looked like we was supposedly going to watch each other do something although I could not now see Istra as she was too far away and without my visual aids I am blind beyond about 4 feet max. I was learning fast as I knew why there was a huge gap between the huge wheels on the walls and its because someone wants to use bullwhips either between both slave Istra and myself or individually but both at the same time and there was numerous connotations that could be worked in this way then for the first time ever they put what looked like plastic eye protective shielding goggles of a clear plastic. That's new I thought, but when the wheels started to rotate it figured it must be in case someone missed their targeting as a bullwhip can pluck and eye clean out of its socket if caught in the wrong way, Master told us about this a long time back when he explained that our body targets were from base of neck to toes and that is all very well when standing vertical like. Then in true statement ship Master Musson appeared with his favorite 10 foot bullwhip and as always he would air crack it, but now not once but twice in two different angles which could only mean one thing he was going for both of us and they could land just about anywhere. I had not at first realized there was an upper balcony all round the room about two feet above the top of the wheel and that was the floor level then 5theree was a solid fence type wall about 4 foot high I guess and thee holiday makers could watch. It reminded me of those motorcycles that raced around a tubular wall and people could watch from the top another sort of balcony mainly fun fairs, the wall of death was most popular name, well this was just like that but in a square and I could just see imagines of faces when I was looking up from an inverted position and that was helped because they had lights above the heads of these people, had they been in the dark I would never have known as the woodwork in this room seemed to go from floor to ceiling and you very easily miss it if there was no faces looking down. But then my concentration was distracted when there was this stinging of pain sort of diagonally across my right breast I think but I was disoriented as inverted at the time, even though the wheel was spinning at a speed I could not calculate and as is typical with Master he tends to speed up and so the impacts come fast and furious and I was at my peak as I realized I had snot in my nose and wet eyes but it was all flying in different directions and I started to lose control of my breathing, and I had blood splattered on the plastic goggles from somewhere but it was a fair bet that Master had covered our fronts in welts cuts and grazes as per normal and you could tell he loved every minute of it because he was not thinking of business. Then the Doctor and the two paramedics appeared and we was eventually released to two waiting stretchers and a Doctor anxious to plaster his yellow smelly iodine on our fronts which would sting like there no tomorrow.

Then I heard one of the Masters say "Master Musson Sir what about their backs?" and he replied "another day I have something else planned for these two and their lovely backs!" and then Added "Doctor See they are cleaned up for this evening please!"

Then Master left thee room and so did Master Ahmed, but Master Niobi stay to watch over me I guess. The two paramedics laid us both on separate stretchers and I could see Istra was well cut up in front and so I knew I would be as well as master does keep an equilibrium between two slaves. I could no longer see the faces above but now I was looking straight up rather than at an angle. Soon the paramedics a plus one Guard that was by the door lifted Istra's stretcher and went off to I assume the medical wing here as one paramedic and Master Niobi at my head end lifted my stretcher and we was off on the same trip.

Then sure enough we arrived at an area with a room marked with a red cross on a white background all across its two swinging doors and we was then transferred to hospital beds to rest. I need a box full of tissues to clear my nose though much of it was all on my breasts and stomach and the Doctor wanted to wash it all off and the re paint the smelly yellow iodine back on. Then it dawned on me that there was no music throughout the whole establishment just in the areas that we alone would venture into, so the breakfast room only had a low hum of whispering holidaying slaves whom maybe allowed to talk in the open, we had to just not get caught doing it though was ok in the presence of some Masters like Master Robert and now Master Ahmed and now Master Niobi whom has calmed down towards me now. And soon I dropped off into sleep escape which is good for healing these wounds for the next time.

The sounds of people rushing about awake me with a stir and a bit of a cold sweat of fear, probably other bad times past rearing their heads, then the Doctor said "Ahh good your awake Musson slave Aureus, it would seem that the master has you lined up for a commencement demonstration as a way to kick this fun palace off with his showmanship skills, well enough of that shit the Domestics will be here soon to give you the usual bucket bath and hair brushing to make you look pretty!" "Doctor I do believe you are upset with me, now what have I done?" I said, then the Doctor continued with "No my dear its not you, not your fault, it's my stupid thinking that we came here for some rest and recuperation, so you could heal the deeper wounds and get some proper rest. I am just an old fool that believed the Master seriously heeded my expertness, I thought he and I was beginning to get understanding!"

"No Doctor, this place is one of Master Lefthanders ideas to change the Masters Direction just a little!" Istra said, "Yes Doctor!" I added and continued "if you remember when Master Lathander helped us to become turned on to the pain and thus become that, that word Istra I've forgotten?" "Masochistically inclined I think you are trying to grasp Musson slave Aureus!" "Yes Istra that word and that ideology surely must be better than having no set path to travel, ending up nowhere?"

Then the Doctor said "Thank you! You are both good kids and I know you mean well and you have no choice in the matter, but I think your hearts are in the right place, Master Lathander is here now as are most of the key Masters of the consortium that are backing this project, The Master is a rare commodity as he does not really want to destroy your bodies like some of the other slaveries, like those that run prostitution just for the gaining of money wealth, or the drug lords that destroy their slaves by making them into human mules and there are some much worse!" Just then as the Domestic girls arrive with their bucket and brush brigade. Master Lathander stepped in and said "hello my favorite slave girls! I have come with some of the other Masters to help push the boat out on this new adventure that the consortium would like to see be given every chance to become a success, that's thee business talk done with. We do know Doctor how you feel and I fully understand your resentment being a Doctor and your prime understandings to do no harm, but this is still a business and you are getting well paid to be here. It's too late to just release the girls because they have become indoctrinated similarly to institutionalize and would only fall into the hands of the one that will not let dogs lie and give us some peace. Now Doctor I assure you the Master seriously knows he fucked up over the misreading of the situation that I am referring to and you had to take steps to save the mental stability of the Masters youngest pain slave and we all hope that it never happens again, but as humans we are bound to make mistakes. The consortium believe that Master Musson has the best pain slavery operations going in the world and the Colonel is not the only one that would like to get their hands on our stable and its contents so come on Guys and gals have some pride in your work!" By the time Master Lathander had finished his speech that we have heard many times before; the Domestic girls were just brushing and braiding Istra and my long blonde hair. "Are we getting evening grub today does anyone know?" "Yes it's coming up shortly and then time for digestion so that you are on top form for the demonstration!" "Who will be our audience I am wondering?" I said looking at Istra whom is sometimes the font of some of these wisdoms. The Domestic leader said "Now that I do know will be a group from the consortium and some of the guests staying here at this time, some of the security people that work with us on The Masters business end and I believe some special guests but don't know about them!" she said smiling and the turned to the other Domestics and "come on you lot lets get a wiggle on we have a lot more to do before bedtime!"

Then Istra and I laid back on this medical wing's version of a medical wing, though not as good as the one we have back at base and I was sure the one on the aircraft was even better than this set up, but then maybe they will have less need for a medical wing here.

Then the Domestic girls with the delightful lamb stew, potatoes and vegetables and the usual metal cup of milk, something I have grown to love since fate brought me and or us to this family environment.

Again I suddenly awoke with a cold sweat and a bad dream, not realizing that I had dropped of to sleep, but no sleep escapes more like horror movie pictures at the cinema. Istra said loudly "Are you alright Aureus?" and I replied "No Istra I keep having a same bad dream, never had them so clear before and I am scared to say the least, I think I would feel safer back at base!"! "Yes I have sensed something since we got here and I agree, I think we would be better off back at base!" Istra said forthrightly. Then I said "I am literally scared to go to sleep now, so I must have tried to stay awake then dropped off, I am sorry Istra, and I know I have become unbearable it's as if some force is trying to drive me to the loony bin I think." "Loony bin?" "Yes I can understand that with all that is been going on I am worried that we might all end up in such a place before our end!" Istra said in a worried expression that I recognized from the times when she really did worry for someone other than herself. Then I thought no that is wrong none of us worry about ourselves, it's against the orders and the rules to think of ourselves above any others... Then Master Niobi appeared and said "are you two alright?" Istra sat bolt upright and said "No

Master Niobi Sir! Musson slave Aureus is scared out of her mind, waking abruptly with cold sweats and talking in her sleep of what sounds more horrific than I can desire to want to talk about let alone think about it, can we not go home!" Then Master Niobi said "Yes we know! This place is wired for sound too and we are fully aware that slave Aureus is having some mental incursions which must be from past bad times. The Doctor could give her a sleeping draft but in a deeper sleep it might be worse, in a light sleep to wake up at least stops it for a time until we can get to the bottom of it, so I have come to baby sit two slaves!" He said smiling and continued Master thought these dreams were emanating from being at base and thought this trip would be a change of scenery and maybe it would ease, but it would seem to be the reverse. Master Niobi Sir when is this special demonstration due to begin as I think I would rather get it over and done with?" "Yes Master Niobi Sir I feel that to!" Istra said in an emphatic and direct way of expressing herself. "Well you have my vote too but we have to wait for all the guests to arrive, this is not the easiest place for people to get to, but then that is part of the idea as we do not want the locals popping in to borrow a cup of sugar, personally I think it needs more security guys on the perimeters, but they want to keep a low profile as well." "Istra you have known me longer and that I like a lot of security with a rigid structure plus dogs, though it might appear old fashion it's always worked well at base!" Yes Master

Niobi Sir you are so right, wishes we was back there now!" Istra added.

Then Master Robert appeared, "My we are a glum pair of slaves on an inauguration night that might prove to be a good investment for the future of the purposed plans to have more of these places of fun for those that seek another way to live or to just live it for a few days and then return to whatever life they started with!" "The Master sent me up to carry either one that you are not carrying Master Niobi Sir?" Then Master Robert Sir if you would be so kind as to carry Musson slave Istra as I am also Musson slave Aureus bodyguard and I prefer to carry her!"

With all the protocol done on who takes who, we set off on an unknown trip as we do not know this venue so well so its all new to Istra and myself as we glide down a large staircase the leads to the main foyer and then travel through many corridors until we approach some double doors with two Guard Guys outside who both together open the doors so we can glide in and through. Then Masters Lathander and Philips, Ahmed a couple of new faces that may well be from the consortium join in behind Musson slave Istra and Master Roberts and I am wondering why am I in the lead surely Istra should be in front of me, though it's a bit late now as a huge audience begin to clap which reaches such a crescendo anyone would think we was pop stars and not slaves of Master Musson.

I whispered into Master Musson left ear and ask "Master Niobi Sir why are they clapping?" "Master

Niobi whispers back I believe because you are slaves of Master Musson whom is the main creator and director to this operation, they must feel that you are worth a round of applause, I would join in if my hands were free, but I do not wish to drop one of Master Musson pain slaves, just enjoy or we will both be in the dog house!"

We eventually arrive upon a stage much like the one they had on that American airbase, somewhere beyond Boston I believe, though this auditorium is the biggest I have seen yet and as master Niobi mounts the steps up I see a trapeze bar with a centre coupling to a dangling guy wire so we know straight off it's a whipping again, Istra is being taken over to my left where the same setup is waiting for her and its not long before we are both having our wrist first link either side being connected to each end of the trapeze bar so the rest of the chain is dangling down, but as that could be dangerous that is clipped to the middle position. Naturally we automatically had spread our legs, but at this time there was no plan to secure them, then the trapeze bar was raised a little bit so we had outstretched arms, but standing on our feet. And then Master Niobi turned my body to face the audience and I assume Master Roberts was doing the same over there now they was now to my right and the audience was now in front of me, but I could not see them and even less as the auditorium lights went down and the spot lights on us and Master Musson in between us on what I would have called a hotspot. In Disco terms some DJs would have a hotspot that has a an illuminated floor that individual dancers could come a dance on the hotspot sometimes just for fun, sometimes for a free drink at the bar or as a competition for the best hotspot dancers. Obviously the hotspot would have disco lighting and lights would change with the music as did most well set up discos and bands.

Master introduced both Musson slave Istra his first Ms1 and the leader of the group and of course his youngest Musson slave Aureus Ms6, and as we was equally matched in our abilities and our understandings of one another we are paired together, so we train together, get punished together and do demonstrations together and lastly share a cell together.

So it begins though Master is now explaining that we are an enforced Muslim slavery operation that bears no parallels with BDSM operations and they should not be misunderstood that BDSM should always be Safe sane and Consensual. And that he tells them that because he could afford to run a non consensual slavery operation for just 6 Musson slaves and he pays a set of 40 couples to come and the females do the domestics of the cooking and cleaning for the whole operation and as a bonus they get use all our equipment in order to maintain a discipline between their Master /Guard partners and the sub /slave Domestic workers. However they have no options on administering any punishments to my 6 slaves other than maybe as carriers as you have seen tonight. Misunderstandings and so Besides we do not want our paid Domestic couples going to war over misunderstandings so our rules and laws are very precise and if anyone breaks them we have the right to punish those involved. Thank you Ladies and Gentlemen.

Then Master Musson slipped into a curtained cubicle as did Master Lathander and then they both re-appeared bare chested but still wearing Arabic headdress what I used to call a tea cozy. Then Master Musson approached me and air cracked his bullwhip as Master Lathander approached Istra and also then air cracked his whip. Then it begun and the strikes went down my back on each side of the spinal column and across my bottom and Master would do a "Hello" between the legs so the end of the whip would curl upwards and hit my shaved pubic area which was always a tender spot. Then he would progress down the backs of my legs and up the front and the another "hello" strike from the front so my labia lips would feel the belly of the whip and the end of the whip would strike either bottom cheek or if a short strike just remain in the crease. Then up my belly more often up one side and down the other on my front and master was particularly good to catch nipples to make one jump a little. And then they would change targets as I would get Master Lathander and Istra got Master Musson and they would begin again and repeat the sequences that master Musson liked to use. Then when both had completed their tasks we were allowed a water break so we could have a drink of water while the Masters got Masters favorite Lemonade.

Afterwards they may again do it all again or allow

other singletail approved Masters to have a go, so we would have to wait to see who or what came next.

Then it begun again with Master Niobi on I and Master Ahmed of Istra both also bare chested as this was a standard they liked to keep and both wearing Arabic headdress. Then they both followed the same sequences and then changed over so I got to feel the whip of Master Ahmed and Istra got to feel the whip of Master Niobi, then again we had a drink of water while they had lemonade

Both Istra and I could usually handle up to about 6 Masters attacking in this way before we would start to weep, but much also depended on how much pressure each Master applied by adding into his thrusting technique.

Then came Master Roberts the trainer and Master Phillips who had also came before us bare chested and in Arabic headdress even though they were not Arabic, in this case the headdress was pure white with no writing or markings on them and so it begun again and after they each completed their sequences' they changed over and I had Master Roberts whom for some strange reason always had his spell interrupted and so often did not get to finish, but not this time, he did complete it. Now I was noticeably tired and could see that Istra's body was glistening with sweat and blood mixed in so mine would be the same and again we drank water while the Masters drank lemonade. I was thinking that should be the end of it when there is a loud bang outside somewhere and the windows all cracked, so broke and there seemed to be a rush of air as the security guys went out to check and then I felt a sharp blade at my throat and I just managed to see a glint of a flash of a blade looking item at Istra's throat also and I thought this is my bad dreams thing, The auditorium soon fell silent when another stranger stood in front of them and told them not to panic as the building was wired with explosives.

Then when Master Musson approached as did Master Niobi and I could see he was mad with himself for leaving me to see that others were safe. As then Master Musson and Master Niobi got closer I could hear some of the discussion. It seems one of the trio was Master Matt the young Saudi Prince that his Father begged Master Musson to train his one son into the ways of modern slavery of females, but young Matt wanted to be the playboy spend money, do no work, laze about all day long and spend the nights in the casinos. Then he accepted a bribe from the Colonel to sneak some Men aboard Master DC 10 aircraft with a view to hijack it and take us back to the Colonel for a measly $50, 000 US dollars. But like so many other badly laid plans it all went wrong and Master let the Irish Military Police deal with him. His father was not happy and cut off his allowances and told him to go get a job.

Now he wants his revenge and has got some mates to assist, one I know to be a Nasty piece of work and used to be on the Colonels Military staff and he was at my throat with his sharp knife. Somewhere in the audience are supposed to be some of the UK's security guys and the police were on hand as well but this did not deter these guys. Then Matt says to Master Musson "The Colonel sends greetings and suggests that if he cannot have the prize he seeks then no Man shall have her and then he spoke in Arabic and the guy behind me stepped back and picked up one of Masters prize bullwhips and laid into us, I could see Master trying to press forwards but was held back as another Man had a gun to his head. And all Arabs are pretty good with singletails and it was not long before we was crying in silence and the snot was all down our front then the last thing I saw was Master Niobi make some move to the sound of a loud bang. That must have been a gun going off as I was lost into unconsciousness, or it was me someone shot.

I awoke once again to the sounds of something being dropped and it was hard for me to open my eyes as if they was glued shut, but then I heard the Doctors voice "Aureus listen to me, you are quite safe we all are. We are all back home at base!" Then I realized I could not move at all and became frightened as I herd the Doctor say "get the Master in here quick. Time seemed to be slow and I was not sure if I was conscious or unconscious. Then I heard the Masters voice even though I could not see him I knew the sound of his broken English voice and he said "Musson slave Aureus listen to me! The Doctor has had you in a drug induced coma for two weeks and he administered a spinal block so you will not feel much for a while. Master Niobi tried your old trick and dropped to the floor and someone shot Matt, that enraged the one that was whipping you at the time and he would not stop and in the end Master Niobi attacked him and the police then moved it, so we are all fine except you, your body was very badly swollen and cut to ribbons that seemed to anger Master Niobi and he flew at that guy Shaster. We are sure you will mend, just needs time and you need to sleep my good slave, and Master Niobi will be here in a few moments as he has been on Guard next to your bed and just went to take a shower. Here he is now; I will come back later as I have business to attend to!"

"Hello Musson slave Aureus, Doctor she's crying!" I know she is in trauma, her mind now has a lot to deal with, she should be in a hospital but she will only be safe here with us, obviously the Colonel is untouchable because he was remote and until someone names him in the affair he remains free and thus will be her greatest danger. As you know Master has tripled the outside Guards and added Dogs. Now we shall all have to spend some serious time with her so she knows in her heart or hearts we are her family. So I take it you will be here for today Master Niobi Sir?" "Yes Doctor I should never have left her!" "They did kill some of the Guards to get into the building so you might have been killed too, Master Niobi Sir you cannot think that way. When they got to the girls no more were injured or killed except Musson slave Aureus and she was like a buffer, became a distraction and it was clear to most people they never would have got one of both out to their car. You should know as an army man that collateral damage happens in love and WAR, be thankful you are alive, she is alive and she will mend. If there is any real serious damage its her mind as she will now never stray from the mental status of Musson slave Aureus, a slave for life and possible forever, if she had not been broken she would not have survived, its only because of her training here and her state of mind which she spoke those words a month or so back she knew she was Master's slave then. You mark my words she will in our lifestyle fare much better than any civilian, now I have things I must attend to see you later Master Niobi Sir."

Then Master Robert entered the room and I could hear all these conversations but not engage in responsive dialogue to the conversations either because of the drugs or mental blocks, but I could hear

"How is our favorite pupil today Master Niobi Sir?" "She was crying earlier on, the Doctor says that her mind has a lot to come to terms with because of the trauma and he claims she could never go back to civilian life because now the imprint of being Musson slave Aureus has gone too deep!"

"Yes he is correct, slave Aureus had already turned a corner into that mode of thinking when she spoke those words about seeing the Male species being above her species, though she can only claim for herself, but the others here understand that." Master Robert said

"However the important thing is she will never ever be able to see the Colonel in her life because his Men destroyed her ability to choose. He might even back off, though I would not bank on that." Master Niobi said

"Let me know when you want a breather as I will sit with her a while!"

"We will all have to take turns sitting with her for close protection while she remains in enforced sleep coma!"

"As we will all have to, as she will need more protection than ever?" Master Niobi said.

Then Master Robert left the room.

The following is a statement by the second in command of the operation on how the captivity environment came to an end. Normally this would have been in the last book, however the writer Miss Marie Clair Orman has been diagnosed with Lung Cancer and she can not be sure as to how many of the 6 books it would take to cover the whole 18 months of captivity, so this statement will be in every book from now on. So readers are not left in the dark wondering.

ENDGAME STATEMENT

Master Lathander phoned today to say he is terminally ill and as slave Aureus have one book in publication and a second in hand. He wanted for slave Aureus to know how it ends in the event that Lathander can not tell slave Aureus when slave Aureus gets closer to the end or cannot write more books.

It seems one of the Domestics was seeing the Colonel for money, she leaked much about what was going on and in the end the Colonel lost the plot in his greediness to grab slaves Istra and Aureus. Master Mussons most prized possessions. As they could handle tremendous amounts of pain from a bullwhipping plus get turned on by it, plus would heal very fast, so he could do it again.

The Colonel sent in his military to level the Tripoli compound so he could walk in and take both slaves Aureus and Istra's, but it went wrong because the leak had friends within and she warned the compound security and they sounded the alarm. Most of the personnel were out in quick time bar slave Aureus whom was injured in a premature explosion. Master Musson had to send his security men back to search for slave Aureus and they did, she was taken to the DC10 aircraft, which was headed for Master Mussons secondary compound in the USA. On the flight over the Atlantic slave Aureus health got worse the Doctor made claim if we wait for US Soil slave Aureus could be dead on arrival so they dropped back to Stanstead London UK. They dropped slave Aureus off naked chains and all, as an ill individual with a plan in mind to recover her later. Then the aircraft took off for their new home in the USA.

However there was also a verbal agreement with a UK politician that slave Aureus would be transported to a private hospital and treated there where slave Aureus could remain naked and in her chains. When fit to travel the DC10 would return to Stanstead UK aerodrome as the known as UK's security airfield to be collected and returned to the USA, But that never took place.

Had slave Aureus not been injured her new home would have been the USA, several attempts to recover slave Aureus failed because no one explained their intentions, all was assumed wrongly it was the Colonel behind it

Because slave Aureus was an embarrassment if it leaked out so she was headed for Broad-moor, but a clerical person got the orders mixed and sent slave Aureus to next of kin P. J. C. of M. Electronics of Selsey

Sussex, the Guy it all began with had an original plan with the Colonel to have the girl he made his life with taught to be more submissive that he could control better. However then Peter was offered £100,000 for Marie to stay and the Peter Gentleman accepted because he loved money more than relationships this would have been through the Colonels friend Master Musson and his operations.

Now the deal was to get slave Aureus to Gatwick where the Colonels private jet would come, for now £250,000 however whatever personality was at this time in command of slave Aureus mind or brain was so frightened she found one of Mr. P.J. C. guns, and then got a taxi to Grayling well Mental Hospital, Chichester. Sussex. Where she knew a specific Dr B.V. and held him at gunpoint to explain events whilst overdosing on pills and vodka.

Police talked slave Aureus out of the room and they pounced and she was sectioned for 12 months.

There was some talk of still going to broad-moor but the ward stopped their night meds for slave Aureus to take in a last ditch to carry out standing order 4

Slave Aureus failed that but did not go to Broad moor, then Maggie Thatcher closed all such hospitals to save money and that is when standing order 1 kicked in and slave Aureus then sought to complete standing orders and the Master she wanted to serve.

Endgame statement by Euan Lathander

Printed and bound by CPI Group (UK) Ltd, Croydon, CR0 4YY

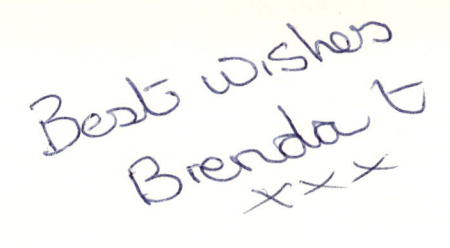

I Peeked in Heavens Gate

by
Brenda Thurlbeck

authorHOUSE®

AuthorHouse™ UK Ltd.
500 Avebury Boulevard
Central Milton Keynes, MK9 2BE
www.authorhouse.co.uk
Phone: 08001974150

© 2007 Brenda Thurlbeck. All rights reserved.

No part of this book may be reproduced, stored in a retrieval system, or transmitted by any means without the written permission of the author.

First published by AuthorHouse 11/1/2007

ISBN: 978-1-4343-0559-6 (sc)

Printed in the United States of America
Bloomington, Indiana

This book is printed on acid-free paper.

TABLE OF CONTENTS

I PEEKED IN HEAVEN'S GATE	1
MY DREAMS	2
THE BUTTERFLY	3
LETTER TO HEAVEN	4
YOU HAVE IT ALL!	5
GOLDEN WEDDING ANNIVERSARY	6
FIND THE SUN	7
GODS GOOD GRACE	8
GUARDIAN ANGEL	9
DO YOU WONDER	10
WOULD YOU SWAP?	11
BE READY	12
AN ANGEL	13
MIRACLES DO HAPPEN	14
FOOTPRINTS IN THE SNOW	15
MY HEARTS PLEA	16
DREAMS	17
WALKING IN GARDEN'S	18
BE GRATEFUL	19
THE VOW	20
SOME FOLK	21
MEMORY	22
SWEET MEMORY	23
FIND THE SPARK	24
HEAVENS PLAIN	25
BLUEBELL WOOD	26
I DID MY BEST	27
I LOVE THE RAIN	28
IN MY MEMORY	29
PERFECT PEACE	30

THE DREAM	31
ONE MOTHER	32
GOD IS THERE	33
LOST YOUR SPARKLE	34
IN YOUR HEART	35
ALWAYS THERE	36
FORTY YEARS WED	37
IF DREAMS CAME TRUE	38
A SMILING FACE	39
LAUGHTER.	40
TOMORROW	41
FIND THE ANSWER	42
IF ONLY.	43
HEAVENS GATE	44
GOD'S PLANS	45
RESTING PLACE	46
THE DOOR BELOW	47
CONTENT	48
MY GRANDSON	49
WORDS OF COMFORT	50
MOTHER LOVE	51
GARDEN OF DREAMS	52
HAVE FAITH	53
IF DREAMS CAME TRUE	54
THE WORLD STOPPED	55
LIGHT ME A CANDLE	56
FIRST IN THE QUEUE	57
BONUS OF HAPPINESS	58
EVERYWHERE	59
THE BLINDFOLD	60
MY PRAYER	61
MOTHER I LOVE YOU	62

SWEET BLISS	63
THE BEST	64
MEANT TO BE?	65
ONLY A DREAM	66
NO ONE KNOWS	67
SHINE YOUR LIGHT	68
SITTING ON THE SEASHORE	69
A NEW DAY	70
BED OF ROSES	71
SOMETIMES	72
LIFE	73
DEEP IN MY HEART	74
LIFE IS ALL	75
IMAGINE	76
JUST THINK	77
THANK YOU LORD	78
IN DREAMS	79
LOVE	80
TIME	81
HOPE	82
MOTHERS ARE ANGELS	83
HARD TO UNDERSTAND	84
TELL HIM NOW	85
LAST NIGHTS DREAM	86
WINNING COMBINATION	87
TWILIGHT	88
DESTINY	89
YOUR OWN ANGEL	90
NEVER FORGET	91
HAVE PATIENCE	92
CHEER UP	93
SO LUCKY	94

GIVE IT AWAY	95
GOD IS ON YOUR SIDE	96
BEST WONDER OF ALL	97
SMELL THE FLOWERS	98
BE HAPPY	99
TREASURES FOR LIFE	100
IN MY HEART	101
SMELL THE ROSE	102
CLOUDS WILL LIFT	103
THE JOURNEY	104
A LIFE SO SPECIAL	105
YOU'RE NOT GONE	106
WISHES	107
MEET AGAIN	108
IMPOSSIBLE DREAM	109
NEVER PART	110
ANGELS GATHER	111
SILVER LININGS	112
SAY YES	113
LET HIM IN	114
MY BROTHER	115
LETTER TO GOD	116
LIFE'S SECRET	117
BAD DREAMS	118
MESSAGE FROM MY HEART	119
TRUE WORD	120
HAPPY BIRTHDAY	121
A MILLION STARS	122
JEALOUSY	123
HEAVENS GATE	124
THE GIFT	125
FIFTY GOLDEN YEARS	126

SIMPLY THE BEST	127
OUR TENTH ANNIVERSARY	128
RICH INDEED	129
A PRAYER FOR HEALTH	130
DREAMS WILL COME TRUE	131
IF ONLY	132
ANGEL IN BLUEBELLS	133
STAIRWAY TO HEAVEN	134
IF	135
YOU'RE CHARKA	136
KIM DEAREST PAL OF MINE	137
IT WILL TAKE FOREVER	138
GOLDEN MEMORIES	139
MY SON	140
I'VE BEEN THERE	141
GOD VISITED	142
ONE WAY	143
JOURNEYS END	144
THE SECRET	145
THE VISION	146
THANK YOU	147
SO PERFECT	148
TOMORROW	149
LIKE A JIGSAW	150
CONGRATULATIONS	151
HAND OF FRIENDSHIP	152
MISSING YOU	153
ENJOY XMAS	154
TODAY TOMORROW FOREVER	155
THANK YOU LORD	156
GO WITH A KISS	157
MY FAMILY BLESS	158

BUTTERFINGERS	159
MY MOTHER'S MAGIC MIXTURE	160
FOREVER	161
WHEREVER YOU ARE	162
THE LONG ROAD	163
THE SECRET	164
HER BEST FRIEND	165
RETIREMENT	166
GARDEN IN HEAVEN	167
LORD	168
A GARDEN IN SUMMER	169
LIFE'S FLOWERS	170
HEALING MY HEART	171
POPPIES	172
IS IT LOVE	173
SPECIAL ANGEL	174
JUST WHISPER	175
FOREVER AND A DAY	176
MY MOTHERS LOVE	177
DO IT ALL	178
FOND RECOLLECTIONS	179
THE GREETING	180
MY SISTER NANCY	181
LEFT THE DOOR AJAR	182
HIS PROMISE	183
OUR SOULS MEET	184
IN OUR MEMORY	185
MOTHERS DAY	186
FOR ETERNITY	187
IF'S AND ONLY'S	188
GOD IS THERE	189

I PEEKED IN HEAVEN'S GATE

Walking Alone One Morning,
Crying In The Rain.
How Could I Go On Living,
With My Heart In So Much Pain.
When I Turned The Corner,
I Heard A Laugh I Knew.
I Felt A Mist Surround Me,
It Was Then I First Saw You.
Standing In A Beautiful Garden,
With Bright Flowers All Around.
Angels Were All Singing,
It Was The Sweetest Sound.
I Saw My Mother And Father,
With Loved Ones Who Had Gone Before.
They Looked So Well And Happy,
I Could Not Have Asked For More.
I Wandered Off The Pathway
I Peeked In Through The Gate.
I Knew It Was Too Early,
That I Would Have To Wait.
Then It Started Fading,
The Scene Just Went From View.
My Heart Had Stopped Its Aching,
It Had Stopped Raining Too.
I Often Walk Along That Road,
But Cannot Find You Again.
God Let Me Peek In Heavens Garden,
To Take Away My Pain.

MY DREAMS

My Love Was In My Dreams Last Night,
We Laughed And Cried Together.
Reminisced For Hours And Hours,
About Love, Life, And The Weather.
My Heart Felt Light As A Bird In Flight,
To Have Him So Close So Near.
With His Hand Enclosed In Mine,
This Whole World Held No Fear.
We Kissed And Said Farewell,
Just As The Dawn Broke Through.
But In My Dreams When Night Falls,
I Am In Heaven With My Love So True.
We Meet On Gods Bridge Of Love,
Walk By A Sparkling Stream.
Wander In Fields Of Flowers,
Where We Just Sit And Dream.
One Day I Will Stay There Forever,
When The Key To Heavens Door, I Obtain.
Our Souls United For Eternity,
Never To Be Lonely Again.

THE BUTTERFLY

Sitting In My Garden,
On A Beautiful Summers Day.
The Birds Were Sweetly Singing,
Every Flower Was Bright And Gay.
A Thought Of You Just Trickled,
So Gently Though My Mind.
Often When I Think Of You,
I Always Seem To Find.
That You Come So Close To Me,
You Are Never Far Away.
I Sense You In Our Garden,
On A Warm And Sunny Day.
It Was Then I Saw A Butterfly,
It Landed On My Hand.
It Fluttered Until It Settled,
Upon My Wedding Band.
It Stayed There For A Moment
Opened Its Wings, Then Flew Away.
My Love Was In Our Garden,
On That Bright And Sunny Day.

LETTER TO HEAVEN

I Wish I Could Send A Letter,
To You In Heaven Above.
I Would Give You All My Prayers,
Send You All My Love.
Ask If You Were Happy,
If You Were, Free From Pain.
Tell You I Would Give The World,
To Have You Home Again.
Have You Met My Mother And Father?
Plus The Dear Friends We Once Knew?
Tell Them That I Miss Them,
My Love I Send Them Too.
I Wish I Could Mail This Letter,
But Heaven Has No Address.
So I Will See You In My Dreams Tonight,
Ending This Letter By Saying
God Bless

YOU HAVE IT ALL!

If God Would Grant You One Wish,
A Dream That Could Come True.
Would You Ask Him For Years Long Past,
To Turn Back Time For You?
If You Could Pick The Best Moments,
Maybe Choose When You Were Small.
Perhaps The Day You Were Wed,
Or The Most Special Years Of All.
When You Had Your Children,
How Quickly They Were Grown.
So Soon Were Adults,
Now From Your Nest Have Flown.
Now You Feel Redundant,
But Proud You Surely Must Be.
You Gave Your Best, You Did Succeed,
To Raise Your Dear Family.
You Have Good Health,
Plus The Love Of Your Life,
So Cheer Yourself Up And Stand Tall.
No Use In Wishing What You Can't Have,
Just Realise "You Have It All"

GOLDEN WEDDING ANNIVERSARY

I Awoke Up Feeling Restless,
One Bright And Sunny Morn.
The Birds Were All Singing,
Preparing For The Dawn.
It Was Far Too Early
To Get Up Out Of Bed.
Then I Remembered,
It Was Fifty Years
Since We Were Wed.
After Breakfast In The Garden,
I Could Not Help But Shed A Tear.
Wishing Like A Million Times Before,
That My Love Was Here.
I Felt Oh So Lonely,
Then I Heard Sweet Music In My Ear.
Glancing At The Rose Trees,
I Saw My Love Appear.
Standing With An Angel,
A Smile Was On His Face.
I Felt A Kiss Brush My Cheek,
The Touch Of His Embrace.
He Held Me In His Arms,
Just As He Fade From View.
Told Me That He Missed Me,
His Eyes Held Tear Drops Too.
He Had Not Forgotten,
On Our Special Day, He Proved To Me.
My Love Came All The Way From Heaven,
For Our Wedding Anniversary.

FIND THE SUN

Is Life All Stormy Weather?
Hard To Find The Sun?
Do You Seek Contentment?
Wish You Had More Fun?
Your Body Feels Soar And Weary,
Your Heart An Empty Shell.
You Search For Fulfilment,
Where It Is, You Cannot Tell.
I Found The Aid I Needed,
When My Life Was Getting Rough.
I Turned And Faced The Storm Clouds,
Said "God I Have Had Enough"
Asked The Dear Lord To Help Me,
To Please Show Me The Way.
I Knew He Had Heard Me,
I Grew Stronger Every Day.
I Know This Is Not Easy,
Do Not Let This Chance Pass By.
Give Your Life Some Sunshine,
You Can Do This If You Try.
God Is Waiting For You To Ask Him,
But He Knows You Have Free Will.
If You Ask And Really Mean It,
You're Dreams He Will Fulfil.
So Come On You Can Do It,
Face Your Problems Do Not Run,
With Gods Help And A Little Courage,
Life's Hard Battle Will Be Won.

GODS GOOD GRACE

Loved Ones Leave, Hearts Are Broken,
No Words Of Comfort Can Be Spoken.
Lights Have Dimmed From Eyes And Heart,
No Reason To Live, So Far Apart.
Their Pain Has Gone, Their Soul Is Free.
Remember What "Will Be Will Be."
Together With God And Others, They Love.
Safe In Their Arms In Heaven Above.
You Feel So Lonely, But You Will Find.
They Are Constantly There,
In Heart And In Mind.
Try To Smile And Dry Those Tears,
Be Thankful For The Happy Years.
Dark Days Will Come When You Feel Bereft,
But You Are Not Alone, They Have Not Left.
When Tears Of Sorrow Roll Down Your Face,
Know They Are At Peace In Gods Good Grace.

GUARDIAN ANGEL

God Has A Vast Army Of Angels,
Who Stay With Us From Birth?
They Guard Us, Protect Us,
On Our Journey Here On Earth.
They Will Not Tell Us What To Do,
Angels Know We Have Free Will.
They Try Their Best To Guide Us,
To Teach Us And Instil
Love And Kindness In Our Hearts,
Inspire In Us A Caring Mind…
Help Us Live A Life That's Full,
They Link With All Mankind.
If We Need Them We May Feel,
Warmth As They Draw Near.
Especially When In Danger,
Your Angel May Appear.
You Might Not Believe In Angels,
For Angels Do Not Always Wear Wings.
You'll Know Them By The Peace They Give,
The Love An Angel Brings.
If You Are All At Sea,
Your Angel Will Keep You Afloat.
Even If You Are Drowning,
Your Angel Is Your Lifeboat.
It Does Not Matter How Low You Sink,
If You Need Help, But Can't Break Through.
Ask God To Pull You Out Of The Mire,
He Will Send A Guardian Angel To You.

DO YOU WONDER

Do You Sometimes Wonder,
What Life Is All About?
Keep On Asking Questions,
But Cannot Work It Out.
You Often Try To Find It,
But Seems To Pass You By.
Sit Beside The Seashore,
Watch The Waves Roll By.
Maybe There You Will Find It,
Your Answer Is In Heaven Above,
This Precious Thing You Are Seeking,
You Will Find It In Gods Love.
You Can Tell The Folk Who Have Faith.
They Have Such A Peace Within.
Life At Times May Be A Struggle,
But They Just Never Give In.
What They Possess You Cannot Buy,
Pray To God And You Will See.
What He Gives Will Cost You Nothing.
Love And Happiness Are Free.

WOULD YOU SWAP?

You Often Sit And Dream,
Of Things That Might Have Been
Wonder What You Have Missed,
All You Should Have Done And Seen.
Maybe Been A Rich Man,
With A Bit Of Cash To Spare.
Or A Famous Poet,
Perhaps A Millionaire.
Are They Better Off Than You,
Can You Honestly Say?
You Would Change
The Life You Have, Even For A Day.
Swap Your Faithful Partner,
Who Shares Your Good And Bad.
Don't Forget Your Beautiful Children,
Without Her, You Might Never Have Had.
You've The Deep Love Of Your Family,
Loyal Friends You Can Depend Upon.
Gods Love Is In Your Heart,
Giving You Strength To Carry On.
A Hero To Friends And Family,
For Them All You Did Your Best.
Filled Their Lives With Love And Laughter,
Asked The Lord To Do The Rest.
So Stop This Wishful Dreaming,
Open Your Eyes Soon You Will See.
These Rich And Famous People,
Like You They Would Rather Be.

BE READY

Try To Be Ready,
For What Tomorrow May Bring.
It Could Be Winter In Your Heart,
Or Turn To Life's Bright Spring.
Have You Helped Your Neighbour Out,
Have You Tried Your Best,
If There's Faith In Your Soul,
God Will Help You With The Rest.
At Times, You Need a Helping Hand,
When Life Gets Hard To Bear.
Ask God For Faith And Courage,
He Will Send An Angel There.
The Lord Can Take You By The Hand,
Lead You Onto The Path That Is Light.
Hold Up A Flickering Candle,
When Things Look Black As The Night.
Life Is What You Make It,
With A Little Help From God Above.
Be Ready For Tomorrow,
Protect Yourself With His Love.

AN ANGEL

Once I Saw An Angel,
When I Awoke Up From A Dream.
I've Never Saw Beauty Like It,
The Loveliest Sight I Have Ever Seen.
With Wings The Colours Of Rainbows,
She Embraced Me With Her Smile.
Hair Flowed Like A Fountain,
Her Aura Stood Out A Mile.
Said She Was My Guardian Angel,
As She Melted Away From View.
Her Voice Was As Soft As Velvet,
With Eyes A Sparkling Blue.
As I Gazed I Saw Her Shimmer,
She Left In One Bright Beam.
I Am Sure I Saw An Angel,
Or Was It All A Dream.

MIRACLES DO HAPPEN

Do You Think Miracles Happen?
I Asked My Mother One Day.
Yes I Am Sure They Really Do,
I Heard My Dear Mother Say.
If You Ask The Lord
With All Your Heart,
Go On Your Knees And Pray.
I Am Certain God Will Help You,
But May Not Answer Right Away.
God Knows What Is Best For Us,
Sometimes Is Cruel To Be Kind.
I Only Know With Gods Help,
A Solution You Will Find.
Believe That Miracles Do Happen,
My Child Don't You See,
On The Day That You Were Born,
A Miracle Happened To Me.

FOOTPRINTS IN THE SNOW

I Watched Snowflakes Falling,
Icicles Glistened In The Snow.
I Start To Remember,
Years So Long Ago.
I Recall My Children Laughing,
Playing On A Sleigh.
Little Did I Know Then?
I Would Be All Alone One Day.
Quickly Time Has Gone By,
Years Did Simply Fly.
Days So Filled With Joy,
Now I Often Sit And Cry…
My Children Are Grown And Happy,
For That, I Am So Glad…
I Thank The Lord Every Day,
For The Good Life, I Have Had.
Though My Love Has Gone To Heaven,
He Is Still Here With Me I Know,
For When I Go Out Walking,
His Footprints Follow In The Snow.

MY HEARTS PLEA

My Poor Heart Is Pining,
It Is So Missing You.
So Crushed And Broken,
Feeling Sad And Blue.
It Has Been Like This,
Since You Went Away.
I Feel Its Constant Aching,
Every Single Day.
If You Ignore My Pleadings,
Turn Your Back
On My Hearts Pain.
I Know It Will Sulk Forever,
Never To Love Again.

DREAMS

Many People Have Dreams,
Who Think Will Never Come True.
Give Up Before Trying,
Simply Make Things Do.
Do Not Be Like These Folk,
At Least Give It A Try.
Fail, And What Have You Lost,
Do Not Let This Chance Pass By.
Never Give In, Keep Plodding On,
Get Up Each Time You Fall.
Hold Your Head Up, Soldier On,
One Day You Will Stand Tall.
Never Doubt That You Will Win,
Believe You Will Succeed.
With Gods Help, And A Little Courage,
Your Whole Life Will Change Indeed.

WALKING IN GARDEN'S

I Love To Walk In Gardens,
I Know That God Is There.
When I See Flowers Blooming,
I Feel Him Everywhere.
I Seem To Hear God Whisper,
In The Gentle Breeze.
His Love Often Surrounds Me,
Among The Falling Leaves.
Listen To The Birds Sing,
As They Wake Up At Dawn.
Watch The Bright Sun Rising,
Damp Dew On The Grass At Morn.
If You Can't Find God In A Garden,
Your Soul Must Be Deaf And Blind…
I Only Have To Walk In One,
Where God I Will Always Find.

BE GRATEFUL

Always Be Grateful,
For What You Have Got,
Think Yourself Fortunate,
Realise You Have Such A Lot.
Have You Two Good Ears,
That Hear Skylarks Sing.
And A Pair Of Healthy Eyes,
Seeing Flowers Bloom In Spring.
Do You Have A Heart?
That Has Never Been Broken In Two.
Do You Have Faith In God?
That He Will Get You Through.
Do You Speak The Truth?
When Other Folk Have Lied.
Grass Is Not Always Greener,
On The Other Side.
Do You Envy Others?
When You Have Got All This,
Compared To Many People,
Your Life Is Utter Bliss.
Next Time You Kiss Your Children,
Thank God, For What You Possess.
Millionaires Would Gladly Swap Places,
You Truly Have Happiness.

THE VOW

Vowed You Would Never Leave Me,
Someone I Could Depend Upon.
Stay Always And Forever,
Our Two Hearts Joined As One.
When You Were With Me,
Life Was Rich Indeed…
I Wanted For Nothing,
Had All I Would Ever Need.
This World Was Such A Lovely Place,
So Special When You Were In It.
My Heart Is Broken Now,
I Miss You Every Minute.
In My Dreams, I Often Hear You Say,
My Love I Am Always With You
I 'm Never Far Away.
The Vow That You Made To Me,
Was We Would Never Part.
You Have Kept That Solemn Promise,
You're Still Inside My Heart.

SOME FOLK

Some Folk Are Thoughtless,
While Others Caring And Kind.
Some Sense The Pain You Feel,
Others Are Ignorant
In Heart And In Mind.
Some Have Contentment,
God Tucked Safely In Their Heart.
Many Try And Find It,
But Don't Know Where To Start.
You Will Meet Many Selfish People,
Void Of Love And Care…?
They May Be Rich And Famous,
But You're The Millionaire.
God Not Only Loves The Faithful,
The Black Sheep He Loves The Same.
If They Ask, He Will Find Them.
Everyone He Knows By Name.
Pray For The Folk, Who Have Faltered?
Plead For Them To God Above.
Ask Him To Fill Them With Kindness,
Protect Them With His Love.
If You Do You Will Gain Entry To Heaven,
The Lost Sheep May Get There Too.
God Will Hear Your Pleading,
The Angels Will Be Proud Of You.

MEMORY

I Walked In Meadows Of Daisies,
One Sunny Summer's Day.
Where We Often Strolled Together,
Before You Went Away.
I Made Pretty Daisy Chains,
Like We Used To Do.
Reaching Our Favourite Place,
I Shed Tear Or Two.
Gazing At The Beautiful Scenery,
You Felt So Close To Me.
I Seemed To Hear You Whisper,
Where I Was, You Would Always Be.
Suddenly I Realised,
Plainly, I Could See.
Like This Daisy Chain I Made,
We're Joined Together For Eternity.
I Will Not Be Lonely,
Both My Heart And I Agree.
We Will Never Lose Touch,
You're Locked In Our Memory

SWEET MEMORY

My Heart Was Truly Broken,
The Day You Went Away.
I Knew I Had To Lose You,
I Prayed Most Every Day.
The Angels Took You To Heaven,
My Prayers Were All In Vain.

I Knew That God Was Being Kind,
He Ended All Your Pain.
My Heart Is Now In Torment,
So Sore And Broken In Two.
It Will Never Recover,
From The Sorrow Of Losing You.
I Hid The Heartache That I Felt,
Keeping A Smile Upon My Face.
But Life Is So Empty Now,
In A Vacuum Of Time And Space.
The Light Went Out Of My Life,
When We Said Good-Bye.
But Memories Cannot Be Lost Or Stolen,
Given Away, And Can Never Die.

FIND THE SPARK

Has Life Lost Its Sparkle?
A Damp Squib That Has No Fuse.
Want To Take Off Like A Rocket,
Try To Win But Always Lose.
You Wake Up On A Morning,
Just Want To Stay In Bed?
Simply Give Up Trying,
A Sheep That's So Easily Led.
Watch Your Reflection In A Mirror,
Face Problems Fair And Square.
Say Life Will Get Better,
Never Believe God Does Not Care.
Every Day You Will Get Stronger,
You Will Feel Your Life Improve…
So Eager Now You're Running.
Yesterday You Could Hardly Move.
Do Not Waste A Precious Moment,
Life Will Not Come Around Again.
Opt For Joy, Love And Laughter,
Say Good-Bye To Doubt And Pain.
Everyone Has It In Them,
If They Only Find The Spark.
Glow Like A Roman Candle,
Light Your Life Up From The Dark

HEAVENS PLAIN

Do You Know I Miss You?
Now You My Love Have Gone.
I Try To Hide My Grief,
Do My Best To Struggle On.
God Knows My Torment
My Heart Is Broken In Two.
I Never Will Get Over,
The Hurt Of Losing You.
I Try To Keep My Chin Up,
Few Have Seen Me Weep.
I Cry Into My Pillow,
When The World Is Fast Asleep.
You Meant Everything To Me,
Were My Best Friend Too.
My Life Feels So Lonely,
So Empty Without You…
Before You Went To Heaven,
You Told Me To Be Strong.
To Do The Best I Can,
Until Life's Battles Won.
When My Journeys Over,
I Will Hear You Call My Name.
Walk Hand In Hand Together,
Over Heavens Golden Plain.
We Will Be United,
Just As We Were Before.
Holding You In My Arms Again,
Weeping For You No More.

BLUEBELL WOOD

Sprawled Beneath A Blossom Tree,
Watching Bluebells Grow.
My Thoughts Began To Wander,
To Days So Long Ago.
Walking In Fields Of Flowers,
Both Our Arms Entwined.
Love Birds Were Jealous Of Us,
Simply Two Of A Kind.
Rambling Through An Orchard,
To Reach A Sparkling Stream.
Lazing Among Bluebells,
Where We Would Sit And Dream.
Many Years We Spent Contently,
Our Two Lives Joined As One.
Sharing Each Dream Together,
Then One Day You Were Gone.
My Heart Yearns For You,
When The Bluebells Are In Bloom.
My Eyes Fill Up With Teardrops,
For The Love, I Lost Too Soon.
They Say Heaven Is Not Far Away,
Like Stepping Through An Open Door.
We Will Walk Again In Bluebells Then,
Together For Evermore.

I DID MY BEST

I Watched My Children Grow Up,
Saw Their Dreams Unfold.
Did My Best To Guide Them,
Sheltered Them From Damp And Cold.
Nourished Them When Hungry,
Comforted Them When Sad.
Filled Their Lives With Laughter,
Gave Them All The Love I Had.
They Are Grown And Happy Now,
Alas, I Am Growing Old.
I'm So Grateful For My Memories,
They Mean More To Me Than Gold.
I Want To Enjoy This Time Of My Life,
Make The Most Of Every New Day.
Take Pleasure In My Grandchildren,
Help Them To Find Their Way.
One Day I Will Knock On Heavens Door,
When My Soul It Longs For Rest.
When God Asks What I Have Achieved,
I Will Say, I Did My Best.

I LOVE THE RAIN

I Was Standing At The Bus Stop,
In The Pouring Wet,
One Lady Stood There Also,
Very Much To My Regret.
She Moaned For Half An Hour,
Was Sick Of All The Rain?
And Would Not Be Bothered,
If She Never Saw Rain Again.
She Asked Me What I Thought,
If I Did Agree.
I Mumbled All Need Water,
Every Person, Flower And Tree.
I Told Her That I Loved The Rain,
I Did Not Want To Lie,
That If It Never Rained Again,
This Earth Would Surely Die,
Think About All The People?
Without A Drop Of Rain.
Their Land Had Turned To Desert,
Once Fertile Now Barren Plain.
Multitudes Of People, Searching For A Drink.
Many Children, Lost Through Thirst,
I Could See This Made Her Think
We Are So Very Lucky,
To Have Rain Clouds In The Sky,
With Out Them Every Living Thing,
Would Shrivel Up And Die.
I Tried To Make Light Of It,
Asked Her What Was Worse?
Scratch In The Sand
When You Want A Drink,
Or Turn The Tap On
To Quench Your Thirst.

IN MY MEMORY

God Waited So Patiently
I Could Not Let You Go.
Did Not Want To Lose You,
Because I Loved You So.
I Had To Let Him Take You,
You Were In Too Much Pain.
I Asked The Lord To Take Your Hand,
To Make You Well Again.
God's Angels Flew You To Heaven,
Far Away From Me.
Now You're Soul Soars Like An Eagle,
Like This Bird, You're Spirits Free.
I Miss You But I Cannot Change It,
What Will Be Is Meant To Be.
Though I No Longer See You,
You're A Beautiful Thought,
In My Memory.

PERFECT PEACE

My Sweetheart Is In Heaven,
How I Loved Him So.
I Did Not Think The Day Would Come,
When I Had To Let Him Go.
I Knew I Was Soon To Lose Him,
The Angels Came One Day.
Wrapped Their Wings Around Him,
Took His Pain Away.
I Asked The Lord For Mercy,
For A Miracle, I Did Pray.
Would Give All I Had And More,
If God Would Let Him Stay.
I Knew His Life Was Over,
God Hushed His Heart To Sleep.
Content Now In Gods Heaven.
Leaving Me Alone To Weep.
But I Have Sweet Memories,
Until We Meet At Heavens Gate.
It May Be Sooner Or Later.
Left In The Hands Of Fate.
For The Rest Of My Life I Will Miss Him,
My Love Will Never Cease.
Although I Want Him Back Again,
I Know He Has Found His Perfect Peace.

THE DREAM

I Dreamt Last Night, I Was
Strolling In Gods Gardens Above.
I Heard Sweet Voices Singing,
Melodies Of Peace And Love.
Then I Saw You Standing,
Beside A Blossom Tree.
Encircled By Gods Angels,
Smiling Over To Me.
Delighted I Ran To You,
Placed A Kiss Upon Your Face.
You Whispered That You Missed Me,
I Felt Your Warm Embrace.
The Angels Let Us Meet,
For One Night In My Dreams.
To Let Me Know You Are With Me,
No Matter How Hard Life Seems.
It Was Important To Tell Me,
That Our Love Lives On.
Content With This Knowledge,
It Helped Me To Stay Strong.
Soon I Had To Say Farewell,
The Scene Just Fade From View.
Each Night I Pray To God,
That Dream I Had Will Come True.

ONE MOTHER

You Only Have One Mother,
If You Search Your Whole Life Through.
There Will Never Be Another Like Her,
She Would Give Her Life For You.
Nourished You In Childhood,
Tenderly Watched You Grow.
Worried When You Got Home Late,
Loves You More Than You Could Know.
She Has Done Her Duty Well,
From Your Mothers Nest You've Flown.
Do You Think Of That Special Lady?
When She Is Sitting On Her Own.
A Simple Act Of Kindness,
Perhaps A Bit Of Praise.
Would Lighten Up Her Life,
Brighten Up Her Days.
But If You Can't Be Bothered,
Too, Busy Rushing With The Crowd.
Your Mother Will Still Love You Forever,
You Are Her Child Whom She's So Proud.

GOD IS THERE

God Is In Everything,
In The Gentle Breeze.
There In Every Flower,
In All The Birds And Bees.
He Can Be In Every Person,
If They Only Let Him In.
There At The End Of Life,
Is There When It Begins.
God Is There In Good Times,
More So In The Bad.
Cheers When Your Heart Aches,
Comforts You When Sad.
God Will Give You Hope,
When In Life's Tempests
You Are Tossed.
Rescues You From Stormy Waters,
When You Feel That All Is Lost.
He Will Be Your Friend,
If You Find Yourself Alone.
If You Stray Too Far Away,
The Lord Will Bring You Home.
Just Have A Bit Of Faith,
Believe That You Can Win.
God Will Give You Happiness,
With Joy And Peace Within.

LOST YOUR SPARKLE

When Feeling Down Hearted,
Disappointed Too.
If Life Has Lost Its Sparkle,
This Is What To Do.
Sit In The Countryside,
Let Your Thoughts Be Still.
With Nature All Around You,
Your Soul Will Soon Refill.
Listen To The Bird's Song,
The Whispering Of The Trees.
Your Spirit Will Soon Be Buzzing,
Like The Bumble Bees.
Watch All Gods Creatures,
Content With Their Lot.
Perhaps You Will Realise,
What A Good Life You Have Got.
Have You A Healthy Heart?
A Pair Of Eyes That See.
Ears That Hear Bird's Song,
Faith That Can Set You Free.
Think Of The Folk Who Are Lacking These.
Plus The Gifts That You Possess.
Recharge Yourself In The Countryside,
Get Rid Of Your Emptiness.

IN YOUR HEART

Have You Found The Answer?
What Life Is All About.
Sometimes You Hit The Jackpot,
Your Heart Soon Fills With Doubt.
Some People Seem To Find It,
Say It Is Easy As Can Be.
I Asked My Friends If They Knew,
But They Were No More Wiser Than Me.
I Asked The Lord This Question,
Hoping His Answer To Receive.
I Seemed To Hear Him Whisper,
My Child Do You Believe..
If You Do Your Sure To Find It,
You Will Never Lose Your Way.
Have Faith And Believe In Me,
I Will Help You Come What May.
Stop This Endless Seeking,
I Have Been There From The Start.
The Answer To Your Question Is,
You Will Find Me In Your Heart.

ALWAYS THERE

Alone With My Memories,
One Cold Winter's Night.
The Snow Gently Falling,
The Fire Was Burning Bright.
My Heart Had A Longing,
Wanting You With Me.
If You Were Home Again,
How Happy Life Would Be.
I Wiped Away A Teardrop,
One Of Many That Still Fall.
I Seemed To Hear You Whisper,
That You Have Never Left At All.
Always There Beside Me,
Helping Me To Be Strong.
Comforting Me In Sad Times,
Urging Me To Carry On.
As I Gazed Into The Embers,
I Seemed To See Your Face.
The Look Of Love I Saw There,
Time Never Will Erase.
I Fell Asleep In Your Arms,
In Dreams You're There With Me.
Saying My Love Where I Am,
You Will Always Be.

FORTY YEARS WED

I Do Not Say It Often,
But I Think You Know.
You Mean The Whole World To Me,
That I Love You So.
Forty Years Since We Were Wed,
How Quickly Time Has Flown.
You Are So Very Special To Me,
My Heart Is Yours Alone.
Our Children Are All Grown Now,
On Their Feet They Firmly Stand.
Tried Our Best To Guide Them,
Gave Each One A Helping Hand.
A Little Rain Must Fall In Life,
We Have To Give And Take.
We Wish We Could Have Sunshine,
Every Day That We Awake.
You Know How Much I Love You,
How Much I Truly Care.
Living Only For Each Other,
With Love That Is So Rare.
I Hope That God Is Kind To Us,
Bless Us As He Did Before.
Keeping Us Together,
With Each Other For Evermore.
So Thank You For Choosing Me,
For Making Me You're Wife
I Will Love You Forever And Ever,
And For The Rest Of My Life.

IF DREAMS CAME TRUE

If Dreams Came True,
You Would Be In My Arms Again.
If Dreams Came True,
I Would Have Joy Instead Of Pain.
If I Had Only One Wish,
I Know What It Would Be.
That I Could Visit Heaven,
To Bring You Home With Me.
We Were So Very Fortunate,
To Have Known The Love We Had.
Laughing With Me In Good Times,
Cheering Me In The Bad.
I Leaned On Your Shoulder,
The Best Friend I Ever Knew.
I Am So Lonely, So Empty Without You.
Friends Say My Heart Will Mend,
They Just Don't Know How I Feel.
My Poor Heart Is Truly Broken,
It Will Never Heal.
If Dreams Came True,
There Would Be Laughter Instead Of Tears.
Looking Forward To Tomorrow,
Forgetting The Wasted Years.
If God Could Grant Me One Wish,
A Dream That Could Come True.
I Would Pray With All My Heart,
For Yesterday And You.

A SMILING FACE

Friends Think I Am Over You,
They Can't See My Heart Is Torn.
My Eyes Are Not Always Weeping,
So They Think I Am Not Forlorn.
No One Knows How Much I Miss You
I Would Give The World And More.
Just To See You My Love,
Come Smiling Through Our Door...
I'd Give My Life In A Moment,
For Five More Minutes With You.
If Only You Were With Me,
My Dreams Would All Come True.
I Am So Empty, Feel So Hollow Inside,
I Tell My Friends I Am Fine,
But My Heart Knows I Have Lied.
I Can't Show The Pain I Feel,
Heartaches I Cannot Erase.
For Many A Broken Heart Is Hidden,
Behind A Smiling Face.

LAUGHTER.

Laughter Is Contagious,
It Starts To Spread Around.
It Is So Infectious,
The Best Tonic I Have Found.
If You Are Feeling Gloomy,
Can't Keep Up The Pace.
You Might Meet A Friend
Who Makes You Laugh?
Puts A Smile Back On Your Face.
You Might Walk A Little Further,
Bump Into Someone Else, You Know.
They Are Not Looking Very Happy,
But Smile Before You Go.
Try This And You Will Find,
That Laughter Can Pass On.
If Everybody Did This,
All Sadness Would Be Gone.
This World Would Be A Better Place,
If Everyone Gave A Bit Of Cheer.
Doom And Gloom Would Vanish.
Making You Feel Glad
That You Are Here.

TOMORROW

Is Your Life Empty?
Haven't Got A Friend.
Are You Feeling Lonely?
Your Heartache Just Won't Mend.
At Night You Try And Slumber,
But Find You Cannot Sleep.
Creep Out Of Bed At Morning,
One Time You Would Wake And Leap.
Get Yourself Together,
Hold Your Head Up High.
Say Life Will Get Better,
Prepare To Do Or Die.
Fix A Smile On Your Face,
Smile At Others Too.
Never Settle For Second Best,
Don't Just Make Things Do.
When You Meet Other Folk,
Who Feel The Same As You.
Hold Out Your Hand In Friendship,
Make Them Welcome Too.
Do This And You're Sadness,
Will Lift And Fade Away.
Remember Tomorrow Is Always,
The Start Of A Brand New Day.

FIND THE ANSWER

I Watch The Sunset Disappear,
As It Slowly Sinks From View.
When The Moon And Stars Appear,
My Thoughts Go Back To You.
I See A Shooting Star So Bright.
Soaring In The Sky.
I Feel An Ache In My Heart,
A Tear Is In My Eye.
What Is Life All About?
Did God Really Make This Earth?
Does He Watch Our Every Step?
Is He With Us From Our Birth?
Sometimes I Doubt Since I Lost You,
Especially In Despair.
I Think Of The Love We Shared,
Then I Know That God Is There.
In Life's Plan We Are Apart Just A Moment,
Soon To Be Together Once More.
Finding Out All The Answers,
When We Next Meet At Heavens Door.

IF ONLY.

If Prayers Could Come True,
Dreams God Would Fulfil.
I Know What I Would Ask Him,
For You, And Always Will.
I Would Wish You Home Again,
To Be With Me Once More.
Life Would Be Worth Living,
With My Love That I Adore.
We Would Be Content And Happy,
Like In The Years Gone By.
I Can't Get Used To Losing You,
No Matter How Hard I Try.
So I Will Keep On Praying,
Wishing Just Like Before.
I Will Be With You In Paradise,
In Your Arms Forever More.

HEAVENS GATE

It Is Years Since I Lost You,
But The Ache In My Heart Is The Same.
My Eyes Still Fill With Teardrops,
When Someone Speaks Your Name.
I Often Glimpse A Face Like Yours,
But Quickly My Eyes See.
It Is Only Wishful Thinking,
I Realise It Cannot Be.
For You Have Gone To Heaven,
Not To Be Seen On Earth Again.
Never To See Your Lovely Smile,
Never To Be Rid Of This Pain.
So Wait For Me My Dear One,
Be It Soon Or Be It Late.
God Will Guide Me To You,
Waiting At Heavens Gate.

GOD'S PLANS

If God Would Grant Wishes,
He Could Make Come True.
There's One Wish I Long For,
That I Still Had You.
If God Offered Me The World,
Giving Out Riches And Wealth Untold.
I Would Refuse Them All,
Just Wanting You To Hold.
If God Turned, Back The Hands Of Time,
So I Was In Your Arms Again.
Life Would Be Like Heaven,
Tears Vanishing With The Pain.
I Am Forever Dreaming,
I Want Life Like It Used To Be.
It Can Never Happen,
But I Still Have Your Memory.
So If You Have A True Love,
Do All That's In Your Power,
Tell Him How Much You Love Him,
Every Minute Of Every Hour.
Sometimes We Do Forget,
Too, Busy To Even Smell The Flowers.
Time Runs Out So Quickly,
Remember,
God's Plans Are Not Always Ours.

RESTING PLACE

I Wander To Your Resting Place,
To Spend Some Time With You.
Arranging Your Pretty Flowers,
Remembering The Love, We Knew.
I Did Not Think The Time We Had,
Could So Abruptly End.
I Would Be Apart From You,
My Partner, My Best Friend.
We Used To Laugh With Joy,
Were So Content Together.
Thought We Were Inseparable,
Side-By-Side Forever.
Time And Tide Wait For No One,
A Hard Lesson For Me To Learn.
When You Left Me Lonely,
Never To Return.
I Wish You Peace, I Wish You Joy,
My Love I Send You Too.
As I Slowly Walk Away,
I Wish I Still Had You.

THE DOOR BELOW

There Are Many Good People,
Others Who Have No Heart.
They Like To Hunt With Dogs,
To Tear The Fox Apart.
Some Like To Kill The Whales,
Others Club The Seals,
Do They Ever Think?
Of How Much Pain It Feels.
If They Were Hunted,
Fleeing For Their Lives,
Maybe It Would Make Them Think,
They Might Realise.
All Life Is Precious,
God Said Protect The Small And Weak.
Do Not Kill For Killings Sake,
Or Just For Pleasure Seek.
When Their Life Is Over,
And For Paradise, They Strive
The Good Lord Will Ask Them,
Did You Help The Weak Survive?
God Will Know The Hurt They Caused,
And Sadly Shake His Head.
You Cannot Enter Heaven,
Try The Door Below Instead.

CONTENT

Each Step I Take,
You Are There With Me.
I Did Not Want You To Leave,
God Said It Had To Be.
When I Am Out Walking,
Or In A Crowded Place.
I Seem To Sense Your Presence,
I See Your Smiling Face.
Even When Sleeping,
You Are In My Dreams.
Telling Me To Stay Strong,
No Matter How Hard Life Seems.
In My Dreams, You Are So Happy,
At Peace And Content Too.
I Know I Will Feel The Same,
When I Am In Heaven With You.

MY GRANDSON

Now You Are Growing Up,
I Want To Tell You This.
Since The Day You Were Born,
My Life's Been Utter Bliss.
For Years I Have Loved You,
Tenderly Watched You Grow.
Praying To God To Keep You Safe,
Because I Love You So.
A Love That Is So Special,
More So Every Day.
Nothing Will Replace It,
It Can Never Be Taken Away.
My Grandson I Am So Proud Of You,
May All Your Dreams Come True?
You Gave Me Lots Of Hugs And Kisses,
Filled My Life With Happiness Too.
I Try To Help And Guide You,
Lewis Do The Best You Can.
I Am Sure I Will Be Just As Proud,
When You Have Grown Into A Man.

WORDS OF COMFORT

I Am Writing You This Letter,
    Dear Friend.
To Show How Much I Care.
I Would Like To Help You With,
This Cross-You Have To Bear.
Hoping God Is Good To You,
Easing Your Hurt And Pain.
You Are Someone Special,
I Will Never Find Again.
I Send You My Good Wishes,
My Prayers I Send You Too.
Hoping The Peace God Can Give,
He Will Bestow On You.
Know That I Love You.
How Much I Truly Care.
When Reading These Words Of Comfort,
Remember I'm Forever There.
Thank You For Being a Special Friend,
For Sweet Memories,
I Will Always Possess.
So I Will Just End This Letter To You,
With All My Love And Say
    God Bless.
        X

MOTHER LOVE

Now You Are A Mother,
For Your Children You Do Your Best.
Working Your Fingers To The Bone,
Just To Feather Their Nest.
You Comfort And Nourish Them,
Protect Them From All Harm.
Shade Them In The Summer,
In Winter Keep, Them Warm.
You Would Gladly Die For Them,
Giving Them Your Last Breath.
For Your Children
You Would Face The Devil,
Doing Battle To The Death.
No Other Love Is Stronger,
You'd Give All That You Possess.
But What You Wish Most For Them,
Is Good Health And Happiness.

GARDEN OF DREAMS

I Was Dreaming
You Were In A Garden.
In Heaven Up Above.
Standing Among Red Roses,,
Surrounded By Gods Love.
You Were All Aglow In Sunshine,
As Was All The Rest.
God Knew You Were Special,
He Always Chooses The Best.
You Know How Much I Miss You,
My Love So Strong And True.
I Never Will Get Over,
The Hurt Of Losing You.
When I Saw You In Gods Garden,
With That Smile Upon Your Face.
I Knew That You Were Happy,
At Peace In Gods Good Grace.
I Hope To Meet You Again,
Rekindle The Love We Once Knew.
Then I Can Spend Eternity,
In Paradise With You.

HAVE FAITH

Folk Say Have Faith,
If Life's Going Down The Drain.
Where Do You Find It?
You're Hearts In So Much Pain.
Church Is Not The Only Place,
If Faith You Wish To Seek.
At First You Might Not Find It,
Keep On Trying To Make The Leap.
If You Open Up Your Heart,
It Does Not Matter Where.
Sitting In A Garden,
Or In A Comfy Chair.
Ask The Lord To Help You,
He Will Enter In.
He Is There For The Asking,
Your New Life Will Begin.
Over Rough Roads, He Will Guide You.
Along Life's Winding Path.
God Will Ease Your Heartache,
Disperse Your Pain And Wrath.
Want To Know Where Faith Is,
It Lives Deep Inside Your Soul.
If Feeling Lost and Empty,
Faith In God Can Make You Whole.

IF DREAMS CAME TRUE

Last Night I Had A Dream,
I Was Safe In Your Arms Again.
My Teardrops Had All Vanished,
Just Like The Bitter Pain.
I Awoke And Found You Missing,
It Was Hard To Carry On,
I Finally Realised That Morning,
That You Were Gone.
I Did Not Think The Time Would Come,
When We Would Be Apart.
The Day You Went Away,
You Also Took My Heart.
We Had Our Ups And Downs,
Like All Couples Do
Life Is So Lonely,
So Empty Without You.
I Have Our Beautiful Children,
For That, I Am So Glad.
Have My Feet Firmly On The Ground.
Through All The Good And Bad.
I Will Always Love You,
No, Matter What I Do.
At Night When All Is Silent,
I Remember The Love We Knew.
I Will Pray To God To Help Me,
As He Has Done Many Times Before.
Till Then Hold Me In You're Arms My Love,
In Sweet Dreams Forever More.

THE WORLD STOPPED

To Your Resting Place I Wandered,
Each Flower I Placed With Care.
As I Looked Up At The Horizon,
A Rainbow Was Reflected There.
As I Gazed At Its Beauty,
The Colours Dazzled Bright.
It Cheered My Heart Up,
It Was Such A Lovely Sight.
Then I Felt A Raindrop,
And As I Turned Around.
Nothing Was Stirring,
Not One Single Sound.
I Thought I Sensed Your Presence,
I Seemed To Feel Your Touch.
I Heard You Softly Whisper,
I Love You Very Much.
I Have Not Left You Sweetheart,
I Am Never Far Away.
I Will Stay Beside You,
Forever And A Day.
In An Instant You Were Gone,
The Birds Began To Sing,
The World Stopped For A Moment,
So A Greeting You Could Bring.
You Came With The Rainbow,
Now All Loneliness Has Gone.
You Gave A Message To My Heart.
That Love Goes On And On.

LIGHT ME A CANDLE

Light Me A Candle,
Lord Show Me The Way.
Lead Me Out Of Darkness,
To A Brand New Day.
Give Me Something To Live For,
A Reason To Go On.
Grant Me Faith In My Soul,
To Build My Dreams Upon.
Give Me Strength And Courage,
Just As Brave As All The Rest.
So When My Life Is Over,
I Can Say I Did My Best.
Give Me Joy And Fulfilment,
Let Peace Soothe My Fevered Brow.
Will You Help Me To Succeed?
Would You Show Me How?
Give Me A Purpose In Living,
Let Me Know You Are There.
Help Me With My Burdens,
When The Cross-Is Hard To Bear.
Shine Your Light Upon Me,
Ease My Hurt And Pain.
Brighten This Dark Tunnel,
So My Eyes See The Light Once Again.

FIRST IN THE QUEUE

If Miracles Do Happen.
If Dreams Can Come True.
I Would Be So Delighted,
Because I'd Still Have You.
If Broken Hearts Were Mended,
Once Again Made Whole.
I Would Have A Reason For Living,
Content In Heart And Soul.
All I Desire Would Come True,
I Would Forget Those Wasted Years.
Sorrow And Anguish Would Vanish,
Along With Millions Of Tears.
Can I Be First In The Queue Dear God?
If A Miracle You Could Give.
I Would Never Ask Another Favour,
For As Long As I Live.
Until This Miracle Happens,
Till My Sweet Dreams, All Come True.
I Will Cherish My Beautiful Memories,
Of The Times, I Spent With You.

BONUS OF HAPPINESS

If You Have Love, You Are Lucky.
It's The Best Thing You Will Own.
So Many Lonely People,
Have To Exist All Alone.
Do You Have Children Who Love You?
A Loving Family Too.
Have You A Faithful Partner?
Who Would Give Their Life For You.
You Also Have What God Gives,
If You Open Your Eyes, You Will See.
With This Love So Freely Given,
Ten Times A Millionaire You Could Be.
Hold Onto This Gift That's So Precious,
Fill Your Heart And Soul With This Love.
Realise You Have Been Blessed,
Thank The Dear Lord Up Above.
Why Do You Seek Wealth And Power?
When You Own The Trophy,
All Want To Possess.
You Can't Buy Love And Kindness,
Love Comes With The Bonus Of Happiness.

EVERYWHERE

I Asked God A Question,
Was He Always There?
Why Did He Not Answer?
Does The Lord Not Care?
That Night While I Lay Sleeping,
God Told Me In A Dream.
My Child I Will Always Answer,
No Matter How Long It May Seem.
I Have My Reasons,
Patience You Need To Learn.
If A Favour You Ask Of Me,
Give Something In Return.
Do Not Think It Is Easy,
You Have To Do Your Part.
If You Want Me To Help,
Believe With All Your Heart.
Never Doubt I Am With You,
Do The Best You Can.
I Will Help Solve Your Problems,
Help Guide You Through Life's Plan.
Love Every Living Thing,
Just As I Love You.
Then All You Are Seeking,
Tomorrow May Come True.
Do Not Shout I Can Hear You,
Just Need Whisper I Will Be There.
Be Patient I Will Answer,
Know I Am Everywhere.

THE BLINDFOLD

Do You Go Through Life Blindfold?
Look But Do Not See.
Summer Flowers Blooming,
In The Spring A Budding Tree.
Deaf To Earths Sweet Music,
The Songbirds That All Sing.
Never Hear Sounds Of Laughter,
Or Feel The Peace All Nature Can Bring.
Your Heart Feels Numb And Frozen,
Your Soul So Tightly Closed.
Ask God And It Will Open,
To See The Sun, And Smell The Rose.
Hear Laughter of Little Children,
Feel Faith Stirring In Your Soul.
Your Life You Thought Was Ended,
God Can Help You Make It Whole.
Ask Him, You Will Not Regret It,
Gods The Key To That Padlocked Door.
The Lord Will Remove Your Blindfold,
To Live In Sunshine For Evermore.

MY PRAYER

Thank You Lord
For The Love You Give,
For All That You Have Done.
Your Comfort When I Have Lost,
Your Joy When I Have Won.
Thank You For My Blessings,
For The Happy Life, I've Had.
Cheered With Me In Good Times,
Carried Me In The Bad.
There When I Needed You,
Made Me Laugh Instead Of Frown.
When The Path Got Rough For Me,
Picked Me Up If I Fell Down.
At Times, Life Got Too Much For Me,
When I Felt, I Just Wanted To Flee.
Each Time I Ran Away From You,
You Followed On After Me.
Now I Am In My Twilight Years,
Most Of My Dreams Came True.
Thank You Once Again Dear God,
For Being A Friend So True.
If I Could Ask One Last Favour,
Please Look After My Family,
Be Their Best Friend Also,
Just Like You Were To Me.

MOTHER I LOVE YOU

Dear Lord I Miss My Mother,
More And More Each Day.
It's Been Years Since I Lost Her,
But This Hurt Won't Go Away.
I Am Lonely Since She Left Me,
This Heartache Will Not Heal.
Those Who've Lost Their Mother,
Will Know Just How I Feel.
The Selfless Love She Gave Me,
I Never Can Replace.
If Only I Could See Her,
To Kiss Her Dear Sweet Face.
Dear God Give Me Five Minutes,
Or Maybe Two Will Do,
Enough Time To Hold Her In My Arms
To Say Dear Mother, I Love You.

SWEET BLISS

I Watched The Sunset Disappear,
Until The Moon Came Into View.
Twinkling Stars Appeared,
With Fond Memories Of You.
Those Precious Times We Had,
So Easy To Recall.
The Life We Shared Together,
Were The Happiest Days Of All?
In My Memory, I See Your Smile,
I See Your Lovely Face.
Cannot Hold You In My Arms,
Or Feel Your Warm Embrace.
I Can't Hear The Words Of Love,
You So Often Said To Me.
Our Love Was So Special,
Everything I Hoped It Would Be.
I Remember The Love Between Us,
Especially On Nights Like This.
Stored Safely Away In My Heart,
Sweet Memories Are Truly Bliss.

THE BEST

She Was One In A Million,
Worth Much More Than Gold.
I Think When God Made Her,
He Must Have Broken The Mould.
Her Love Was So Precious,
A Treasure I Will Not Find Again.
When God Took Her From Me,
My Loss Was Heavens Gain.
God Needed A New Star In Heaven,
A Beautiful Light To Shine.
I Did Not Think The Day Would Dawn,
When He Would Take
That Dear Mother Of Mine.
God Make My Mother Happy,
You Have An Angel More Fair Than The Rest.
Let Your Light And Love Surround Her,
Without Doubt, She Was
One Of The Best.

MEANT TO BE?

The Light Went Out Of My Life,
The Day You Went Out Of Mine.
My Heart Knows That I Lie,
When I Tell My Friends, I Am Fine.
I Think Of What We Once Shared,
The Special Love We Knew.
I Never Will Recover,
From The Hurt Of Losing You.
I Have Our Lovely Children,
Memories Time Will Not Erase.
But Many A Broken Heart Is Hidden,
Behind A Smiling Face.
If God Could Grant A Wish For Me,
A Dream That Can Come True.
I Would Go On My Knees And Ask Him,
For Yesterday And You.
I Will Leave It In The Hands Of God,
I Hope He Hears My Plea.
Giving Me Strength To Cope
With Problems What Come My Way,
Accept What Is Meant To Be.

ONLY A DREAM

I Awoke And Saw An Angel,
She Was Such A Lovely Sight.
Her Wings Shone Like A Rainbow,
Her Eyes Were Shining Bright.
A Face Aglow With Sunshine,
Moonlight Was In Her Hair.
She Was A Stunning Vision,
Beautiful Beyond Compare.
I Blinked And She Vanished,
I Sat In Shock And Awe.
The Image Of Her Beauty,
Is With Me Forever More.
In My Prayers That Night
I Told The Lord,
That I Needed Him Was He There.
If He Really Loved Me,
To Help With This Cross I Bear.
Give Strength To Me To Go On,
Ease My Stress And Strain.
God Must Have Sent An Angel,
So I Would Never Doubt Again.

NO ONE KNOWS

I Cry Into My Pillow,
Bed Is My Best Friend,
Twilight Hides My Teardrops,
I Dread Each Night To End.
My Grief Is Overwhelming,
Will I Ever Smile Again?
How Do You Go On Living,
When You're Heart
Is Racked With Pain.
Lord Give Me Some Courage,
Help Me To Carry On.
So Many Years Spent Together,
It's Hard Now He Has Gone.
No One To Give Me Comfort,
No One To Urge Me On.
No One To Live My Life For.
To Pin All My Hopes Upon.
In My Dreams When I Am Sleeping,
My Heart Is Free From Pain.
As Dawn Peeps Through The Curtains,
My Grief Starts All Over Again.

SHINE YOUR LIGHT

Give A Helping Hand Dear Lord,
I Find This Life's Road Tough.
I Do My Best To Struggle On,
But My Soul Has Had Enough.
I Look For Sunny Weather,
Dark Clouds Hang Overhead.
From Waking On A Morning,
Until Time To Go To Bed.
Tomorrow May Be Better,
My Prayers I Hope You Heed.
Folk Say If I Ask You Lord,
You Will Give Everything I Need.
I Do Not Want Fame Or Riches,
Just Peace Within My Heart,
With A Little Bit Of Contentment,
To Make A Brand New Start.
Maybe I Could Rise And Shine,
Just Like The Morning Sun.
Enjoy Every Single Minute,
Until My Life Is Done.
I Am Begging You Dear God,
Hear My Heartfelt Plea.
Inspire Hope In My Heart,
Shine Your Love And Light On Me.

SITTING ON THE SEASHORE

Sitting On The Seashore,
Gazing Out To Sea.
Tears Fall Like Raindrops,
As I Remember All You Meant To Me.
We Often Strolled On This Warm Sand,
Happy And Content Together,
Thought We Were Invincible,
Side-By-Side Forever.
But God Willed It Not To Be,
I Am Alone And Broken Hearted.
I Have Wept A Million Tears,
Since The Sad Day, We Were Parted.
But My Faith Is Strong, I Do Believe,
We Will Meet Again Once More.
Walking Hand In Hand In Paradise,
On Heavens Golden Shore.

A NEW DAY

Night Time Ends, Day Begins,
Darkness Turns Into Light.
Dawn Has Arisen,
The Sun And Sky So Bright.
This Day Could Be The Start Of,
A Brand New Way Of Life.
Perhaps A New Beginning,
Releasing Stress And Strife.
Aim To Make Folk Happy,
I Am Sure That If You Do.
A Smile Or Cheerful Greeting,
Will Rebound Back To You.
Spread A Little Happiness,
Live This Day Like It Was Your Last.
Your Life Could Be So Wonderful,
But Time Runs Out So Fast.
Try This For One Day,
Maybe You Will See.
The Special Way You Are Feeling,
For The Rest Of Your Life You Could Be.

BED OF ROSES

Life's Not A Bed Of Roses,
To All A Little Rain Must Fall.
Everyone Has Bad Times,
Their Backs Up Against The Wall.
Sometimes As We Grow Older,
Our Ailments Multiply,
Our Body Has Slowed Down,
Where Once We Used To Fly.
Think What You Have Learned,
How Fortunate You Have Been.
Blessed With This Life You Have,
The Things You've Done And Seen.
A Faithful Partner Who Loves You,
A Beautiful Family Too.
Wisdom From Living A Life So Full,
Plus The Love God Has For You.
Put One Foot In Front Of The Other,
My Friend Do The Best You Can.
Worry Will Get You Nowhere,
Only God Knows Our Life's Plan.
No One Could Ask More Of You,
For Your Family You Did Your Best.
Gave Them Love In Abundance,
Taught Them To Stand
Proud With The Rest.
Give Your Worries To God,
No Matter How Big Or Small.
Remember To Live In Roses,
A Little Bit Of Rain Must Fall.

SOMETIMES

Sometimes You Slipped,
God Reached And Caught You.
Sometimes You Strayed,
God Brought You Back.
At Times, You Doubted,
He Still Loved You.
God Will Always Grant,
The Faith You Lack.
If You're Heart Ached,
The Lord Would Comfort.
If You Hurt, You're Pain He Eased.
In Your Worst Times, You He'd Carry.
All Your Suffering He Appeased.
God Laughed With You
When You Were Happy.
Cried With You When You Felt Sad.
Gave You Courage, When You Crumbled.
God Is The Best Friend You Ever Had.
Don't Let Him Be Disappointed,
Make Him Proud, Do The Best You Can,
If You Strive To Do Your Utmost,
God Will Guide You In Life's Plan.
When Your Stay On Earth Is Over,
God Will Take You By The Hand.
Place His Loving Arms Around You,
Welcome You To His Heavenly Band.

LIFE

Life Goes By So Quickly,
Like A Race Time Gallops On.
You Stop To Take A Breather,
Suddenly Realise It's Nearly Gone.
Make The Most Of Every Minute,
Pray To God Each Time You Doubt.
Cherish Every Special Moment.
Find What This Life Is All About.
You Are Here For A Reason,
Life Is Not Just A Song And Dance.
Every Life Has A Purpose,
Grasp It While You Have The Chance.
Fill Your Heart With Kindness,
To The Brim With Light And Love.
Know There Is A God That Loves You.
Leads And Guides You From Above.
Do Your Best To Help Gods Creatures,
Try To Aid You're Fellow Men.
Live For Every Precious Moment,
Life Will Not Come Around Again.
When You Shed This Mortal Body,
God Will Give You What He Vowed.
Grant You The Keys To Heaven,
What You Did In This Life,
Has Made Him Proud.

DEEP IN MY HEART

It Is A Beautiful Morning,
White Clouds Floating In A Blue Sky.
Birds So Sweetly Singing,
Yet All I Do Is Cry,
Thoughts Return To Times Before,
Days That Used To Be.
It Seems Like A Lifetime,
Since You Shared That Life With Me.
This World Was Mine, When I Had You,
Life Felt Oh So Dear.
Never Believing The Day Would Come,
When You Would Not Be Here.
Tears Fall Like Raindrops,
My Heart Is Broken In Two.
It Will Never Recover,
From The Hurt Of Losing You.
My Memories Are So Precious,
With Them, I Will Never Part.
I Keep Them Where I Store Your Love,
Deep Within My Heart.

LIFE IS ALL

Walking In The Countryside,
Planning My Life's Dreams.
Gazing At The Bluebells,
Dotted Along Sparkling Streams.
I Watch All Gods Creatures,
Merrily Dashing About.
I Suddenly Wondered,
What Is This Life About?
I Seemed To Hear God Whisper,
Do All That's In Your Power,
Live Each Precious Moment,
Bloom Just Like A Flower.
Hurt Not A Living Thing,
Help Your Fellow Man.
If You Believe In Me,
I Will Guide You In Life's Plan.
Give Aid Where It Is Needed,
Keep Faith In Your Heart.
Give Out Love And Kindness,
Then We Will Never Part.
I Will Not Desert Or Pass You By
Blessings I Will Give To You.
Be a Good Samaritan,
Make Your Neighbours
Dreams Come True.

IMAGINE

Imagine Life's A Flower,
Opening In Full Bloom.
Glowing Radiant Colours,
Sweet As A Roses Perfume.
At Times It Fades And Withers,
Petals Droop And Fall.
If This Happens Pray For Courage,
God Will Make You
Grow Six Feet Tall.
      Wait,
    Have Patience,
      Persevere,
Just Like Flowers,
Depend On The Rain.
Storm Clouds Sometimes
Enter Our Lives,
To Give Us Strength
To Blossom Again.

JUST THINK

Do You Believe In Destiny?
Put It Down To Fate.
Think Its Pointless Trying,
Leaving It Far Too Late.
God Gave Us Free Will,
We Can Change Life If We Choose.
Decide What Path To Take,
Whether To Win Or Lose.
God Knows Our Destination,
It's How We Get There
That Counts So Much.
Strive To Help Our Fellow Men,
Never Lose That Common Touch.
Be Kind On Your Life's Journey,
Abstain From Cruelty And Greed.
Do Not Covet Wealth Or Riches,
God Provides You With All You Need.
Never Think You Are Better,
Than The Folk Who Live Next Door.
Do Not Tolerate Avarice,
Asking God For More And More.
Give Love Unselfishly,
Aid The Sick And Poor.
When Feeling Sorry For Yourself,
Think What Innocent Children Endure?
You Are Free To Smell The Flowers,
Wander In Fields Under A Clear Blue Sky.
When You See All This Suffering,
              "Think"
There But For The Grace Of God Go I.

THANK YOU LORD

To Natalie, Lewis, Aaron, Jessica, Ellie and Leia

When My Beautiful
Grandchildren Were Born,
I Thanked The Lord Above.
I Asked Him To Stay Close To Them,
Fill Them With Light And Love.
To Always Keep Them Healthy,
With Kindness In Their Heart.
Faith Deep Within Their Soul,
From Which They Will Never Part.
I Asked God To Make Their Burdens,
Only Very Small.
Prayed The Lord, Would Grant Them,
The Most Precious Gifts Of All.
Peace And Contentment,
Their Souls Forever Bless.
Give His Love Unending,
Filling Their Lives With Happiness.
Love From Nana xxx

IN DREAMS

Sitting In My Armchair,
Pondering Over Life.
Thinking Of My Children,
Thinking Of My Beautiful Wife.
My Mind Went Back
To The Day We Met,
Feels Like Only Yesterday.
Sweet Memories That Fill My Heart,
Time Can Never Take Away.
When I Reflect On My Life,
Plus Happy Times Recall.
The Years We Spent Together,
Were The Happiest Days Of All?
When Folk Ask If I Miss Her,
I Say Life's Not Half
As Bad As It Seems,
Whenever I Feel Lonely,
I Just Meet Her In My Dreams.

LOVE

Peacefully You Slumbered,
Tired Eyes Closed In Sleep.
I Feel So Lucky To Have You,
That A Tear Rolled Down My Cheek.
A Smile Was On Your Lovely Face,
Content With What You Had.
 I Hope Our Love Will Last Forever,
Through All The Good And Bad.
You Are My Life My Soul Mate,
My Best Friend You Will Always Be.
I Could Never Thank You Enough,
For Being In Love With Me.

TIME

Time And Tide Wait For No One,
That Is What They Say.
You Can Never Change It,
Once It Has Passed Away.
God Could Not Ask More Of You,
If You Have Done Your Best.
If You Have Helped Others,
You Have Passed His Test.
So Many People,
Just Let Life Pass Them By.
Give Up At The First Hurdle,
Before They Even Try.
So Seek Determination,
You Will Find It If You Look.
Do Not Keep Secrets,
Be Like An Open Book?
Give Out Only Kind Thoughts,
For Thoughts Are Living Things.
Pray To God In Heaven,
Take What This Life Brings.
Time Is So Precious,
Go Along With The Flow.
Remember God Is With You,
More Than You Will Ever Know.

HOPE

Do You Forever Doubt?
Wonder How You'll Cope.
You Will Always Manage,
With A Thing Called Hope.
You Can Easily Find It,
It Lives With Faith,
Deep In Your Heart.
Once You Have Found It,
A New Life Will Begin To Start.
Hope Is A Small Word,
But It Can Mean So Much.
You Cannot See It,
But Often Feel It's Touch.
Hope Can Bring Other Things,
Like Courage Faith And Love.
Maybe You Will Realise,
There Is A God Above.
Once You Have Found It,
Hold On To It So Tight.
Hope Will Fill Your Life With,
Gods Pure Love And Light.

MOTHERS ARE ANGELS

We All Have A Special Angel,
Happy Warm And Bright.
Making You Feel Special?
Filling Your Heart With Light.
Their Words Give You Courage,
They Chase Away All Doubt.
Make You Glad That You're Alive,
Help Sort Your Problems Out.
When You Look Into Their Eyes,
You See Deep Inside Their Soul.
Love And Faith You Find There,
To Spread Happiness Is Their Goal.
It Is Not Just A Lucky Few,
Who Have Someone Who Cares Like This?
Each Has A Special Angel,
So Thank You're Dear Mother With a Kiss.

HARD TO UNDERSTAND

Sometimes It's Hard To Understand,
The Meaning Of Gods Ways.
Why He Takes The Ones We Love,
Shattering Our Happiest Days.
We Try And Find A Reason,
Why Bitter Tears Must Fall.
Feel We Are Left With Nothing,
Where Once We Had It All.
That Is Where Faith Comes In,
If We Would Just Believe.
Our Loved Ones Are Still With Us,
All Fears And Doubts Would Leave.
They Are Free And Happy Now,
God Has Eased All Hurt And Pain.
You Can Be So Certain,
One Day You Will Meet Again.

TELL HIM NOW

I Lost My Soul Mate,
I Loved Him Like No Other.
He Was My Life's Companion,
My Best Friend And My Lover.
The Day That We Met,
My Dreams All Came True.
A Lifetime Together,
Best Years I Ever Knew.
God Broke My Happy Bubble,
When He Took My Love One Day.
But Could Not Take My Memories,
They Will Never Go Away.
Make Each Moment Special,
Tell Him How Much You Care.
You Never Know The Heartache,
Until He Is No Longer There.

LAST NIGHTS DREAM

I Had A Dream Last Night,
I Was In Your Arms Again.
My Heart Felt So Happy,
Free From Hurt And Pain.
So Content Together,
As If Never Been Apart.
Said You Missed Me So Much,
Loved Me With All Your Heart.
Would Wait For Me In Heaven,
Know You Were Never Gone.
To Live A Life That's Full,
Ask For Strength To Carry On.
If I Started Doubting,
To Pray To God Above.
He Will Never Leave Me,
I Am Circled By His Love.
I Do Believe That God Is There,
Forever By My Side.
Though I May Falter Sometimes,
His Love Is Still My Guide.
When I Awoke This Morning,
My Heart Could Feel No Pain.
Because You My Love Are With Me,
I Will Never Doubt Again.

WINNING COMBINATION

We Ask The Same Questions,
From Days When Very Small.
Sometimes Live A Lifetime,
The Answers Still Elude Us All.
Some Lucky People,
Know Just Where To Start.
They Feel The Solution,
Is Somewhere In Their Heart.
Faith And Hope Live In There,
Grows Just From A Seed.
With Plenty Of Kindness To Flourish,
Giving All You Will Ever Need.
With These Come Close Companions,
Courage, Strength And Love.
Following On Later, There Comes
          Peace,
A Gift From God Above.
With This Winning Combination,
Life's Puzzles You'll Finally Workout.
Realise What's Important,
Find Out What Life's About.
Do Not Seek Fools Gold,
Have No Room For Envy, Or Greed.
Faith And Hope, Bring Contentment,
You Will Be Very Rich Indeed.

TWILIGHT

I Long For The Night Time,
For I Meet You In My Dreams.
When I Am Safe In Your Arms,
Life's Not Half As Bad As It Seems.
We Shared So Much Together,
Now I Am Completely Alone.
Feeling So Sad And Lonely,
Since God Took You To His Home.
I Know He Has His Reasons,
I Try To Accept What Is Meant To Be.
So I Welcome In The Twilight Hours,
For In My Dreams,
You Are There With Me.

DESTINY

Do You Believe In Destiny?
A Friend Asked Me One Day.
Is Our Life Mapped Out For Us?
Will It Happen Come What May?
I Said I Was No Expert,
God Gave Us All Free Will.
We Can Sit And Wait Of Fate,
Or All Our Dreams Fulfil.
We Can Sit And Suffer In Silence,
Or Finally Find The Voice.
Challenge The Hardship This Life Brings,
We Alone Must Make That Choice.
We Can Turn Our Backs And Run From It,
Or Face It Head On, It's Up To You.
Waste This Chance God Gave To Us,
Or Make Our Dreams Come True.

YOUR OWN ANGEL

Everyone Has An Angel,
Who Is With Us From Our Birth.
Helping As We Travel,
On Our Journey Here On Earth.
They Come To Protect Us,
Make Us Strong, When Feeling Weak.
Guide Us To The Right Path,
If God We Wish To Seek.
We Very Rarely See Them,
Maybe Sense When They Are There.
We Never Should Be Lonely,
They Are With Us Everywhere.
They Cheer With Us In Good Times,
Wipe Away Tears When We Weep.
Ease Us Through Our Sorrows,
Soothe Us When We Sleep.
If Life Gets Too Much For You,
Sometimes Hard To Bear.
Ask The Angels To Give You Strength,
Remember They Are Always There.

NEVER FORGET

No Dawn Breaks, Sun Sets,
Without Sweet Thoughts Of You.
Words Of Love You Whispered,
Kind Things You Used To Do.
Nothing Was Too Much Trouble,
Treat Me Like A Queen.
Put Me On A Pedestal,
Fulfilled My Every Dream.
Very Much To My Regret,
The Lord Took You Away.
Nothing Can Console Me,
I Miss You More Each Day.
I Will Not Find Another Like You,
Someone So Kind So Good.
I Never Bother Looking,
For I Know, I Never Would.
The Next Time We Meet,
Will Be At Heavens Door.
Greeting Me With Open Arms,
Together For Evermore.

HAVE PATIENCE

God Answers All Our Prayers,
Maybe Not Straight Away.
Some Take Years To Reply To,
Others Just A Day.
God Has His Reasons,
Patience We May Need To Learn.
If You Expect To Always Get,
Giving Nothing In Return.
Sometimes He Gives Us
High Mountains To Climb,
Making Life's Journey Tough.
But Never Gives Us
More Than We Can Bear,
Knows When We Have Had Enough.
So Do The Best You Can,
Let God Help With The Rest.
He Will Be So Proud Of You,
If You Have Passed His Test.
When Your Life Is Over,
And To Heaven You Succeed.
God Will Shake You By The Hand,
Saying You Have Done Very Well Indeed.

CHEER UP

There Is No One In This World,
Who Does Not Have A Care.
Millions Of People Have Burdens,
Problems They Would Like To Share.
Many Hide Their Worries,
Behind A Smiling Face.
Concealing Tears In Their Heart,
Where No Human Eye Can Trace.
Sit Down And Write A Letter,
Go On The Telephone.
Speak To A Friend, Who Is Lonely,
Living On Their Own.
Maybe Just A Few Words,
Will Brighten Up Their Day,
A Little Bit Of Laughter,
Might Chase Their Cares Away.
You Might Enjoy It So Much,
You Don't Want This Chat To End.
It Gives You So Much Pleasure,
That You Phone Another Friend.
Try To Make Folk Happy,
I Am Sure That If You Do.
One Day When You Are Lonely,
They May Phone And Cheer You Too.

SO LUCKY

I Am So Lucky,
With This Life, I've Got,
Never Had Much Money,
But I Have Such A Lot.
Love And Contentment,
Plus Faith In My Heart,
God And I Have An Agreement,
That We Will Never Part.
A Partner Who Truly Loves Me,
A Beautiful Family Too.
Life Has Been So Good To Me,
How Has It Been For You?
I Was Not Always Like This,
Stress Had Taken its Toil.
Could Not Find My Way,
Life Was As Black As Coal.
I Was All For Giving Up,
God Heard My Desperate Plea.
Sent His Angels To Help,
Who Took Good Care Of Me.
If You Feel Like I Did,
Please Do As I Say.
Ask God To Send His Angels,
To Chase All Your Cares Away

GIVE IT AWAY

Can't Take Money With You,
That's What Folk Say.
Have You Too Much To Spend?
Why Not Give It Away.
So Many People Lacking,
In Shelter Food And Drink.
So Many Children Homeless,
Does That Not Make You Think?
If You Could Save Just One Child's Life,
By Offering, What You Can.
You Would Feel Much Better,
Making You A Finer Man.
When Work On Earth Is Over,
And You Knock On Heavens Door,
The Lord Will Gladly Bid You Enter,
To Live With Him For Evermore

GOD IS ON YOUR SIDE

The Sky's The Limit,
If God Is Your Guide.
There Is Nothing You Can't Do,
If He Is On Your Side.
Climb Life's Highest Mountains,
Sail Life's Roughest Sea.
Cross Over Barren Deserts,
Making All Your Doubting Flee.
Your Spirit Will Soar Like An Eagle,
Up In A Clear Blue Sky.
Nothing Will Defeat You,
Open Your Heart And Try.
Ask God To Be Your Helper,
Do It Without Delay,
With God Forever On Your Side,
All Fears Will Soon Melt Away.

BEST WONDER OF ALL

I Sat In My Garden Of Flowers,
One Warm Summer's Night.
Gentle Breezes Were Blowing,
In The Suns Last Rays Of Light.
Their Petals Slowly Closing,
Just Earlier They Were In Full Bloom.
Though Soundly Sleeping,
I Could Still Smell Their Sweet Perfume.
Birds Settled In Their Nests,
Tired From Their Long Day.
Not Long After The Sun Set,
The Moon Came Out To Play.
Twinkling Stars Appeared,
Stretched Far Across The Milky Way,
Trying To Outshine Each Other,
Chasing The Last Remnants Of Day.
Who Doubts When They See All This,
That God Is Really There.
You Can Feel Him In All Nature,
Sense Him Everywhere.
Only God Could Create This Wonderful World,
I Thought As I Went To Bed.
The Best Wonder Of All He Gave To Me,
As I Tenderly Kissed My Childs Sleepy Head.

SMELL THE FLOWERS

Take Time To Pause,
And Smell The Flowers.
Often Plans God Makes For Us,
Sometimes Are Not Ours.
We Cannot Halt The Hands Of Time,
Or Live Again The Past.
We Very Seldom Notice,
The Years Are Passing Fast.
Stop Your Frantic Rushing,
Think What Life's About.
Breathe In Deeply Just Relax,
Get Yourself Sorted Out.
Life Is What You Make It,
It's Your Choice How You Live,
      Not Ours.
Life Can Be So Wonderful,
If You Just Take Time,
To Smell The Flowers.

BE HAPPY

Are You Feeling Happy?
Is Your Life Worthwhile.
Does Your Heart Lift Up,
When You See A Baby Smile.
Do You See Flowers Blooming,
Hear Songbirds Sing.
See The Climate Changing,
From Winter Into Spring.
Do You Stand In Awe,
At The Beauty Of It All.
Does Life Still Give You Pleasure,
Even When Teardrops Fall.
Does Loving Friends And Family,
Stand By You Come What May.
Do You Know That Sunshine,
Always Follows A Rainy Day.
Have You Found The Answer?
If So You Have Been Blessed.
Nothing More Is Needed,
For You Truly Have Happiness.

TREASURES FOR LIFE

Have You Priceless Treasures?
You Guard With Your Life.
Is This Prize Your Children?
Also, You're Beautiful Wife.
Now You Have A Family,
Treat Them With Special Care.
Teach Them Love And Kindness,
Make Them Glad You're There.
Tell Them That You Love Them,
That God Loves Them Too.
I Am Sure That If You Do This,
Love Will Rebound Back To You.
Thank The Dear Lord Often,
For The Life That You Possess.
If You Love And Care For Others,
God Will Bless Your Life
With Happiness.

IN MY HEART

Loving You Was Easy,
A Heart As Good As Gold.
I Thought We Would Stay Together,
Until We, Both Grew Old.
We Planned For Our Future,
Though God's Plans Were Not Ours.
Now I Wander To Your Resting Place,
Giving To You Your Favourite Flowers.
All I Have Left Are Memories,
Since We Had To Part.
God Has You In His Keeping,
I Have You In My Heart.

SMELL THE ROSE

God Is Forever With You,
Perhaps You Don't Agree.
Do You Ever Hear Birds Song,
See A Blossoming Tree.
Is Your Heart Firmly Locked,
Eyes So Tightly Closed.
You Don't Hear Children Laughing,
Feel The Sun Or Smell The Rose.
Rushing Back And Forwards,
These Simple Pleasures Pass You By.
Beauty Is In The Eye Of The Beholder,
You Can See Them If You Try.
God Is Always With You,
In Life's Highs And Lows.
Open Up Your Heart To Him,
Then You Too, Will Smell The Rose.

CLOUDS WILL LIFT

It Seems A Lifetime,
Since We Had To Part.
Leaving Lots Of Tears,
Plus A Broken Heart.
Every Day Is Lonely,
Every Day I'm Blue.
Every Moment Of My Life,
Longing Just For You.
Joy Does Not Come Easy,
No One Sees Me Weep.
I Cry Into My Pillow,
When The World Is Fast Asleep.
Clouds I Hope Will Lift From Me,
My Heart Will Be Free From Pain.
Hoping Time Will Come Around,
When I Am Safe In You're Arms,
Once Again.

THE JOURNEY

My Loves Gone On A Journey,
Where Everyone Must Go.
He Was My Life And Soul Mate,
But One Thing I'm Certain I Know.
That He Is So Happy,
Now He Is Free From Pain.
Although I Miss Him So Much,
I Don't Wish Him Back To Suffer Again.
Love Does Go On Forever,
It Can Never Die.
One Day I Will Make That Journey,
Never Again To Say Goodbye.

A LIFE SO SPECIAL

Tears Fall Like Raindrops,
As Past Years, I Tenderly Recall.
Those Years We Spent Together,
Were The Happiest Times Of All.
We Built A Life So Special,
A Loving Family Raise.
But God Took You From Me,
Shattering My Happiest Days.
I Am So Very Grateful,
But I'm Sure We Will Meet Again.
God Was Only Being Kind,
When He Ended All Your Pain.
Now You Are In His Heaven,
An Angel You Surely Must Be.
While You Lived Upon This Earth,
You Were A Beautiful Angel To Me.
So Stay Close To Me My Dear One,
Wipe The Teardrops That Still Fall.
Few Have Had A Love So Precious,
Once We Had It All.

YOU'RE NOT GONE

Memories Keep Me So Close To You,
I Think Of All You Said To Me,
The Things You Would Always Do.
I Know I Was So Lucky,
To Find A Love Like This.
Now All I Have Are Memories,
But Sweet Memories Are Bliss.
Night Time When All Is Silent,
I Seem To Feel You There.
Just Like Before You Left Me,
Sat In Your Favourite Chair.
Sometimes When I Go To Bed,
I Sense That You Are Near.
Softly Cradled In Your Arms,
Soothing My Every Fear.
When I Awake On Morning,
I Know You Are Not Gone.
And In My Weakest Moments,
I Feel You Urge Me On.
One Day We Will Be Together,
Just Like, We Were Before.
Wrapped Safely In Your Arms,
Weeping For You No More.

WISHES

Since Losing You My Angel,
Millions Of Teardrops Fall.
You Were Everything To Me,
My Love, My Life, My All.
If God Could Grant Me One Wish,
A Dream That Could Come True.
I Would Pray With All My Heart,
For Yesterday And You.
I Would Climb The Highest Mountain,
Cross The Roughest Sea.
Walk All The Way To Heaven,
To Bring You Home With Me.
But This Miracle Could Never Happen,
For God He Loves You Too.
I Know When I Reach His Heaven,
My Wishes Will All Come True.

MEET AGAIN

God Came In A Dream
Said "I Know You're Oh So Sad."
Your Heart Is Truly Broken,
Now You Have Lost
The True Love That You Had.
I Want To Tell You He Is Happy,
Freed From All Hurt And Pain.
Living With Angels And Loved Ones,
Until You, Are United In Heaven
Once Again.

IMPOSSIBLE DREAM

Do You Dream The Impossible?
Or A Sheep That Has To Be Led.
Do You Look Forward To Each New Day?
Or Content To Stay In Bed.
Have You Worries That Bother You?
And Just Cannot Make Go Away.
Open You're Heart, Ask The Lord,
Go Down On Your Knees And Pray.
God Will Always Help You,
In Ways, That He Thinks Best.
He May Not Answer Right Away,
Faith Sometimes He Will Test.
Your Doubts Will Evaporate,
From All Mortal Bonds Set Free.
With God Forever On Your Side,
All Fears From You Will Flee.
Do You Creep Through Life,
God Can Make You Fly.
You Can Reach Life's Impossible Dream.
Don't Let This Chance Slip By.

NEVER PART

My Eyes Are Forever Weeping,
Since God Took You Away.
My Broken Heart Yearns For You,
Every Single Day.
Mornings When I Wake Up,
Thoughts Go Straight To You.
Kind Words You Used To Say
Special Things You Used To Do.
You Were My Lifetime Partner,
Best Friend I Have Ever Known.
Life Is So Lonely Without You,
Since Left On This Earth All Alone.
Your Memory Is Here With Me,
And You Still Have My Heart.
When They Are Both United Again,
We Will Never Be Apart.

ANGELS GATHER

Angels Gather Around You,
When In Deep Despair.
Wings Gently Enfolding,
You Sense Them In The Air.
If Weak, You They Will Carry,
Until Strength Is Yours Again.
Do Their Best To Comfort You,
Pour Balm Upon Your Pain.
Giving Hope In Your Heart,
Faith Deep Inside Your Soul.
Angels Will Never Leave You,
Until You Are In Control.
Angels Are Not Only Beautiful,
But Full Of Goodness Too.
Trying Their Best To Instil,
Gods Love Inside Of You.

SILVER LININGS

Storms Always Have Silver Linings,
Open Your Eyes And See.
If You're Soul Feels Trapped,
The Good Lord Can Set It Free.
Do Dark Clouds Often Surround You,
See Nothing But Turmoil Ahead.
Do Not Try To Fight It,
Think What The Good Book Said,
Peace That Passes All Understanding,
God Can Bestow On You.
Believe And He Will Help,
Have Faith That Dreams Can Come True.
    "Oh Just Think"
To Have Peace And Contentment,
Both Are Riches Indeed.
Add A Little Luck To These,
Then You Will Have All
You Will Ever Need.

SAY YES

Stuck Between A Rock
And A Hard Place,
Which Way Can I Go?
Should I Say Yes To God?
Or Should I Say No?
Do I Ask Him For Help?
Or Should I Stay Lost?
Keeping My Foolish Pride,
No Matter What The Cost.
I Heard A Voice Say Clearly,
Do Not Let Pride Get In The Way.
God Will Guide You Safely,
You Only Have To Pray.
No Need To Be Saints Or Martyrs,
For God To Listen In.
He Helps All Who Ask Him,
If You Only Have Faith Within.
God Will Give You Confidence,
Show You The Way To Go.
Open Up Your Heart To Him,
Just Go Along With The Flow.

LET HIM IN

You Know It Is Wrong,
But You Do It Just The Same.
Do You Have No Conscience,
Think Life Is Just A Game.
Do You Not Care Who You Hurt,
As Long As You're Alright.
Think The World Owes You A Living,
Always Ready For A Fight.
If You Feel Like This,
Open Up Your Heart.
Ask God To Help,
Make A Brand New Start.
It Will Not Be Easy,
Let God Shine His Light Within.
Your Life Can Change In A Moment,
If You Only Let Him In.

MY BROTHER

My Brother Was A Brave Man,
A Hero Through And Through.
He Did Not Have Much Money,
But Would Give His Last To You.
He Was A Special Person,
All Who Knew Him Felt The Same,
Faced The End With Courage,
Battled Bravely Through His Pain.
His Family Were His Treasures,
Worked His Fingers To The Bone.
Never Heard Him Grumble,
Never Once Heard Him Moan.
Life To Him Was Precious,
Made The Most Of Every Day.
Right Up To The Last Moment,
When The Lord Took Him Away.
My Brother Was Small In Stature,
But Massive Was His Heart.
Though Living With Angels Now,
We Will Never Be Far Apart.
He Left Behind A Loving Family,
Plus A Beautiful Memory.
Not Only My Big Brother,
But The Dearest Friend To Me.

LETTER TO GOD

Dear God My Mother Was Special!
I Am Sure You Thought So Too.
You Gently Hushed Her Heart To Sleep,
So She Could Go To Heaven With You.
I Pray That She Is Happy,
Since You Have Eased Her Pain.
Living With The Angels,
Until We Are United Once Again.
I Try To Do The Best I Can,
Accept What Is Meant To Be.
Treat Folk With Love And Respect,
The Way That She Taught Me.
Thank My Dear Mother For Me Lord,
From The Rest Of Her Family Too.
Bestow On Her Special Care,
Now She Is In Paradise With You.
She Helped Us More Than We Deserved,
Filled Our Lives With Happiness.
Till We Meet Again In Heaven,
I Will Just End This Letter By Saying
   God Bless.

LIFE'S SECRET

I Sat And Drank A Coffee, At A Café In Town One Day.
I Looked At All The Faces, Of Folk Who Passed My Way.
Some Relaxed And Smiling, Others Very Sad.
Carrying Heavy Burdens, With Problems That They Had.
An Old Lady Sat Next To Me, As I Glanced Up, I Could See.
Her Body Looked So Feeble; But Her Eyes Were Aglow With Glee.
She Said She Was So Happy, Fortunate For The Life She Had.
Lived Many Blissful Years Contently, With Just A Hint Of Bad.
When I Asked Her Secret, She Just Start To Laugh.
Said That Many Years Ago, Prayed God Would Guide Her Path.
Life Was Not Ideal Or Perfect, Had Its Highs And Lows.
But Knows God Is With Her, Everywhere She Goes.
The Best Advice She Said, I Can Give To You.
Open Up Your Heart To God, He Will Help You Through.
Be Grateful For The Life You Have, Plus All That You Possess.
Ask God For Contentment, And Then You'll Find Happiness.
I Thanked That Dear Old Lady, As I Walked Away.
Decided I Would Change My Life, From That Very Day.
As I Turned To Wave To Her, She Was No Longer There.
Did God Send Me An Angel? So Life's Secrets I Could Share!

BAD DREAMS

Loving You Was Easy,
I Did It Every Day.
The Hardest Part About It,
Was When You Went Away.
I Think I Must Be Dreaming,
Cannot Believe Its True.
That I Can Go On Living,
When No Longer I Have You.
My Days Are Dull And Dreary,
Nights Are Lonely Too.
Life To Me Is Empty,
Its Nothing Without You.
Lord Wake Me From This Nightmare,
Please End This Bitter Pain.
Send My Love From Heaven,
So I'll Never Have Bad Dreams Again.

MESSAGE FROM MY HEART

Absence Makes The Heart Grow Fonder,
That Is What Folk Say.
I Know Its So True,
I Miss You More Each Day.
From Dawn Breaking At Morning,
To The Setting Of The Sun.
My Thoughts Will Be
With You Forever,
Until My Life Is Done.
I Was So Lucky To Have You,
Making My Every Dream Come True.
A Love That Will Last A Lifetime,
Your Memory Will Get Me Through.
Come Close To Me My Dear One,
Each Time I Reminisce.
Till We Meet Again In Heaven,
I Will End This Message With A Kiss.
         X

TRUE WORD

Many A True Word Is Said In A Joke,
Most Folk Will Agree With Me.
We Don't Think, And Go For Broke,
We Just Can't Let Things Be.
Maybe We Say Words
We Cannot Take Back,
Jumping In At The Deep End.
Ignorant Of How Others Are Feeling,
Our Actions Might Lose Us a Dear Friend.
Stop Awhile And Ponder,
Treat Folk With Love And Respect.
Don't Put Your Foot In It,
Think How Your Words Will Effect.
Count To Ten Before Being Unkind,
Hold Onto Your Tongue Don't Bite.
Take A Deep Breath, Pause And Smile,
Even Though You Know, You Are Right.
Don't Think If You Do This, You Are Weak,
Carry On With Your Life's Plan.
If You Can Turn The Other Cheek,
The Boy Will Have Finally
Grown Into A Man.

HAPPY BIRTHDAY

Today Is Your Birthday,
Dearest Pal Of Mine.
We Might Celebrate This Special Day,
With A Few Bottles Of Sparkling Wine.
We May Get So Tipsy,
That We Will Not Have A Care.
Meet Someone Down The Town,
Perhaps A Millionaire.
If Not That Lucky,
We Will Have A Song And Dance.
Making The Most Of Your Birthday,
As If, It Was Our Last Chance.
Years May Come And Years May Go,
One Day It All Will End.
So I Want You To Know
On This Special Day,
You Will Always Be My Best Friend.
      CHEERS

A MILLION STARS

Millions Of Stars Were Out Last Night,
But Thoughts Were Just Of You.
The Moon Tried It's Best To Cheer Me,
My Poor Heart Stayed Sad And Blue.
Eyes That Could Not See The Wonder,
The Beauty Of It All.
So Busy Weeping,
Sore From Teardrops That Still Fall.
If God Could Grant A Miracle,
Let Me Hold You Once Again.
Just To Be In Your Loving Arms,
Would Take Away This Pain.
The Stars Would Then All Twinkle,
Like They Have Never Done Before,
The Man In The Moon
Will Be Laughing Too,
When I Am Safe
In You're Arms Once More.

JEALOUSY

Some Folk Are So Envious,
Take All And Do Not Give.
Want More Of Their Share
Of Everything,
Can't Just Live And Let Live.
Why Are They So Jealous?
So Green With Envy Because You Try.
Think The World Owes Them A Living,
Golden Chances Passing Them By.
Begrudging Your Good Fortune,
Don't They Realise Life's Only On Loan.
Few Get A Second Chance,
There's No Time To Moan And Groan.
Treat Folk, As You Want To Be Treated,
This I've Often Found.
If You Treat Others Badly,
What Goes Around,
Will Come Back Around.

HEAVENS GATE

Mornings When I Wake Up,
My Thoughts Are All Of You.
I Often Have To Pinch Myself,
To Realise That It's True.
You Are No Longer Here With Me,
I Can't Believe You're Gone.
I Try And Face Up To It,
But Heartaches Linger On.
Our Lives We Shared Together,
My Sweetheart, My Best Friend.
Never For A Moment,
Did I Think It So Soon Would End.
God Took You From Me,
Spoilt Our Happiest Days.
Leaving Me To Ponder,
On His Mysterious Ways.
He Must Have His Reasons,
Why We Had To Part.
Shattering My Life's Dreams,
Breaking My Poor Heart.
I Am Sure We Will Meet Again,
Until Then I Will Have To Wait.
Hoping To Find The Answer,
When Next We Meet At Heavens Gate.

THE GIFT

A Lot Has Happened My Darling,
Since You Went Away.
Special Things You Would Have Loved,
If God Had Let You Stay.
Dreams We Shared Together,
I Now Do On My Own.
Trying To Make You Proud Of Me,
As I Bring Up Our Children Alone.
You Left A Firm Foundation,
For The Ones You Loved So Much.
I Miss Your Love Around Me,
Long For Your Tender Touch.
Folk Say It Is Better To Have Loved And Lost,
Then Never To Have Loved At All.
But Do They Know A Heart Can Break?
When A Million Teardrops Fall.
I Know I Will Not Be Lonely,
The Best Thing You Did For Me.
Was Give Me A Gift So Precious,
A Beautiful Family.

FIFTY GOLDEN YEARS

Fifty Years Since Your Wedding Day,
How Quickly Time Has Flown.
You Are The Nicest Couple,
That I Have Ever Known.
Everyone Has Bad Times,
Each One Knows Worry And Pain.
Every Time Life Knocked You Down.
You Sprang On Your Feet Again.
You've Had So Many Good Years,
With A Little Bit Of Bad.
Many Happy Times Together,
With Just a, Trace Of Sad.
God Has Been On Your Side,
This I Know For Sure.
Always There In Good Times,
The Bad Spells Helped You Endure.
Wishing You Many More Years Together,
May All Your Dreams Fulfil?
Wishing You Both,
Health, Wealth And Contentment.
Hoping Gods Love Surrounds You Now
And Always Will.

SIMPLY THE BEST

I Love You Dear Mother,
I Miss You So.
My Heart Was Broken
When You Had To Go.
A Better Friend I Never Knew,
If I Was Happy, Then So Were You.
You Lifted Me Up When I Felt Down,
Made Me Laugh When I Wore A Frown.
Shared My Joys, My Worry's Too,
A Mother In A Million That Was You.
God Bless You Dear Mother,
You've Earned Your Rest.
For When On This Earth,
You Were Simply The Best.

OUR TENTH ANNIVERSARY

Our Wedding Anniversary,
A Special Time For Me And You.
Is It Really Ten Years,
Since We Said "I Do"
Ten Years Of Love And Laughter,
With Just A Spray Of Tears.
Many Happy Moments,
Sprinkled With A Few Doubts And Fears.
I Hope God Will Be Kind To Us,
As In The Years Before.
Love And Cherish Both Of Us,
Now And Forever More.

RICH INDEED

If God Could Grant One Wish,
I Wonder What It Would Be.
Would You Ask For Riches,
Or To Win The Lottery.
Perhaps You Won't Be Greedy,
Just A Bit Of Cash To Spare.
Maybe Go The Whole Hog,
Ask To Be A Millionaire.
Those Who Are The Wisest,
Who Know What Life's About,
They Ask For Contentment,
Finally Working It Out.
It's Not How Much Wealth You Have,
But What's In Your Heart And Soul.
The World Could Be Your Oyster,
If God Is In Control.
It's In Your Power To Have It All,
Everything You Need.
If God Is On Your Side,
You Will Be Very Rich Indeed.

A PRAYER FOR HEALTH

Dear God In Heaven, If You Are There?
Please Help Me With This Cross-I Bear.
Stay Near To Me Until I'm Well Again.
Ease Me Through All Hurt And Pain,
Give Me Hope And Courage Too,
Give Back The Health That I Once Knew.
Most Of All Keep My Faith Strong,
Give Me Strength To Carry On.
So Dear Lord, Hear My Prayer,
Keep Me Always
In Thy Loving Care.
  Amen.

DREAMS WILL COME TRUE

Treat Life As A Treasure,
Cosset It With Care.
Even If Funds Are Low,
Know You're A Millionaire.
Can You Hear Birds Sing?
Watch Beautiful Flowers Grow.
Have Dear Friends Around You?
A Family Who Love You So.
Do You Have Hope In Your Heart?
Faith Deep Inside Your Soul.
Take What Life Throws At You,
Are You Are In Control?
If You Have These Things,
Hold Your Head Up High.
Live For Every Moment,
Never Let A Chance Slip By.
Help Where It Is Needed,
Aid Those Worse Off Than You.
Fill Your Life With Gods Love,
Then Every Dream You Have
Will Come True.

IF ONLY

There Are Two Words,
We All Know,
That Are The Saddest Words Of All.
They Often Come With Regret,
When Bitter Teardrops Fall.
They Also Come With Heartache,
When Dreams Collapse
And Troubles Call.
I Truly Believe" If Only"
Are The Saddest Words Of All

ANGEL IN BLUEBELLS

You Did Not Want Pearls,
Or Expensive Perfume.
You Loved Simple Pleasures,
Like Bluebells In Bloom.
Since You Have Been Gone,
I Miss You So Much.
I Long For Your Love,
Yearn For Your Special Touch.
If I Was Happy, You Were Too.
Nothing Was Too Much Bother For You.
Our Children Were Your Jewels,
You Did Not Need Gold.
Just A Family That Loved You,
To Have And To Hold.
When I Go To Heaven,
Be It Late Or Soon.
I Will Look For An Angel,
Among Bluebells In Bloom.

STAIRWAY TO HEAVEN

You Have Climbed The Stairway To Heaven,
An Honour That Was Your Due.
I Hope One Day To Follow,
On Those Golden Steps
That Me Lead To You.
You Are Living With The Angels,
At Peace And In Gods Glow.
I Believe You Are Happy Now,
But Still Miss You More
Than You Could Know.
So God Bless You My Dear One,
Be At Peace And Free From Pain.
Wait For Me In Paradise,
Until We Meet Once Again.

IF

Busy Bees Were Buzzing,
Sun Was Shining Bright.
God Was In His Heaven,
Everything Seemed Right.
Some Part Of Me Was Missing,
A Big Piece Of My Heart.
It's Been So Very Lonely,
Since We Had To Part.
If God Would Grant A Miracle,
Hear My Heart Felt Plea.
If My Prayers He'd Answer,
You Would Still Be Here With Me.
I Would Still Feel The Suns Glow,
Hear The Buzz Of The Bumble Bee.
I Too, Would Be In Heaven,
If You Were Home
Once Again With Me

YOU'RE CHARKA

Blue Is For Healing,
Bright Yellow Is For Energy.
Green Often Means Balance,
Giving You The Strength
Of An Old Oak Tree.
If Sweet Pink Surrounds You,
Then Loves Not Far From You.
This Colour Though Delicate,
Means A Love So Strong And True.
Vibrant Orange, Like Its Neighbour Red,
Bestows On You Vitality.
Maybe Your Life's Force Is Sapping!
Colours Give Power To You And Me.
The Last Two Shades In Our Charka,
Almost Mean The Same.
From Light Lavender, To Dark Purple,
Opening Spiritual Pathways Is Their Aim.
Letting Us Know That Gods Love,
Is Always Around.
If Colours Of Mixed Purples Surround You,
You Are Very Special I Have Found.
You Are Lucky If You Can See These Auras,
Means Your Third Eye Is Opening Wide.
Like A Flower, You're Spirit Will Flourish,
With God Forever By Your Side.

KIM DEAREST PAL OF MINE

I've Lost A Special Pal Of Mine,
The Best Friend I Have Known.
No One Knows The Heartache,
As I Go On Walks Alone.
Her Little Tail Will Wag No More,
While Waiting At The Gate.
No Cheerful Bark Or Greeting,
When I Get Home Quite Late.
Sometimes I Think I See Her,
Walking Aside Of Me.
But It Is Only Wishful Thinking,
I Know It Can Never Be.
I Thought She Would Stay Forever,
But Years Had Taken Their Toil.
I Tried My Best To Help Her,
Asked God To Make Her Whole.
Too Soon Her Life Was Ended,
God Hushed Her Heart To Sleep.
I So Miss That Dearest Pal Of Mine,
But Sweet Memories I Will Always Keep.
Farewell My Faithful Companion,
Until One Day, We Meet Again.
Hoping We Will Walk Together,
Down Heavens Leafy Lane.
I Pray That You Are Happy Now,
Running In Heavens Fields Above.
God -Bless You My Dearest Pal Of Mine,
Go With All My Love.
     Xxx

IT WILL TAKE FOREVER

I Loved Our Lives Together,
Never Wanting This Time To End.
But God Took You From Me,
My Partner My Best Friend.
Days Are Long And Dreary,
Nights Are Lonely Too.
I Never Will Recover,
From The Hurt Of Losing You.
If God Could Grant A Miracle,
Turn Back The Hands Of Time.
A Second Chance With You Again,
Would Heal This Heart Of Mine.
More Special Years Together.
More Time To Show I Care.
Another Lifetime Together,
Just Knowing You Are There.
My Empty Arms Long For You,
Since The Sad Day We Had To Part.
It Will Take Forever, My Love,
To Mend My Broken Heart.

GOLDEN MEMORIES

I Have A Bunch Of Memories,
Tied With A Deep Red Bow.
How Much It Meant To Lose You,
Know One Will Ever Know.
Special Golden Memories,
Of A Love So Warm So True.
I Only Have To Pick One Out,
To Recall The Joy We Knew.
The Many Years I Spent With You,
Are The Best I Have Ever Known?
Love We Shared Between Us,
Are Mine And Mine Alone.
These Are My Sacred Treasures,
I Am So Lucky To Possess.
Memories Wrapped In Love,
Bound Together With Happiness.

MY SON

My Dear Son I Miss You So,
It Broke My Heart
When You Had To Go.
I Do Not Show The Pain I Feel,
With You Not Here Life Is Unreal.
There Is A Space Inside Of Me,
A Gap In My Heart,
Where You Used To Be.
I Long To See Your Dear Sweet Face.
To Kiss You're Cheek,
You're Warm Embrace.
Five More Minutes Or Two Will Do.
Just To Say How I Miss You.
If I Could Hold You Once Again,
Would Free Me From This Hurt And Pain.
Just Enough Time To Whisper Low,
Goodbye, My Son I Love You So.
Please Dear God Hear My Prayer,
Keep Him In Thy Loving Care.
Love Forever +Always.

I'VE BEEN THERE

I Know That You Are Suffering!
For I Have Been There Too.
In Fact, I Have Worn The Tee -Shirt,
Know The Hell You Are Going Through.
Ask God To Help You?
Please Just Call His Name!
He Will Aid And Guide You,
Easing Your Hurt And Pain.
Feel Life's Fire Is Just An Ember?
But The Smallest Spark,
Can Become A Flame.
Try To Cast Your Mind Back,
To When Sunshine Always Followed The Rain.
One Day The Clouds Will Disappear,
The Sun Will Come Out Again.
No One Knows What Joy Is,
If They've Never Felt Sorrow Or Pain.
Keep Walking Onward,
Know Friends And Family Really Care,
Believe You Will Recover,
I Am Certain You Will,
For I Have Been There.

GOD VISITED

God Came Down To My Garden,
To Sit Awhile With Me.
He Tried So Hard To Comfort,
Did His Best To Help Me See.
He Had To Take You To Heaven,
As Your Pain Was Hard To Bear.
He Eased All Your Suffering,
Banished Your Every Care.
You Are Now Living With The Angels,
At Last, You're Spirits Free.
You Are Always Near,
Watching Over And Guiding Me.
When My Time On Earth Is Over,
God Will Come And Take Me Too.
Then I Hope To Spend Forever,
In Paradise With You.

ONE WAY

Is Your Heart Breaking?
Feel You Have Had Enough?
When Reaching Rock Bottom,
The Only Way To Go Is Up.
Are Skies Forever Gloomy?
Hope All Dwindled And Gone?
Pray To A God Who Loves You,
He Will Give You Strength To Carry On.
Dark Clouds Have Silver Linings,
Time Will Ease Your Bitter Pain.
The Day Will Soon Come Around,
When The Sun Shines
For You Once Again.

JOURNEYS END

Do You Believe That God Is There?
Helping You With Each Cross-You Bear.
Walking With You, When Life's Road Is Tough,
Carrying You If You Have Had Enough.
Comforts Your Heart When It's In Pain,
Soothes Your Soul Until You're Well Again.
On This Journey We All Must Trod,
You Are So Fortunate If You Believe In God.
He Will Ease Your Hurt And Tears,
The Lord Will Calm All Doubt And Fears,
Just Call His Name When Hope Is Gone,
His Shoulder You Can Lean Upon.
You Will Never Have A Better Friend,
God Will Stay With You
To Your Journeys End.

THE SECRET

Have You Time On Your Hands?
Plus Plenty Of Love To Share,
For This World Needs It Desperately.
Maybe Just A Dime To Spare?
Give What You Have Unselfishly,
To The Ailing, Sick And Poor.
Help The Homeless People,
Think Of The Hardship
Some Children Endure.
Smile To The Folk Who Are Lonely,
It Is So Easy If You Try.
Just a Kind Word Is Needed,
To Those You Usually Pass By.
If You Help When You Are Able,
And Pray For All Mankind.
If You Do This Often,
Very Soon, I Am Sure You Will Find.
Your Heart Will Feel Much Lighter,
Free From All Strain And Stress,
What You Have Given Away.
You Will Never Miss,
It's The Secret To Happiness.

THE VISION

Seeing Is Believing, People Often Say.
I Saw Something Wonderful,
When I Awoke The Other Day.
A Bright And Beautiful Angel,
Stood In Front Of Me.
Her Wings Shone Like The Sunshine,
I Did Not Believe What My Eyes Could See.
As I Began To Focus,
I Felt Overwhelmed With Awe.
With A Smile My Angel Vanished,
My Stunning Vision Was No More.
God Must Have Sent An Angel,
Knowing My Life Was Hard To Bear.
To Let Me Know I Am Not Alone,
That He Is Forever There.

THANK YOU

Now We Have Retired,
I Just Want To Say To You.
Thank You For The Love You Give,
For Your Special Friendship Too.
My Thoughts Go Back So Often,
To The Day We Said "I Do"
You Promised To Make Me Happy,
Your Words Have Proven True.
My Life Has Been So Wonderful,
With Just a Sprinkle Of Tears,
Helping Me Through The Bad Times,
Chasing Away All Doubts And Fears.
I Thank God For My Blessings,
Giving Me A Husband That I Adore.
Hoping That God Will Grant To Us,
Maybe Just A Few Years More.

SO PERFECT

This World Was So Perfect Then,
So Special When You Were In It.
Now That You Have Left Me,
I Miss You Every Single Minute.
The Sound Of Your Laughter!
The Smile On Your Dear Face!
I Miss Your Arms Around Me,
The Touch Of Your Embrace.
You Were My Guiding Light,
An Angel In Heaven, You Surely Must Be.
For While You Lived Upon This Earth,
You Were A Beautiful Angel To Me!
I Thank God For The Life We Had,
Full Of Joy, With Just A Tinge Of Pain,
I Know One Day It Will Be Perfect,
When We Are United Once Again.

TOMORROW

If Tomorrow Never Comes,
Did You Try Your Best?
Have You Done Your Utmost?
To Try To Pass Gods Test.
Did You Give Those You Met In Life,
The Same Respect,
That They Showed You.
Treating All Gods Creatures,
With The Same Love And Caring Too.
We All Have Our Faults,
I Admit That I Have Many.
The Time To Worry Is,
When You Think You Haven't Any.
Open Up Your Heart Today,
Let God Enter In.
You Will Not Regret It,
A New Life Will Begin.
If You Really Mean It
You Will Surely See.
God Will Clear Your Heart,
Of All Doubt And Misery.
Do Not Fret About Tomorrow,
Whether Or Not You
Have Passed Gods Test.
When Reaching The Door Into Heaven,
Just Say, "Lord I Did My Best"

LIKE A JIGSAW

Life Is Like A Jigsaw,
That Slots Into Place.
It Is Not The Winning,
But How You Run The Race.
Would You Cheat Others?
To Prove That You're The Best.
Would You Tell Lies?
To Be Ahead Of All The Rest.
Would You Hurt People?
Who Do No Harm To You.
To Swell You're Ego,
To Make Selfish Dreams Come True.
If You Help Folk,
Who Fall Down In Life's Race.
Pick Them Up Cheerfully,
With A Smile Upon Your Face.
Just Give Out A Kind Word,
As You Go On Your Way.
Why Worry If Overtaken,
You Will Still Get There One Day.
Treat Others With Respect,
With Kindness Too My Friend.
God Will Be There To Thank You,
When You Reach Your Journeys End.

CONGRATULATIONS

Congratulations Is A Word,
I Would Like To Say.
So Glad Your Precious Baby,
Is Really On Its Way.
Welcoming This Little Treasure,
When It Joins Your Family.
A Special First Child
For Its Mother And Father,
To Love For Eternity.
Bestowing On This Little Angel,
All The Love You Have To Give.
Guiding It Through Life's Journey,
For As Long As You All Live.
So I Will Say "Congratulations"
Thanking The Good Lord Too.
For Giving You This Blessing,
Making Your Dreams Come True.

HAND OF FRIENDSHIP

Do You Feel Regret?
As The New Years Drawing Nigh.
Things You Wished You Had Done,
But Were Too Afraid To Try.
Did You Help Your Neighbours Out,
When They Wanted A Friend.
Did Someone Need Your Solace,
Maybe A Prayer You Forgot To Send.
Feel You Should Have Done More?
Now This Year Is At An End.
Maybe You Still Have Time?
A Shoulder To Lean On You Could Lend.
Hold Out Your Hand In Friendship?
Assist When Needed Too.
Make A New Years Resolution,
Help Make Other Peoples,
Wishes Come True

MISSING YOU

My Love How Much I Miss You,
Now That You Are Gone.
I Feel So Lost And Lonely,
How Can I Still Go On?
In Spring When Flowers Are Budding,
Or Summer In Full Bloom.
In Autumn No One To Walk With,
Where Bluebells Cast Their Perfume.
In Winter No Happy Christmas,
The New Year
All Are Making A New Start.
As I Smile And Give Out My Good Wishes,
Trying To Hide My Poor Broken Heart.

ENJOY XMAS

Try To Enjoy This Christmas,
As Though It Was Your Last.
Make The Most Of Every Moment,
As Time Flies By So Fast.
Be Kind To Everybody,
Every Moment Of Your Day.
Help Where It Is Needed,
When Troubles Come Their Way.
Give Out Only Kind Thoughts,
For Thoughts Are Living Things.
Don't Fret About Tomorrow,
Just Take What Each Day Brings.
I Am Sure That If You Do This,
Your Kind Deeds
Will Come Back To You.
Not Only For This Christmas,
But For All Of Next Year Too.

TODAY TOMORROW FOREVER

There's Many Things I Need To Tell You,
Such A Lot I Want You To Know.
Just How Special You Are To Me,
How Much I Love You So.
Pleasures That You Bestow On Me,
Comforting Me When I've Had Enough,
Sharing Troubles Come What May,
Guiding, When The Way Is Rough.
Wiping My Eyes When Sorrow Calls,
There Through Good And Through Bad.
Our Lives Were Filled With Laughter,
With Just a, Hint Of Sad.
You Always Kept Your Promise To Me,
That You Would Leave Me Never.
Hoping We Will Stay Like This My Love,
Today, Tomorrow, Forever.

THANK YOU LORD

You Gave Me So
Many Blessings Lord,
Thank You For Them All.
Always There When Needed,
You Picked Me Up Each Time I'd Fall.
At Times I Did Not Listen,
Sometimes From You I'd Turn.
But You Knew I Was Only Human,
There Was A Lot I Had To Learn.
Now Older And Much Wiser,
I Realise How Much You Care.
No Matter What Life Throws At Me,
I Know You Will Be There.
At Times My Life Is Hectic,
As Through This Busy Life, I Dart.
I Never Will Forget You Lord,
You Are Here Inside My Heart.

GO WITH A KISS

Into Your Hands Oh Lord,
Come The Sick And Weak.
From A Life Of Pain And Suffering,
To A Land Of Perfect Peace.
Reaching The Place All Are Seeking,
After Searching A Lifetime For.
Living In Heavens Sunshine,
With Gods, Love For Evermore.
So Do Not Be Heartbroken,
Though Your Loved One's
You Will Surely Miss.
God Gave His Promise,
You Will Meet Again,
Let Them Go Now With A Kiss.

MY FAMILY BLESS

I Beg You Lord My Family Bless,
Fill Their Lives With Happiness.
Give Them Faith And Courage Too,
Onto The Path That Leads To You.
When Troubles Call As Come, They Will,
Help Them Climb Life's Highest Hill.
Finally, When Having Reached The Top,
Let Them Survive Each Blow And Knock.
Teach Them What Life Is All About,
Keep Them Free From Want And Doubt.
Protect This Family That I Adore,
Please Stay With Them Forever More…

BUTTERFINGERS

I Had Butter Fingers,
I Let You Slip Away.
I Took Your Love For Granted
Every Single Day.
You Often Tried To Warn Me,
But I Walked Away From You.
My Pride Would Not Let Me Beg,
Though I Desperately Wanted To.
Nothing In This Whole Wide World,
Means More To Me Than You.
When I Said I Did Not Care,
My Heart Knew It Was Not True.
I Must Not Waste A Minute,
Time Is Precious I Must Not Wait,
To Beg You To Come Back To Me,
Before It Is Too Late.
Say You Do Forgive Me!
End This Hurt And Pain.
I Promise I Will Never,
Have Butterfingers Ever Again

MY MOTHER'S MAGIC MIXTURE

There Is Light At The End Of A Tunnel,
My Mother Would Often Say.
One Day The Sun Will Come Out,
Chasing The Darkest Clouds Away.
There Is Always A Silver Lining,
Though Your Path Seems Bleak And Rough.
Bad Fortune Won't Last Forever,
Tell God When You Have Had Enough.
Some Folk Say You Make Your Own Luck,
With That, I Do Agree.
Add A Bit Of Faith And Patience,
Never Accept What "Will Be Will Be"
What We Need For This Magical Mixture,
Are Patience, Faith And Love.
Is There Anything I Have Missed Out,
Oh, Yes I Forgot,
Add A Prayer To God Up Above.

FOREVER

Lord My Heart Pleads To You,
Please End This Bitter Pain.
Eyes So Raw From Weeping,
Lips That Will Never Smile Again.
Life Is Not Worth Living,
Since You Took My Love Away,
Skies Are Dark And Gloomy,
Every Single Day.
As I Lay Upon My Pillow,
I Get No Comfort When I Sleep.
Slumber Only Brings Me Nightmares,
No Sweet Dreams To Cherish And Keep.
My Heart Is Broken And Aching,
But One Thing That Nothing Can Sever.
Precious Thoughts I Have Of My Loved One,
Memories That Will Comfort
And Stay Forever.

WHEREVER YOU ARE

At Night When All Is Silent,
My Eyes Fill Up With Tears.
Thoughts So Often Wander,
To The Joyous, Happy Years.
I Have So Many Golden Memories,
Of a, Love So Warm And True.
But I Did Not Want Just Memories,
I Only Wanted You.
I Will Do All You Asked Of Me,
Before We Had To Part.
But It Is Hard To Keep Your Chin Up,
When You Have A Broken Heart.
So Stay Close To Me My Dear One,
Give Me Strength When Teardrops Fall.
I Know I Was So Lucky,
Once I Had It All.
God Will Keep His Promise,
We Will Surely Meet Again.
One Day On Heavens Pathway,
You Will Hear Me Call Your Name.
When Life Gets Too Much For Me,
And I Wonder If You're Near Or Far.
I Seem To Hear You Whisper,
I Am Wherever You Are.

THE LONG ROAD

Body Sore And Weary,
As I Crept Into Bed Last Night.
I Tossed And Turned For Hours,
My Bedroom Filled Up With Light.
A Beautiful Glowing Angel,
Appeared In Front Of Me.
I Thought I Must Be Dreaming,
But My Eyes Could Clearly See.
With Wings The Colour Of Rainbows,
Sunshine Shone On Her Face.
She Wrapped Her Arms Around Me,
I Felt Her Warm Embrace.
With A Voice As Soft As Velvet,
She Told Me To Be Strong.
Bad Times Won't Last Forever,
Be Brave And Carry On.
Remember I Am With You,
The Dear Lord Is With You Too.
Have Faith You Will Get Better,
Believe You Will Get Through.
With A Smile My Angel Vanished,
But My Problems Still Were There.
Knowing God Sent Me An Angel,
Made My Troubles So Easier To Bear.
At The Moment My Life Is All Uphill,
Life's Road Seems Rough And Much Longer.
But I Remember
What My Mother Once Told Me.
What Doesn't Kill You
Will Make You Much Stronger.
This Path That I Walk Is A Hard One,
But Alone I Never Will Be.
Every Step That I Take In This Life Of Mine,
The Dear Lord Will Be Walking With Me.

THE SECRET

Have You Found
What You Are Looking For,
Or Does It Hide From You.
Have You At Last The Answer,
Your Wildest Dreams Coming True.
Can You Find What Is Good In Life,
Or Do You Search In Vain.
Just When It Is In Your Grasp,
It's Snatched Out Of Your Hands Again.
Why Not Do What I Did,
After Searching High And Low.
I Prayed To The Lord To Help Me,
To Show Me The Best Way To Go.
Once You Have Found Him,
He Will Never Leave.
God Is The Secret To Happiness,
If You Truly Believe

HER BEST FRIEND

A Little Old Lady Dozed In Her Chair,
Her Best Friend Was By Her Side.
A Cat That Kept Her Company,
Fussing Her When She Laughed Or Cried.
All She Had Left Of Her Hard Life,
Were Some Photos On The Wall.
Of Her Children Laughing,
From Very Young To Grown Up Tall.
Just Five Minutes Of Their Time,
A Letter Or A Call,
Would Mean The World To Their Mother,
Who For Them She Gave Her All.
Is That A Knock She Could Hear,
As She Hurried To The Door,
It Was Only A Postman With A Bill,
Her Wobbly Legs Feeling Stiff And Sore.
Most Of Her Days She Spent Dreaming,
Of Her Life So Long Ago.
Recalling The Time She Was Married,
To Her Handsome Beau,
At Least She Has These Memories,
Many People Don't Even Have That.
She Smiles As Her Best Friend
Settles On Her Knee
Her Dearly Beloved Old Cat

RETIREMENT

Life Is What You Make It,
Most Of My Friends Said.
Try And Get Some Living Done,
Do Not Laze All Day In Bed.
Get Up Bright And Early,
Force Your Legs Along.
Go For Walks In The Park,
Listen To Natures Song.
Get Some Fresh Air In Your Lungs,
Feel the Sunshine On Your Face.
Put A Smile Upon Your Lips,
That Nothing Can Erase.
You Might Meet Someone,
Who Will Have A Gossip With You?
Minutes Might Turn To Hours,
Maybe Share A Good Laugh Or Two.
Do This Very Often,
Then Alone You Never Will Be.
Think Tomorrow Will Get Better,
Maybe You Might See.
Though You Have Reached Retirement,
There Is Still A Lot To Do.
Help Those Less Fortunate,
Aid Them Worse Off Than You.
Take The Bull By The Horns,
Go Try Something New.
Life Is What You Make It.
You Have A Lot More Living To Do.

GARDEN IN HEAVEN

A Million Stars Came Out Last Night,
As The Moon Came Into View.
I Start To Dream And Reminisce,
Of My Happy Life With You.
If I Was In Your Arms Again,
Or Could Feel Your Tender Kiss.
My Time Would Not Be Wasted,
On Such A Lovely Night Like This.
Thinking About The Love We Shared,
How We Used To Laugh And Tease.
I Imagine Your Dear Sweet Face,
As Trees Sway In The Gentle Breeze.
Perfume Enveloped My Garden,
Though The Flowers Were Fast Asleep.
Heaven And Earth Are Between Us,
But You're Memory I Will Always Keep.
We Will Meet Again, My Loved One,
When My Life On Earth Is Through.
Walking Hand In Hand Together,
In Gods Garden Paradise With You.

LORD

Walk With Me When My Path Is Lonely,
Give Me Strength If Life's Road Is Rough.
Soothe My Soul When Doubts Enfold Me,
Ease My Mind When I Have Had Enough.
Hold My Hand When I Am In Darkness,
Bestow On Me Hope If I Am Feeling Lost.
Fill My Heart With Love And Kindness,
To Do My Best No Matter What The Cost.
When My Life On Earth Is Over,
And My Soul Just Longs For Rest.
Wrap Your Loving Arms Around Me,
At Long Last I'll Have Passed Life's Test.
Absent Loved Ones All Will Greet Me,
Friends And Family Who Have Gone Before.
Never Again To Be Parted,
Patiently Waiting At Heavens Door.
I Will Find Out All The Answers,
All The Things I Want To Know.
Why We Have Pain And Heartache!
Why Some People Suffer So!
No More Weeping, No More Sorrow,
Safe With The Ones That I Adore,
All So Happy I Have Joined Them,
Living With God Forever More.

A GARDEN IN SUMMER

I Sat In My Garden Of Roses,
Air Filled With Their Sweet Perfume.
It Seemed Like Only Yesterday,
We Were Surrounded
By These Flowers In Bloom.
We Laughed That Whole Long Summer,
But In The Autumn God Took You Away.
Now I Feel It's Always Winter,
With Dull Skies Ever Cloudy And Grey.
Just When Our Lives Were Settled,
In The Midst Of Our Happiest Days.
This Life We Shared Was Shattered,
By Gods Mysterious Ways.
I Still Sit In Our Garden Of Roses,
Imagine You're Still There with Me.
Sometimes I Can Hear You Whisper,
"Where You Are I Always Will Be"

LIFE'S FLOWERS

Walking In Gardens Of Flowers,
I Start To Reminisce.
Of The Happy Life, I've Had.
The Years I So Sorely Miss.
As A Child In Meadows In Springtime,
So Happy Among Tulips In Bloom.
I Remember From My First Sweetheart,
Gifts Of Carnations With A Heady Perfume.
I Met The Love Of My Life One Summer,
Deep Red Roses Were My Favourite Flowers.
My Thoughts Go Back
To This Special Time,
I Can Reminisce For Hours And Hours.
Every Day I Thank The Dear Lord,
Thinking Of My Life That's Past,
Nothing To Rue Or Regret,
Except Time Went A Little Too Fast.
From When I Was Born, To Seventy Years
As a Child, A Sweetheart And Wife.
Following On Came Beautiful Children,
I Have Had Such A Wonderful Life.
Now In Life's Winter Time,
I Have Learned What Will Be Will Be.
As I Lay White Lilies
On My Loved Ones Grave.
Sweet Memories All Flood Back To Me

HEALING MY HEART

If God Would Grant A Miracle,
Turn Back The Hands Of Time
If Wishes Could Come True,
You Would Still Be
In These Arms Of Mine.
The Sun Then Would Come Out
The Birds Again Would Sing.
This Life I Have Would Change
From Winter Into Spring.
All My Tears Would Dry Up,
My Heart Would Sing Again.
When God Grants Me A Miracle,
Freeing Me From Doubt And Pain.
I Would Wrap My Arms Around You,
Like We Have Never Been Apart.
Never Again To Be Lonely,
Healing My Poor Broken Heart.

POPPIES

When Poppies Are Blooming,
Tears Fill Up My Eyes.
Putting On A Brave Face,
But My Heart Knows Its Just Lies.
Thoughts Wander Back So Often,
To Before You Went Away.
Never For A Moment,
Did I Think You Would Not Stay.
Memories Of The Springtime,
With Daffodils In Full Bloom.
Hot Summers When We Had a Picnic,
Flowers Emanating Their Perfume.
Many Years We Spent Contently,
Sharing Hopes And Dreams Together,
Lives Spent Like A Fine Forecast,
With Just A Hint Of Very Bad Weather.
Then Came The Storm Clouds,
God Deemed That We Must Part.
He Chose You To Be An Angel,
In The Process, He Broke My Heart.
When I See Poppies In Autumn,
Colours So Vibrant And Gay.
I Believe God Must Have His Reasons,
We Will Meet Again One Day.

IS IT LOVE

A Smile Comes On My Face,
Then A Tear Is In My Eye.
My Emotions Are All Mixed Up,
Not Sure Whether To Laugh Or Cry.
My Heart Feels As Light As A Feather,
I So Want These Feelings To Last.
Why Does Time Go Far Too Slow,
Other Times It Goes Too Fast.
My Soul Feels Like It's Flying,
Like A Bird Soaring On The Wing.
Suddenly Dropping Down To Earth,
Making My Spirit Sing.
I Have Such Wonderful Feelings,
What On Earth Am I Thinking Of.
Has God Actually Sent Me
What I Have Always Wanted,
A Magical Thing Called Love.

SPECIAL ANGEL

I Once Had A Special Angel,
Who Stayed With Me On Earth?
Who Loved Me From The Moment,
From The Day She Gave Me Birth.
I Wanted For Nothing,
Only The Best Would Ever Do.
My Life Was Filled With Laughter,
As From A Child, To a Woman I Grew.
Now I Too Have Beautiful Children,
And A Bond That Nothing Can Sever,
Plus Loving Thoughts Of My Dear Mother,
Safely Locked In My Heart Forever.

JUST WHISPER

Do You Believe God Exists,
Or Think That Its Not True.
Pushing Back Longings, In Your Heart.
Doubting The Small Voice Inside Of You.
You Can Have What You Are Seeking,
This Is What To Do.
Trust That God Can Help,
 Miracles Do Come True.
You Will Feel The Warmth Of Gods Love,
If You Ask Him To Come In.
Just Need Whisper,
He Will Hear You,
A New Life Will Begin.
You Will Find That You Are One,
With All Things On This Earth.
Everything Will Have New Meaning,
Your Life Will Have Rebirth.

FOREVER AND A DAY

Do not Cry Because I have Left You,
Be Happy I Am In Heaven Above.
Living With The Angels,
Surrounded By Gods Love.
Free From Pain And Suffering,
All Sleepless Nights Are Past
Though I Sorely Miss You,
I Have Found Sweet Peace At Last.
Though Heaven And Earth Divide Us
And The Distance Seems So Far,
I will Never Leave You Lonely,
I Am Wherever You Are.
Time Means Nothing In Heaven,
Lifetimes Like A Blink Of An Eye.
One Day We Will Be Together,
Never Again To Say Goodbye.
When You Gaze At The Moon On An Evening,
Or Wish On A Shooting Star,
I Will Be Watching From Gods Heaven,
Keeping The Door For You Ajar.
So Do Not Weep For Me My Dear One,
Just Call And I Will Be There,
I Will Wrap My Arms Around You
Making Our Parting Much Easier To Bear.
You Will Always Sense My Presence,
Feel Too My Tender Touch.
Perhaps You Will Hear Me Whisper,
I Love You So Very Much.
The Love We Shared Between Us
No One Can Take Away.
Remember I Will Always Love You,
Forever And A Day.

MY MOTHERS LOVE

My Mother Loved Me So Much,
From The Moment, She Gave Me Birth.
She Cherished And Protected Me,
Since I Arrived Here On Earth.
My Childhood Is A Treasured Memory,
Brought Up In Loves Bright Glow.
My Mother Often Told Me,
She Loved Me More Than I Could Know.
Comforted Me When Needed,
Shed Tears Of Joy When I Was Wed.
I Still Remember Her Words,
When On My Wedding Day She Said.
My Child I Have Tried My Best,
Now The Rest Is Up To You.
Have Trust In Yourself And In God,
And He Will Guide You Through.
Give Love And Care To Your Family,
If With Children, You Are Blest.
Listen To What Your Heart Tells You,
Then You Will Truly Find Happiness.
My Dear Mothers Gone To Heaven Now,
All Her Hard Work Is Done.
I Am Sure She Is With The Angels Now,
For Here On Earth She Was a Special One.

DO IT ALL

Life Is For Living
Enjoy it While You Can.
Try To Do Your Utmost,
Fulfilling Every Plan.
Climb Life's Steepest Mountains,
No Matter How High Or Far
Having Reached The Summit.
Head For The Nearest Star.
Make The Most Of Every Moment,
Enjoy Each Minute Of Each New Day.
Shine A Light From Your Heart,
To Chase Dark Fears Away.
Live Every Dream You Have,
Make Special Ones Come True.
When Your Spirits Weary,
Ask God To Help You Through.
He Will Grant You Courage
Pick You Up Each Time You Fall.
Then When Your Life Is Over,
You Can Say Yes
 I Did It All

FOND RECOLLECTIONS

I Have Fond Recollections,
I Bring Out When I Am Sad.
They Come When I Remember,
The Good Life That I Had.
When We Were Together,
The Years Flew All Too Fast.
Never For A Moment,
Did I Think It Would Not Last.
I Have Fond Recollections,
Imprinted In My Heart,
To Stay With Me Forever,
No Matter How Long Apart.
During The Day When I Am Lonely.
Or Night Time While I Sleep,
They Are There To Comfort,
To Soothe Me When I Weep.
Sadly Gods Plans Were Not Ours.
He Took My Love One Day.
But Left Me With Special Memories,
Death Can Never Take Away.

THE GREETING

I Would Like To Send This Greeting,
Hoping God Will Let You Know.
Telling You I Still Love You,
That I Miss You So.
No Smiling Face To Cheer Me Up,
Or Strong Arms To Hold Me Tight.
The Only Time I Am Happy,
Is When You Are In My Dreams At Night?
Thank You For The Love We Shared,
For The Sweet Memories That I Possess.
Most Of All Thank You For Giving Me,
All The Years Of True Happiness

MY SISTER NANCY

You Were Always There Dear Sister,
Sharing The Good And Bad.
In Grief And Joy, My Companion,
My Anchor When Life Was Sad.
Ears That Would Always Listen,
To Problems That Did Call.
Like A Second Mother To Me,
Picked Me Up Each Time I'd Fall.
You Might Think I Have Forgotten,
But Believe Me I Have Not.
I Have Always Loved You,
So Grateful For The Bond We've Still Got.
You Were Born First, I Followed On.
Sharing Our Dreams Together,
Each Having A Shoulder To Lean Upon.
Holding Hands Through Life's Stormy Weather.
When Our Lives Are Over,
And The Key To Heavens Door We Obtain.
Links We Have Lost In Our Family Chain,
Will Join Up Together Again.
Just Think Of The Joy In Heaven,
How Happy We Both Will Be.
Mother, Father, And Loved Ones,
In Paradise With You And Me.

LEFT THE DOOR AJAR

Last Night As I Lay Sleeping,
You Whispered In My Ear.
I Thought I Felt Your Presence
Then Your Voice Said "I Am Here."
I Promised I Would Come Back,
To See You Once Again.
To Let You Know I Am Happy,
Since God Has Eased My Pain.
It Is So Beautiful In Heaven.
But I Miss You Oh So Much.
I Long For Your Arms Around Me,
Yearn For Your Tender Touch.
Heaven Is Such A Lovely Place,
It Is Filled With Love And Light.
I Will Let Nothing Hurt You
You Are Always In My Sight.
I Am Close Beside You,
Closer Still When Teardrops Fall.
It's Far Better To Have Loved And Lost,
Than Never To Have Loved At All.
Farewell! For Now My Dear One,
Know I Am Not Gone.
In Your Weakest Moments,
You Will Feel Me Urge You On.
I Will Stay Near You,
I Have Not Travelled Far,
Just Entered Gods Beautiful Garden,
And Left The Door Ajar.

HIS PROMISE

When First Seeing A Rainbow
Some Folk Long
For A Pot Of Gold.
But I Wish I Had You,
Just To Have And Hold.
When I See A Shooting Star,
I Don't Want Wealth Galore.
I Would Be Content In Your Arms,
Close To You For Evermore.
Folk Say Its Just Wistful Dreaming,
But I Pray My Dreams Come True,
Hoping God Will Keeps His Promise
And I Will Spend Eternity With You.

OUR SOULS MEET

There Is A Face I Want To See,
A Voice I Would Love To Hear.
I Long For That Special Hand To Hold,
To Calm My Every Fear.
I Miss A Pair Of Loving Arms,
To Soothe Me Through The Night.
Plus Words He Used To Whisper,
To Make My World Seem Right.
This Man I Loved More Than Life
Has Gone To Heaven Above.
Missing Is The Heart That Beat With Mine,
Giving So Much Care And Love.
I Asked God Not To Take Him,
My Pleas Were All In Vain.
I Truly Believe There's A Heaven
And One Day We Will Meet Again.
Though I Miss Him So Much,
I Am Not As Lonely As It Seems,
For When I Fall Asleep At Night,
Our Souls Meet Up In My Dreams.

IN OUR MEMORY

As I Gazed Out To Sea,
My Thoughts Went Back
To You And Me.
Sitting Here On The Same Seashore,
Pledging Our Love For Evermore.
Our Happy Years Went Flying Past,
Believing It Would Always Last.
But God Had Willed It Not To Be,
He Took My Love Away From Me.
Now Watching The Ocean Deep,
Praying To God His Soul To Keep.
As The Soft Winds Blew His Ashes Away,
I Forgot The Words I So Wanted To Say.
I Must Not Weep!
I Must Let Him Go!
Let His Spirit Sore !
With Each Ebb And Flow!
If I Am Brave And Set Him Free,
Our Love Will Live For Eternity.
Even Though He Will Be Sorely Missed,
I Will Bid Farewell With a Loving Kiss.
Trying To Accept What Will Be Will Be,
True Love Lasts Forever
In Our Memory.

MOTHERS DAY

No Mother To Give A Gift To,
On This Her Special Day.
Your Mother Is Your Best Friend,
Not Much More Can I Say.
You Are Her Favourite Person.
She Would Give Her Life For You.
Saying Prayers For Your Happiness,
With A Love So Warm And True.
Those Who Still Have Their Mother,
Here On Earth Are Truly Blest.
Spare A Thought To Us
Who Take Flowers,
To Our Mother's Grave,
Or The Garden Of Rest.

FOR ETERNITY

My Loved One Was Precious,
God Took Him Far Too Soon.
He Was My World,
My Sun And My Moon.
The Day He Was Taken,
All Life's Light's Went Out.
Groping In Darkness,
Sorrow And Doubt.
Not Only Making Me Lonely,
But My Heart Did Destroy.
Nothing Is Left In This Life To Enjoy.
Lord Why Did You Take Him?
Please Give Me A Sign.
If You Needed A New Angel
Why Did It Have To Be Mine?
Please Do Me A Favour
Give Him A Message From Me.
Say That I Will Love Him For Eternity.

IF'S AND ONLY'S

You Went Away
Now I Am So Lonely.
Nothing Left But Ifs And Onlys.
Bitter Tears From Eyes That Cry,
Never The Chance To Say Goodbye.
A Shock Severe, A Broken Heart,
Just Cannot Believe We Are Now Apart.
My Prayers To God Are All In Vain,
Longing To Hold You Once Again.
Losing You Is My One Regret,
The True Love Of My Life,
I Will Never Forget.

GOD IS THERE

This Verse I Think Will Be My Last,
I Have Done What I Set Out To Do.
God Has Helped Me Achieve My Task,
Now The Rest Is Up To You.
I Wrote This Book To Give You Hope,
To Comfort You In Your Loss.
Know God Is Forever With You,
Willing To Carry Your Heavy Cross.
If I Stirred Up Just A Bit Of Faith,
In Your Heart And In Your Soul.
I Will Be Satisfied With This,
Truly Having Reached My Goal.
If The Words In Just One Verse,
Give Your Heart Peace And Rest.
Writing This Book,
Will Not Have Been In Vain,
I Will Feel That I Have Been Blessed.
   God Bless You All.
      Brenda T.
     XXX

ABOUT THE AUTHOR

I Am Now Retired And Live With My Husband Dave,Who I Have Been Married To For Forty Three Years. Our Three Children Are Grown Now With A Family Of Their Own. I Now Have Time To Do The Things That I Am Most Interested In. I Have Always Wondered What This Life Is All About,Why Are We Here? Is There Another Life After This One? I Decided To Find Out. I Tried Different Churches Seeking The Answer. After The Loss Of My Mother I Went To Our Local Spiritualist Church, Looking For Proof That Life Does Go On, And If There Is Life After Our Body Dies. I Find Most Spiritualists I Meet Are Warm Kind People,Who Really Do Care For God. And This Earth We All Live In. I Have Made Many Loving Friends Since I Attended My First Meeting All Those Years Ago.Now I Too Have Developed This Gift, Seen And Heard Spirit Many Times At Long Last I Have Found The Answer I Was Seeking.

With Love

Printed in the United Kingdom
by Lightning Source UK Ltd.
124998UK00001B/13-45/A